B e T
/23/84
13.45

LITTLE FLOWER

BOOKS BY LAWRENCE ELLIOTT

The Long Hunter: A New Life of Daniel Boone (1976)
I Will Be Called John: A Biography of Pope John XXIII (1974)
The Legacy of Tom Dooley (1969)
Journey to Washington (with Senator Daniel K. Inouye) (1967)
On the Edge of Nowhere (with James Huntington) (1966)
George Washington Carver: The Man Who Overcame (1966)
A Little Girl's Gift (1963)

LITTLE FLOWER

THE LIFE AND TIMES OF FIORELLO LAGUARDIA

LAWRENCE ELLIOTT

William Morrow and Company, Inc.
• New York 1983 •

Copyright © 1983 by Lawrence Elliott

Library of Congress Cataloging in Publication Data

Elliott, Lawrence.
  Little flower.

  Bibliography: p.
  Includes index.
  1. La Guardia, Fiorello H. (Fiorello Henry), 1882–
1947. 2. New York (N.Y.)—Politics and government—1865–
1950. 3. Legislators—United States—Biography.
4. United States. Congress. House—Biography.
5. New York (N.Y.)—Mayors—Biography. I. Title.
E748.L23E44   1983   974.7'104'0924   [B]   82-23964
ISBN 0-688-02057-7

Printed in the United States of America

First Edition

1 2 3 4 5 6 7 8 9 10

BOOK DESIGN BY ALLAN MOGEL

This book is dedicated to
Harry Gold, with love

CONTENTS

PART I
ASPIRATIONS

PART II
WASHINGTON, D.C.

PART III
NEW YORK, N.Y.

PART I
ASPIRATIONS

1 &
OVERTURE

Late one evening between Christmas and New Year's Eve, 1945, New York's Commissioner of Investigation, Louis E. Yavner, drove up to a darkened City Hall. The three-term administration of Fiorello H. La Guardia, ninety-ninth mayor of the city, was to end at midnight, December 31, and Yavner, who had served it from the beginning, had some final matters to attend to.

But he wasn't alone. Down the echoing marble corridors came the erratic clacking sound of unskilled typing. Yavner looked at his watch—it was nearly 8:00 P.M. He followed the sound to the office of the mayor's secretary, and there sat La Guardia, pecking away with one finger of each hand and glaring at the keyboard as if it were a political adversary.

"What are you doing, Major?" Yavner asked, addressing La Guardia by his World War I military rank, as did nearly everyone but relatives and strangers.

The mayor looked up, shoving his glasses back to the top of his head in a characteristic gesture. He was a round little man with a marvelously mobile face that couldn't hold secrets. "Oh, hello, Lou," he said. "I've got these letters to get out and there was nobody else around. Say, can you type?"

"As well as that. But can't it wait until tomorrow?"

"Tomorrow there'll be something else to do. Come on, sit down."

So Yavner sat down at the other typewriter in the small room and together he and La Guardia began clearing up the last loose ends of an era. For all at once it struck Yavner that the age of La Guardia was ending in front of his eyes and he felt the loneliness and sudden desolation that goes with the passing of power. This was it: It was all over, the zeal, the melodramatics— and twelve years of the best reform government in American municipal history. And it was going out in the antic La Guardia

11

style: The mayor was squeezing one last effort out of himself and whoever else he could lay hands on.

The wonder is that he was ever elected in the first place. New York had never had a mayor of Italian descent. Moreover, he was a Republican in a city so overwhelmingly Democratic that not for twenty years had the Republicans won anything more nourishing than a few patronage crumbs and an occasional petty office. Not to mention that except for a handful of reformers, not a single member of the political establishment in *any* party supported his nomination.

In 1921, the Republican leader of Manhattan warned him, "Fiorello, this town isn't ready for an Italian mayor." In 1929, when he pried the nomination away from the bosses anyway, they sat on their hands while Jimmy Walker, then in his glory as the Beau James of Broadway, gave "the crazy little wop" the worst beating of his political career. When at last a Fusion party was organized to reclaim City Hall from Democratic corruption and fell to arguing about a nominee, one leader slammed a fist on the table and said, "If it's La Guardia or bust, I say bust!"

There was good reason for the regulars to fear the contentious little maverick. He fitted no political category. He was barely more tolerant of his own party than of the Democrats. "The minority party in any city can afford to be virtuous," he said, and added, "Some men who claim to be exponents of Republican principles know as much about the teachings of Abraham Lincoln as Henry Ford knows about the Talmud."

He was a lawyer who castigated his profession, a champion of honest garment-center labor unions who was not a socialist, a reformer who could play ward politics with the most devious Tammany aldermen, a Republican who periodically went swooping off the reservation, a campaigner with a dazzling gift for languages who walked out into the melting pot and talked to each of the city's ethnic groups in its own tongue—Italian, Yiddish, German, Spanish.

He was called the Little Flower but fought like a nettled wildcat. Forever bristling with indignation, personally aggrieved by the knavish gang that ran New York, he lashed out at every corrupt act, from ticket-fixing to judge-buying, uncovered by his furious energy. On the very day of his election, hearing that his people were not being allowed to vote in some polling places, he rushed out and found one being "watched" by twenty Tammany thugs. "Get out! Get out, you bums," he yelled in that falsetto screech of his, "or I'll mop the floor with you!" When two policemen intervened, he threatened to throw them off the force the day he took office. The area was cleared; the voting went on, and the candidate dashed off to the next embattled election district.

He wielded wit like a bludgeon. Soon after the stock market crash, New York University conferred an honorary degree on Richard Whitney, president of the New York Stock Exchange, and La Guardia immediately wired the trustees, "Through what oversight did you overlook gangster Alphonse Capone of Chicago?" (La Guardia sometimes shot from the hip, but this time he hit the bull's-eye; eventually Whitney confessed to grand larceny and went to prison.) Local Nazis jeered at him as the Jew mayor of New York and La Guardia called in the press to say, "I never thought I had enough Jewish blood in my veins to justify boasting of it." When the German consulate demanded protection from Jewish "hooligans," he assigned a detail of Jewish policemen to guard it.

"La Guardia," wrote a City Hall reporter, "comes in a small package, but so does a bomb." When he had been in office two years, a national publication tried summing him up this way: "The Mayor of the City of New York can play the cornet, cook spaghetti and fly an airplane.... Where he goes, turbulence follows." An instantly famous *New Yorker* cartoon shows City Hall heaving and quaking from the moment La Guardia comes to work in the morning, subsiding, spent, only after his departure.

He was regularly called to task for his histrionic approach to government, but nothing could diminish his zest for taking center stage and calling forth all the spotlights in the house. Some ascribed this penchant for drama and the sometimes exaggerated gesture as the efforts of an honest politician to reach past the bosses with a message for the electorate that there were great wrongs to right and that he, Fiorello H. La Guardia, was the proper man for the job. But most voters knew the truth, that he was just a natural ham—which, paradoxically, only intensified their faith in him.

His friend George N. Shuster, president of Hunter College, thought the mayor's incessant intrusions into non-mayoral realms—he was forever going to fires, answering police calls, and lecturing housewives on cooking and good grocery buys—could be attributed to La Guardia's sense of New York as one big family. He, of course, was the father. "He ought to have had fourteen children," concluded Shuster.

He would have had a hard time supporting them. He was broke nearly all the time. When he became mayor he owned neither an automobile nor an overcoat. He had nothing but contempt for the acquisition of money as a personal goal and once said he was concerned with the nation's destiny, so shooting for small stakes did not interest him. Be that as it may, the fact no one argues is that in an office whose temptations had overwhelmed many a predecessor, La Guardia was incorruptible. For twelve years he walked an arrow-straight line, and no one in his administration who did less lasted beyond the next pay period. But though it was built into his nature to fly into a rage at even a hint of chicanery, there wasn't a trace of sanctimony or self-righteousness about him; he could never long fend off the essential humanity that animated his better self. The case of Jimmy Walker is instructive.

They had been adversaries from the time La Guardia entered politics. Walker, only a year older but Irish and a Democrat in a Tammany-run town, had made a far more promising start. Their first significant encounter came in 1915, when La Guardia was a young deputy state attorney general prosecuting some important meat-packing houses under a new law requiring that all containers be marked with the true weight of their contents. The packers had seriously overstated the weight on the wrappers of their ham and bacon packages. "It looked like a very simple case to me," said La Guardia.

Enter the author of the new Weights and Measures Law, State Senator James J. Walker, to address the court—on behalf of the defendants. The law, he said, was never meant to apply to paper. Glass, wood, tin containers—yes. But not paper wrappers. And of course he *knew*, he concluded with boundless urbanity, since he had written the law.

Case dismissed. La Guardia was still stunned when, afterward, Walker and the judge invited him out for a drink. He asked Walker how in the world he could appear in court to undercut his own law.

"Fiorello, when are you going to get wise?" Walker replied in the friendliest way. "Why are you in the attorney general's office? You're not going to stay there all your life. You make your connections now, and later on you can pick up a lot of dough defending cases you're now prosecuting."

The judge was nodding vigorously, but La Guardia was appalled. "Listen," he protested, "a lot of little storekeepers have been fined for selling the same kind of hams in wrappers."

"Fiorello," said Walker with the solicitude of an older brother, "you stop worrying about those things. What are you in politics for—for love?"

But of course La Guardia could not stop worrying. With his bottomless capacity for indignation, he peppered away at Walker from the sidelines until, in 1929, running against him for mayor, he assailed him and his Tammany sponsors with charges of wholesale corruption and callous indifference to the city's welfare. But it was endless summertime in New York then; stock market prices were at an all-time high and climbing higher. It was clear to everyone but La Guardia, who campaigned his heart out, that New Yorkers believed they could afford the luxury of a playboy mayor. Walker wisecracked his way right through to Election Day and won by a margin of better than two to one. La Guardia didn't even carry a single assembly district. Never in the city's history had a major candidate suffered so humiliating a defeat.

But then the halcyon summer of the twenties ended. With it went the fantasy of an eternal bull market, swept away by the crash and the real-life loss of 32 billion dollars' worth of stock equity, and 12 million Americans were out on the street looking for jobs. In New York, which had been devastated by the Depression, more than 100,000 families were on relief—and relief funds ran out. Mayor Walker, the endlessly appealing ornament of a sunnier city, appeared bewildered by events, pathetic in the bitter winter of the disaster. Echoes of La Guardia's 1929 charges were heard again in the Appellate Division of New York's First Judicial Department, and in Albany, the state capital, and were now seen to be more than campaign oratory. Called to account, first by Judge Samuel Seabury's special investigation into corruption in New York City, then by Governor Franklin D. Roosevelt himself, Walker abruptly resigned his office and sailed away to European exile.

Three years later, inveterate New Yorker that he was, he came back to make his peace. He was a different man, broken in spirit, all but penniless. Plenty of glad hands were thrust out at him, and invitations to sit on the dais at countless banquets. But no one offered him a job. Meanwhile he was threatened with lawsuits and denied a pension by the indignant protests of self-proclaimed paragons of civic virtue. In 1940, when his health was gone and he was about to be divorced by his cherished young wife, when he was down and out and had only a few short years to live, La Guardia quietly appointed him labor arbiter of the women's cloak and suit industry at a salary of $20,000 a year plus expenses.

When La Guardia became the first mayor in New York's 275-year history to be elected to three consecutive terms, he was less than elated, for he saw himself at a political dead end. He had dreamed of becoming mayor of New York but never wanted to believe it would be the capstone of his career. During his first term, Thomas E. Dewey had been an obscure prosecutor; he could never have been elected district attorney without La Guardia's pulling power at the polls. Now Dewey was governor and on his way to winning the Republican nomination for President— and La Guardia was still mayor.

Once, there had been talk of his having a place on the Democratic presidential ticket. "Listen," he told reporters who kept pressing to know when he would announce his candidacy, "I couldn't get a gallery pass to either party's convention." The observation happened to be closer to reality than his aspirations, but he kept hoping lightning would strike nevertheless, and he didn't care who knew it. But it never did, and when he came to the end of his third term as mayor, he had reached the end of his political life—the only one that mattered to him. La Guardia had twenty months to live when he left office; those who knew him best say they were the loneliest months of his life.

Two decades later, Robert Moses, who had been his parks commissioner—while holding down a clutch of other city, state and federal jobs—and whose brilliance and irascibility matched La Guardia's own, rose to make a few remarks at the dedication of a La Guardia bust at the New York airport named for the late mayor. They had not had the easiest relationship. An aide remembers at least one stormy meeting after which La Guardia, livid with anger, said, "Someday I'm going to knock that son of a bitch through the door." And Moses's man, waiting in the Parks Department limousine outside City Hall, reported that Moses would come out wild—"just absolutely wild."

But that December day in 1964, Moses did not speak of their confrontations. Earlier, he had written of La Guardia, "Only those who recall the cynicism of the late Twenties and early Thirties and remember how low the City's credit and civic morale had fallen can properly gauge what this man did to lift us up and to attract to New York the lost respect of the nation." Now, with elegance and legendary wit, he evoked La Guardia, the surging social power plant that had illuminated New York for twelve unforgettable years:

> His motto was "patience and fortitude." He was not equipped with patience by inheritance, temperament or experience, and perhaps he had a premonition that he would not be around long enough to finish everything. As to intestinal fortitude, known in the good American vernacular as "guts," he had far more than his share.
>
> The Little Flower invited caricature but never ridicule. . . . He was a gallant little man, fiercely proud of our town and of our common humanity. Under La Guardia, reform, which had been merely respectable, became popular. . . .
>
> Pause at this bust, traveler, as you hurry from the accelerated pace of the city to a thousand miles an hour in the air. Keep your shirt on. You still have time. Pause and reflect on The Little Flower. Give him a thought. He deserves well of the city. He was quite a man.

2

ACHILLE AND IRENE

Achille La Guardia used to tell his children that the reason they were born in the United States was because, as a boy in Italy, he was forever in trouble at school. He ran away from home at the age of thirteen and spent the next fifteen years wandering the world.

But he was far from the typical Italian emigrant of the time, nearly all of whom were in flight from poverty or political oppression. His father was a civil servant in the southern city of Foggia; he was a solid middle-class *cittadino* and the family means were not insubstantial. Achille could have completed his education and found a place in the government service, too, or gone into one of the respected professions, as had his brothers. But he appears to have been that generation's heir to a certain volatile independence that ran in the La Guardia line, and left home for the simple reason that he felt unable to unfurl his exuberance there.

But there was more to him, a basic seriousness. He was an achiever. He spent some time in the larger towns of northern Italy, as well as in Switzerland, indulging an innate gift for music. He studied, composed, learned to play the cornet, worked at odd jobs when he needed to, but more and more supported himself as a musician. Soon he was traveling all over Europe, mastering German and French, shipping out with the Hamburg Line and once voyaging to the farthest Pacific as a bandmaster. By the time he came to America, aged twenty-nine, he was an accomplished musician and linguist. The year was 1878.

Achille liked America. It suited his free-speaking, freewheeling nature. If he had a wife, he thought, he'd be glad to stay. Early in 1880, he went back to Europe and found one.

His father would have been appalled by his choice, a dark, full-figured girl named Irene Luzzato Coen, who not only was not Italian—she lived in Trieste, then part of Austria—but a Jew.

They met at a dance, an alertly chaperoned one in the custom of the time, but that did not inhibit the smitten Achille. Thereafter the couple saw each other regularly. Irene was twenty-one years old and, though raised in a religious home, was thoroughly Italian in speech and culture, the prevailing tendency among Jews in cosmopolitan Trieste.

Achille pressed his suit hard; Irene was more and more taken with the worldly, good-looking musician and the prospect of an exciting new life in America. On June 3, 1880, barely half a year after they met, they were married by the mayor of Trieste. On the marriage certificate, Irene recorded her religion as *Israelita;* Achille, carrying the memory of indignities heaped on him by his teachers, all priests, put down *nessuna*—nothing. They sailed for New York the same day

Their first home in America was Greenwich Village, an enclave of narrow, meandering streets with a faintly European flavor that seemed to have nothing to do with the surrounding city. Within a year of their arrival they had their first child, a daughter, and named her Gemma. Soon after, they moved from one red brick tenement flat to another, slightly larger one, and it was here that their son Fiorello Enrico (which he later Americanized to Henry) was born on December 11, 1882. The address was No. 7 Varick Place, just two blocks south of decorous Washington Square, where Irene took her babies on sunny days, and barely a mile from City Hall.

They were in the vanguard of one of the greatest migrations of history. In the twenty-four years between 1890 and the outbreak of World War I, an unbelievable flood tide of humanity from eastern and southern Europe, from Italy, Russia, and the dozen nations comprising the Austro-Hungarian Empire, came to America, passing through the immigration station at Castle Garden and—when that was overwhelmed by the torrent—through the big new one in New York harbor, Ellis Island. They numbered 15 million, increasing the population of the United States by 25 percent and trebling the size of New York City. More than any other factor—more than its banks, commerce and arts, more than Wall Street or Madison Avenue—the immigrants, by their sheer numbers, by their aggregate energy and in-

dividual genius, made New York an imperial city. Their sons and
daughters would come to dominate its life and politics.

There was a magnetic fascination about New York in those
years. It was not beautiful as Paris was beautiful, nor stately
and settled as was London. But it was vibrant with its growing
power, rich and lusting to be richer, building buildings to be torn
down and replaced by bigger or different or more magnificent
buildings. Nothing was permanent except the conviction that the
city would grow into its unoccupied areas, filling them with newcomers from the American hinterlands who burned for a share of
its glory and wealth, and with the poor and scorned and homeless
of the Old World, longing for something—anything—better
than what they had.

But in 1882 it was still in turbulent adolescence. The Brooklyn Bridge consisted of two granite piers in the East River; not
for another year would it be open to traffic, the longest suspen-
sion bridge in the world. The Statue of Liberty, gift of the
French people to commemorate the hundredth anniversary of
American independence, was still in France, packed in 214 enormous crates. In October 1886, a suitable pedestal was finally
built for it at the entrance to the harbor and President Cleveland
took the train up from Washington to dedicate the 151-foot co-
lossus that was to become America's best-known and best-loved
piece of sculpture. Inscribed with the haunting sonnet of Emma
Lazarus

> ... Give me your tired, your poor,
> Your huddled masses yearning to breathe free ...

it came to stand as the open door, and more, the open arms, of a
nation of immigrants.

They did not find the streets paved with gold. "I am satisfied
from my own observations that hundreds of men, women, and
children are every day slowly starving to death in the tenements," wrote Jacob A. Riis, the passionate journalist-reformer
in *How the Other Half Lives.* He saw hordes of bewildered,
newly arrived Germans, Irish, Jews and Italians herded into
foul and airless flats at exorbitant rentals, the swelling immi-

grant inflow guaranteeing that someone would be there to pay for every available foot of shelter, no matter how filthy and congested. By 1890, when New York was forging ahead of all other cities in the Western world in its rate of growth, it also had the dubious distinction of leading in arrests, serious illness and deaths per capita. A contemporary history noted that "New York, unfortunately, is becoming in large degree a city of only two conspicuous classes, the rich and the poor."

If landlords of the time were grasping and venal, the politicians accommodated and usually outdid them. Tammany Hall, the Democratic party organization, held a stranglehold on New York and ran it for the benefit of the faithful. The leader, John Kelly, was known as Honest John because he put graft on a sound, businesslike basis; each Democratic candidate for a municipal office, for example, was required to pay an "assessment" to Tammany Hall—which then guaranteed his election. Kelly himself held an unsalaried post, sheriff of New York County, but managed to put by $800,000 during his six-year tenure as leader.

There was, however, a momentous difference between Honest John Kelly and his predecessors at City Hall: He was Irish and had seen to the election of William R. Grace, the first Irishman and the first Catholic to be mayor of the city.

It was not an inconsequential achievement. Historically, Tammany had always been a "100 percent American" organization, with a particular antipathy for Irish immigrants. But if there was one thing a Tammany stalwart responded to even more spontaneously than his prejudices, it was votes. With the Irish population of the city at 25 percent of the total, there was no longer any question of keeping them out, only of keeping them from taking over.

A vain hope. The Irish had a natural gift for the delicate machinery of politics; knowing English, adapting easily to their new surroundings, they seemed to seize on politics as a profitable way to put their innate sociability to work. Many among them started as saloonkeepers and gained a wide circle of customers and friends; this gave them a certain eminence and, in time, considerable influence in their wards and precincts. And so eventually, inevitably, the Irish came to dominate Tammany and in

1880 began a long tradition of sending their own to City Hall. It would be more than fifty years before the first Italian, Fiorello H. La Guardia, reached that high ground.

Among those turning to careers in politics in the 1880s was one, William H. Walker, who paid his "assessment" and became Tammany's candidate for alderman from the Ninth Ward in Greenwich Village. He won handily. In fact, he would run for alderman three times more, and once for the New York State Assembly, without a defeat, ending his political career as superintendent of public buildings in Manhattan, not wealthy but comfortably well-to-do. His glib second son would also choose politics, having first tried his hand as a songwriter, and his path and that of Fiorello La Guardia, both born so close in time and place, would cross with a kind of ironic inevitability. Christened James John, he was sometimes called Jimmy Talker.

The later lives of both would be greatly affected by a third New Yorker, Franklin D. Roosevelt, also growing up in those early 1880s. His upbringing and expectations would be far different from theirs; he lived on an estate about halfway between New York City and the state capital at Albany, a considerable establishment of nearly a thousand acres on a height overlooking the Hudson River, with maids, nurses, cooks, coachmen, gardeners and stable boys. "He was brought up in a beautiful frame," said a governess.

His father, James Roosevelt, considered himself a gentleman of the old school but differed from his patrician neighbors in one respect: He was probably the only Democrat among them. Of course that did not keep him from ensuring that his son would have all the advantages to which his class entitled him. Young Roosevelt was born to be part of the reigning establishment and bound to have opportunities no Irish or Italian immigrant's son could even contemplate. In the summer of 1883, for example, "through the good offices of trustee James Lawrence, the name of Franklin Delano Roosevelt was entered upon the list of those who, at the proper age, would enter Groton School." He had learned to walk only the month before.

Irene La Guardia adjusted easily to life in New York, learning English, making neighborhood friends. Her husband was faring less well. Times had turned hard, marked by strikes and serious unemployment, and apparently Achille La Guardia, who had never been a regular member of any orchestra, went without work for long periods. There may have been other motivations, too, but in any case he came home one day in 1885 to announce that he had enlisted in the United States Army; he was assigned to the Eleventh Infantry Regiment as chief musician. Soon after, the family was on a train bound west for Fort Sully in what was then a barely settled western expanse that would not become the state of North Dakota for four more years. So it was that Fiorello La Guardia, who is so indelibly identified with New York, who is expressly remembered as the quintessential New Yorker, in fact left the city at the age of three. He would not return until he had reached young manhood, twenty-one years later.

The frontier was very much part of American life in 1885, and the past seemed very close. The year's most stirring news was the death of Civil War hero Ulysses S. Grant (people did not dwell on his scandal-ridden presidency). That summer, Sitting Bull, the warrior chief who orchestrated the Sioux massacre of Custer's cavalry at the Little Big Horn, was touring with Buffalo Bill's Wild West Show, but the Apache chief Geronimo was still on the warpath, eluding five thousand federal troops and five hundred Indian scouts. Fort Sully and the dozens of other army posts spotted throughout the western territories had not yet outlived their usefulness.

"I have only a child's recollection of the place," La Guardia wrote, "and from my hazy recollection it was most primitive." His sister, Gemma, almost two years older, remembered a prairie fire, the clanging alarm, women and children ordered to the post hospital for safety and wrapped in wet blankets. It was all very exciting, she thought.

The regimental commander, Colonel Richard Dodge, took a liking to his new bandmaster and assigned him a "charming" hillside house well separated from the company area. At first Achille worried that his young wife would feel isolated there, even that his family might be in danger from the Sioux Indians who lived just outside the fort. But Irene's gift for making friends continued to overcome barriers of language and culture, and as Gemma wrote, she became the Indians' ally:

They brought her all kinds of gifts, such as handmade blankets, moccasins, beads, and, in turn, she gave them sugar and staples. The Indians spoke a Spanish dialect, Mother spoke Italian to them, and in this manner, they understood each other very well. Mother always said, "No one is so well protected here as I am."

In the spring of 1887, the La Guardias' third child, a son, was born and they named him Richard Dodge for Achille's commanding officer; the family was complete. Soon after, in keeping with standard War Department practice of alternating regiments between frontier duty and more congenial surroundings, the Eleventh Infantry was transferred to Madison Barracks at Sackets Harbor, New York, on the eastern shore of Lake Ontario. This was a famous old post, rows of brick and stone barracks and officers' homes lining a long oval parade ground. Grant had been stationed there as a young officer in the 1840s; earlier, Sackets Harbor won a measure of fame when a force of farmers dragged a cannon they called the Old Sow up to a bluff overlooking the anchorage and fired a round that de-masted an invading British frigate. It was the first shot in the War of 1812.

The two older children started school at Sackets Harbor; Fiorello, small, dark, disputatious, left emphatic memories. "He used to torment my girls by pulling their hair ribbons off and such pranks," recalled Mrs. Joanna J. Franklin, wife of the commissary sergeant, whose family lived next door, "but he was honest and truthful and had the instinct to take the part of the underdog. Even in his play, he was a leader, and many an argument was the outcome of his desire for leadership. He may have been the smallest, but he was the most persistent and the other children eventually capitulated and followed."

His first teacher, Mrs. Estella Littlefield, had cause to remember him too. Not that he was her most promising pupil. "He was impetuous and full of fight," she told an interviewer years afterward, "and his English vocabulary was well-stocked with words of profanity which lads of six are not supposed to have at tongue-tip." But she conceded that he was bright and learned quickly, and on Friday afternoons, when the class recited verses and other pieces they had memorized, "Fiorello was the most adept."

Apparently the young Mrs. Littlefield was taken with the stocky first-grader, despite his volcanic personality. She spent extra time helping him over the rough spots small boys encounter in their first days at school; she tried to channel his fire into worthy projects. More than fifty years later they were still in touch. "I search the papers to learn of you and wish for your success in all you do," she wrote him in 1944. To which he replied, "You are certainly mighty energetic for a young woman of eighty-five . . . but you must not work too hard at it. We all have to rest once in awhile."

In 1890, the Eleventh Infantry was transferred back to the frontier, to Fort Huachuca in the Arizona Territory, just north of the Mexican border. It was a dry mudhole of a stockade, set down barren, dusty miles from anywhere else, the sort of posting troops suffered stoically while waiting for their next assignment. To nine-year-old Fiorello La Guardia, it was a paradise: "Our playground was not measured in acres, or city blocks, but in miles and miles. We could ride burros. We talked with miners and Indians. . . . we learned to shoot even when we were so small the gun had to be held for us by an elder." The La Guardias lived in a two-room adobe house with plank sides and flooring and a detached kitchen with a canvas roof. "It sure looked great to a small boy," La Guardia later wrote, but it is unlikely that either Irene or Achille was overcome with regret when the regiment received its transfer orders in May 1892.

The distance it moved was not great, not even 250 miles, and still within the Arizona Territory. But it was another world, a return to civilization—Whipple Barracks, on a breezy, mile-high plateau just outside the town of Prescott, which had been the territorial capital until just a few years before. Both town and fort owed their existence to the discovery of gold in the surrounding pine mountains in the 1860s; farmers and cattlemen followed the miners, and now there were two thousand people in the town, which was built around a large open square and had a sawmill and a brickyard. The railroad was scheduled to reach Prescott the following year.

Fiorello La Guardia would spend the next six years here, perhaps the single most impressionable period of his life. He always considered Prescott his hometown—and later, as New

York's best-known congressman and as mayor, always wore a high-crowned Stetson to emphasize the appealing irony of his wide-open-spaces background. The few pages of his autobiography allotted to his Arizona boyhood are an unqualified paean:

> My memories of Prescott are that it was the greatest, the most comfortable and the most wonderful city in the whole world.... Father was popular in the town.... The setting of Prescott was about as beautiful as any I have ever seen.... I thought [the public school] was grand.... Maybe it is sentiment, but that bunch of Arizona public school teachers still seems to me to be about the best in the whole world.

But there is a paradox between these patent enthusiasms and another, darker side of life at Whipple Barracks. About this, La Guardia writes with uncharacteristic diffidence, but the message is there, between the lines, easy to read. It is that Arizona was also where young Fiorello started working out the important matter of who he was, the place where he began to understand unspoken truths—that there were differences between classes, nationalities, religions, and that some were "better" than others. It was where he first encountered discrimination.

There was, for example, a world of privilege and prerogative between officers and enlisted men. As bandmaster, his father was among the highest noncommissioned officers in the regiment. But neither he nor any other enlisted man could ever cross the invisible social barrier, the separate and unequal housing, mess and recreational facilities, that separated them from the officers. Wrote La Guardia:

> The distinction between commissioned officers (all West Pointers in those days) and enlisted men was great. And that distinction went all the way down to the kids on the post. It never bothered me very much because I did not adhere to such rules. I would just as soon fight with an officer's kid as I would with anyone else.

There is no reason to question that. Evidence of his pugnacity is amply set down by his teachers, his sister, Gemma, and contemporaries like Joey Bauer, who claimed to have "licked him every day," a hyperbolic reference to young Fiorello's obstinate unwillingness to acknowledge that he had been whipped and let it go at that. But one cannot help wondering whether the ten-year-old boy went at these battles as matter-of-factly as his laconic account of later years suggests. Nor does he ever tell us, as others do, that the fights were all about a born firebrand's instinctive eruption at taunts about his size, his Italian name, his dark Latin looks. It was the overt, exuberant Americanism he associated with Arizona that captivated La Guardia—the frontier, the "tough" soldiers, the "real, honest-to-goodness he-man Army food." But how "American" can he have felt, this swarthy, stunted, screechy-voiced son of foreign-born parents, both of whom spoke thickly accented English, one a non-practicing Jew, the other a lapsed Catholic, in a land of God-fearing, church-going Protestants? It is true that Achille and Irene, who did not attend any church, began sending Gemma and Fiorello to the Episcopal Sunday school; but the boy must have wondered whether he really belonged there either.

The only racial wound he specifically admits to is the episode of the organ grinder and his monkey. They "blew into town," as La Guardia put it, promptly attracting the attention of a jostling throng of children. The hurdy-gurdy made sprightly music; the monkey danced and tipped a little red cap whenever someone gave it a penny. Then the jeering began. "A dago with a monkey!" cried the blue-eyed children. And, "Hey, Fiorello, you're a dago—where's *your* monkey?"

"It hurt," La Guardia conceded afterward. "Some of their families hadn't been in the country any longer than mine. What difference was there between us?"

Still, he could fight the slurs. What made it worse, he goes on to tell us in the autobiography—meaning shattering, intolerable—was that his father came along at this precise moment and started to chatter in Italian with the hurdy-gurdy man, everyone watching. "Perhaps he considered him a fellow musician," La Guardia says sarcastically. In any case, Achille invited the organ grinder home for a macaroni dinner—and the son would be taunted about *that* for a long time too.

Forty years later, as mayor of New York, La Guardia, "with a great deal of gusto," banned organ grinders from the streets— and received dozens of protest letters steamy with sentiment, in-

cluding one from actress Cornelia Otis Skinner in which she accused him of having no heart. La Guardia replied with uncharacteristic patience that organ grinders obstructed traffic,
that their city licenses were really licenses to beg, and that the
hurdy-gurdies they cranked with such merriment were rented
from the *padrones* at usurious rates. His logic was unassailable,
but there is also no doubt that he still remembered, darkly, the
long-ago incident in Arizona.

His account of it seems to have said more than he intended.
It reveals an essential insecurity—his sense of having only
an equivocal place in American society, of fitting nowhere except
on the periphery of this star-spangled life he wanted so whole-
heartedly to embrace. Soon he would begin testing himself in the
role of outsider; he found it more comfortable than running with
the crowd. And when he turned to politics, it would be as a maverick—La Guardia the endless dissenter.

Italian was rarely spoken at the La Guardias'; Achille discouraged it on the grounds that they were all Americans now and
he and Irene had to practice their English at home. There probably had never been another home like it in all Whipple Barracks.
The walls were hung with family portraits and Victorian drap-
eries, the floors covered by decorous patterned carpeting; there
were books, newspapers from New York City, and an assortment
of musical instruments which Achille taught the children to
play, Gemma the mandolin and violin, Fiorello the cornet and
banjo, and Richard the piano.

All this contributed to an air of middle-class gentility as
alien to a military post as afternoon tea, and further unhinged
the family's social status, which normally would have derived
from Achille's rank as noncommissioned officer. He was forbid-
den to consort with officers, yet had almost nothing in common
with the other NCOs, who were usually distinguished from the
average recruit only by their stripes and stridency, and whose
off-duty hours were passed in the bars and brothels along Prescott's Montezuma Street. As a result, the La Guardias were
oriented toward families in town, where their musical talents
won them a privileged place; there, Achille, who gave private
music lessons, was called Professor La Guardia. He looked the

part, a compact, handsome man with a full beard now added to the flowing mustaches of his youth. With the three children, he turned up to play at every Prescott benefit and most of its main social functions.

Once, Fiorello, having ridden everything from the regimental donkeys to wild mustangs, declared his intention of becoming a jockey. His father paid no attention. As far as he was concerned, the boy's future was ordained: He was going to become another John Philip Sousa, then at the height of his fame as America's March King, and he, Achille, was going to see to it. Usually relaxed about the children's discipline, he turned into an impassioned taskmaster when they took up their intruments, sometimes bringing tears to Gemma's eyes with his agitation and bawling imprecations against musicianship that fell below his exacting standards. But Fiorello, once he had outgrown his horse-racing aspirations, took it all with paradoxical calm. "Keep on screaming, Papa," he would say. "In this way I'll learn."

But it was already becoming clear that music was not nearest Fiorello's heart, either. It would always be his best-loved and most dependable diversion, but his lifework would take him in another direction, and he seemed to sense it even as a twelve-year-old. One of his teachers, Miss Lena Coover, said he was an insistent and determined speaker, "a real fighter" when it came to expressing his views. These same attributes must have been a pain in the neck to his sister Gemma; Fiorello was regularly interrupting her and her friends at play to announce, "Now I am going to speak." Then he would jump onto the handiest chair or table and begin declaiming about how parents ought to treat their children or how teachers ought to teach, mixing up a batch of pedagogy and morality to hurl back at the most recent source of his ire. If he caught the interest of his audience, as he usually did, all was well; but if their attention wandered, recalled Gemma, "Oh my, it was terrible."

Miss Coover, who was "the prettiest little thing," according to nostalgic La Guardia recollection, was a recent graduate of an Iowa normal school; the Prescott job was her first. In keeping with a lifelong pattern, young Fiorello didn't make things easy for her. Yet, as was also to happen again and again in his life, their formal relationship evolved into warm, long-lasting friendship. In her eightieth year, Lena Coover flew to New York to attend the funeral of her most prized pupil. "I knew he was bound to be someone important," she said then. "He was not only stubborn about having his say, but he also knew what he was talking about. Everything interested him."

The New York Sunday *World* reached Ross's drugstore in Prescott the Friday or Saturday following publication. Fiorello La Guardia would come rushing in almost immediately after. He read the comics section on the spot. It featured a one-panel cartoon called *The Yellow Kid,* the first ever to use color—the Kid wore a yellow shirt. He lives on as an allegory of the bitter circulation wars between *World* publisher Joseph Pulitzer and William Randolph Hearst, owner of the rival New York *Journal;* their stunts and emotional exploitation of the news came to be called "yellow journalism." But the *World,* even at its most flamboyant, hewed to a crusading editorial line: It advocated taxing luxuries and large incomes, supported civil service reform, railed at political corruption, and stood foursquare behind what it called the aristocracy of labor. It was a power in the land.

To a boy like Fiorello, with omnivorous curiosity and innate sympathy for society's losers, its populist ardor was fan to a flame. Once he got the *World* home he could barely contain himself until his father passed it on, so he could spread the pages on the floor and immerse himself in the issues of the day. "I got my political education from Pulitzer's New York *World,*" he said later.

There was a lot to learn, a lot to stir both the rage and compassion that bubbled in his heart. There had been a depression in 1892 which led to a financial panic, the third in two decades. In 1894 the American economy hit rock bottom: unemployment nearing 20 percent of the work force, sixteen thousand business enterprises down the drain, five hundred bank failures. The *World* chronicled not only the grim statistical record of the financial chaos but also the human wreckage in its wake—shattered dreams, lost homes, breadlines, bloody strikes.

That summer the parade of national events pricking Fiorello's forming sense of social justice marched right off the pages of the *World* and into regimental headquarters at Whipple

Barracks. More than 250,000 railroad workers across the nation
had gone on strike to protest a 25 percent wage cut by the Pullman Company of Illinois, immobilizing the entire American rail
network. At the end of June, charging "obstruction of the U.S.
mails," the railroad owners won an injunction in federal court
against any interference with the movement of trains. Some
strikers defied the order; there was violence. On the Fourth of
July, President Cleveland interrupted his holiday to call out the
army. Ten days later the strike was over, broken by the federal
force.

At Whipple Barracks, the Eleventh Infantry, fully armed,
had marched off to protect the property of the Atlantic & Pacific
Railroad in Prescott and Ash Fork. Fiorello watched, shaken. He
recognized the overriding imperative: The mail *had* to go
through. But he did not understand why, in a dispute in which
there was at least theoretical justice on both sides, the full power
of the government—"enforced by bayonets of United States soldiers"—had been brought to bear solely in favor of the owners.
No troops had been sent to protect workers, of whom thirty-four
had been killed; no agent of the United States spoke up for the
thousands of Pullman employees evicted from company-owned
homes by order of the Pullman president.

There was hardship enough close at hand. To the La Guardias, Whipple Barracks seemed to stand in the eye of the economic storms buffeting the nation; at Whipple every man was
guaranteed his pay on the last day of the month, and life followed a consistent, predictable pattern. But in half a dozen
nearby towns, the mines and smelters were shut down and the
railroad, then building its way from Prescott to Phoenix, hired
and fired as it moved south. Idle miners and laborers wandered
into Prescott and, finding neither work nor much sympathy,
drifted on. Those who had jobs hung on to them, even the most
menial ones, such as laying track for the railroad, a bitter, hard-
slogging undertaking beset by accidents and sudden death.
Wrote La Guardia:

> If a laborer was injured, he lost his job. If he was killed, no one
> was notified, because there was no record of his name, address or
> family. As construction moved on, it left in its wake the in-

jured, the jobless, the stranded victims. Even as a young boy, this
struck me as all wrong. . . . this early glimpse of the condition of
working people, of their exploitation and their utter lack of protection under the law . . . prompted me to take an interest on their
side in society.

Fiorello first read about Tammany Hall in 1894, in the
World. New York's Democratic political machine was being in-
vestigated, and all that year newspapers were full of lurid testimony detailing Tammany's venal clutch on the city and
particularly on the police department. Fiorello was morbidly fas-
cinated. "Unlike boys who grew up in the city and who hear from
childhood about such things as graft and corruption," he wrote,
he was genuinely shocked by the disclosures. And of course he
took it all as a personal affront. "A resentment against Tammany
was created in me at that time, which I admit is to this day almost an obsession."

He felt the same way about the professional politician; the
very word left a bad taste in his mouth that never went away.
His unalterable image of the politician was of the small-fry regular, the ward heeler, the party hack—and his prototype in Arizona was the Indian agent, paid off for party loyalty with a
government appointment.

It was, of course, a license to steal. Bands of Indians, once
free-roving, were now herded onto reservations and made dependent on the federal government for the requisites of life, which
were to be dispensed by the government's agent; food, clothing
and shelter were all provided without cost by the Great White
Father in Washington. But Washington was a long way off and
all too often the Indian agent made his own arrangements, selling off the Indians' provisions to miners, ranchers, even general
stores, at excellent discount prices. It was a classic political
swindle: There was something in it for everyone—except the
victim.

For young La Guardia, the image of the politician-as-thief
was self-enforcing: He saw hungry, hollow-eyed Indian children
watching him eat an apple or a cookie his mother had baked and
he thought of crooked politicians. He read about Tammany Hall
and seethed to realize that they had corrupted even "the greatest
city in the country." But none of this circumscribed his view of

politics. He never became cynical, and neither as a boy nor as a man did he ever lose his basic faith that honest public officials could undo the politicians' mess and bring good government to the people. He believed in the American system, and as the thieving Indian agent was his pattern for political iniquity, so Prescott's grizzled, chain-smoking mayor, Bucky O'Neill, became his youthful model of the true and faithful public servant.

Fiorello was not alone in his admiration for Bucky—born William Owen—O'Neill, who had long ago demonstrated his good sense and the essential Western ability to ride and shoot, and was now proving his devotion to the plain, hard-working people steadily filling up the Arizona Territory. Bucky had wandered some, worked at a variety of jobs—typesetter, court stenographer, local judge—done well at all of them, and in 1888 was elected sheriff of Yavapai County, of which Prescott was the only town with more than a general store and a handful of settlers. People remembered how he took a posse three hundred miles across the wilds after four bandits who had robbed an Atlantic & Pacific train; it took two weeks but Bucky brought them in. Then he became tax assessor and went after the A & P itself, levying a bill against them for something close to a million dollars in taxes for the free land, 425 million acres of it, handed over to the railroad by the U. S. government. Eventually someone with more authority settled things to the A & P's satisfaction, so Bucky quit and ran for election as Arizona's territorial delegate to Congress. The trouble was he ran as a Populist and was twice beaten by the regular Democratic and Republican party organizations. In 1897, though, enough people in Prescott shucked the party label to elect Bucky mayor.

Fiorello was elated. Not even fifteen, as absorbed in politics as another boy in that time and place might have been in horses, rifles or girls, he now had a genuine local legend to idolize, a man of action whose political stands wholly accorded with Fiorello's own populist instincts. He kept learning about politics, declaiming at home and at school whenever family, teachers or classmates gave him half a chance. Lena Coover said that he had decided to become a lawyer by then. "Every lunch hour he would bolt his food and dash to the courthouse to listen to cases or even to be in that atmosphere."

On January 28, 1898, his class of six was graduated from Prescott's grammar school. Fiorello was chosen to make the graduation speech (one can almost hear the cries of agony had it been otherwise). He was then ten weeks past his fifteenth birthday, not quite five feet tall and well under a hundred pounds in weight. A contemporary photograph shows him standing slim and serious, dark-eyed, hair parted severely down the middle.

A few days later he began the ninth grade. But he was not to complete the two-year high school course in Prescott. On February 15, the battleship *Maine* exploded in Havana harbor killing hundreds of American seamen, and life took a sharp turning for all the La Guardias.

3

THE YOUNG EXPATRIATE

It was natural for Americans to sympathize with subject people aspiring to be free—they had been revolutionaries themselves. And the long Cuban struggle to shake off the Spanish rule was all the more intensely felt for Cuba's closeness to U.S. shores. But this essentially humanitarian instinct also nourished private ambitions: Businessmen and politicians began to see in an independent Cuba a profitable new sphere of American influence. More than a few clergymen took to preaching the sacred necessity of intervening on behalf of "our little brown brothers," and Hearst's *Journal* and Pulitzer's *World* battened on sensationalized accounts of Spanish atrocities. With the mysterious explosion that sank the *Maine*—immediately but mindlessly blamed on a Spanish conspiracy—the word *war* sprang to everyone's lips.

In the flammable days that followed the disaster at Havana, Fiorello was among those who crowded into the Prescott telegraph office every afternoon to read the Associated Press bulletins that came in over the wire and were posted. A declaration of war was expected momentarily. The Eleventh Infantry was put on alert and made ready to move out. Bucky O'Neill began recruiting a volunteer regiment from among the territory's rugged frontiersmen, appealing to Washington for the immediate induction of "Arizona's rough-riding men." Meanwhile, Hearst and Pulitzer, their circulation booming, kept thundering, "Remember the *Maine*!" and demanded war. Hearst, in fact, had personally guaranteed it. When his famed illustrator Frederic Remington telegraphed from Havana that "there will be no war" and said he wanted to come home, Hearst told him to stay where he was. "You furnish the pictures," he wired back, "and I'll furnish the war."

But days and weeks passed and nothing happened. "There was a feeling in our military circles that President McKinley was hesitating too long," wrote young La Guardia. Then, on March 28, a court of inquiry made public its conclusion that the *Maine* had been destroyed by the explosion of a submarine bomb and McKinley's weakening resolve to stand against war broke down. No one, then or since, ever showed how Spain could profit by blowing up the *Maine,* but the war fever had erupted out of control. "I have exhausted every effort," McKinley reported to Congress on April 11. "... I await your action." The invitation was unanimously accepted; on the 25th war was declared.

A day or so later, Bucky O'Neill addressed the assembled students at Prescott's high school on the meaning of the war. When it was won, he said, no nation would ever again try to dominate another in the Western Hemisphere. This truth, and the absolute justice of the American cause, were unequivocally, even emotionally, accepted in Prescott. The town hero was himself going off to fight and the young students, Fiorello most ardently, wished they were going too. They gave Bucky a ringing cheer.

On the 27th, 210 local stalwarts were mustered into service at Whipple Barracks. There had been more than a thousand volunteers but places had to be saved for others in the territory who applied in overwhelming numbers to serve with Arizona's First U.S. Cavalry Volunteers—already known as the Rough Riders— under Colonel Leonard Wood, Lieutenant Colonel Theodore Roosevelt second in command. On May 4, in a public ceremony, Prescott bade Godspeed to the men of Troop A and presented to its favorite son, *Captain* Bucky O'Neill, a new Colt revolver. Fiorello was no longer there, but he had felt from the beginning that what Bucky really ought to have been given was command of the regiment.

The Eleventh Infantry, with all its dependents, had shipped out in the last days of April. The trains stopped first at Jefferson Barracks, Missouri, near St. Louis, where the men were given a little time, some only a few hours, to settle their wives and children before moving on to a training center in Mobile, Alabama. As soon as his father was gone, Fiorello, determined to follow, marched up to the regimental recruiting officer and tried to enlist. But he looked even younger than his fifteen years, underweight and undersized, and the answer was no.

He was only briefly discouraged, and anyway otherwise distracted. One night a fire broke out in the La Guardias' barracks, and Fiorello dashed into the blazing building for his cornet and blew the fire call, alerting the entire post. Another time he played taps at a soldier's burial. Then, within two weeks of his arrival in this alien place full of strange faces, he walked into the offices of Joseph Pulitzer's St. Louis *Post-Dispatch* and said he wanted a job as a war correspondent.

Probably the editor, cornered by this baby-faced apostle of his own faith, was too stunned to throw him out. And probably Fiorello, with built-in tenacity and burgeoning self-confidence, began talking about his admiration for Mr. Pulitzer, his long experience with the army, his familiarity with military tactics and terminology, and how, once he rejoined his father and the Eleventh Infantry, he would send back an insider's dispatches—that sort of all-fronts assault on a prized objective would mark the future politician. And the editor, wearying, sighing, finally saying all right, he would stake him to a press card and a railroad ticket to Mobile—that sort of thing happened too. In any case, Fiorello got the job and must have been off like a shot; by May 18, under the headline *"Post-Dispatch's* Youthful Correspondent Heard From,"* he had his first article in the paper. It was full of vigorous patriotism, and no censor need have worried that Fiorello was giving anything away to the enemy:

EVERYBODY IN FINE SPIRITS . . . all ready and anxious for the orders to go to Cuba. They are a nice lot of good spirited boys and the right sort of men to defend their country.

The byline was slightly mangled, "F. LaGuardi," and the *Post-Dispatch* chose to run a picture of its Youthful Correspondent holding a cornet and wearing short pants with an enormous white bow on his blouse. But none of that mattered. Fiorello was at the scene of the action, and his father, according to Gemma, was proud to have him there.

In time the Eleventh Infantry and its young *Post-Dispatch* reporter moved on to the sweltering embarkation center at Tampa, Florida. Arizona's First Cavalry Volunteers, the Rough Riders, had preceded them and were already in Cuba—unfortunately, without their horses, which had to be left behind for lack of transport. Fiorello constantly sought news of them, especially of Bucky. But it was not until much later that he learned of the high regard in which his idol had been held by Colonel Roosevelt, a former New York City Police Commissioner and Assistant Secretary of the Navy who cut quite a figure himself. Captain O'Neill, Roosevelt wrote in his journal, alone among all the Rough Riders, had the "soul and imagination" to speak of "the nearing future, with its chances of death, honor and renown." On the night their troopship crossed the Gulf, the two men stood together at the rail, and searching the dark sky, Bucky said, "Who would not risk his life for a star?"

It was a remark TR would have cause to remember. Two weeks later, as the Rough Riders hugged the ground in the shadow of San Juan Hill, a last terrible hail of Spanish gunfire between them and their moment of everlasting glory, Bucky, smoking a cigarette, strolling before his troop as though they were on the parade ground back at Whipple, was hit full in the face with a rifle shot and was dead before he hit the ground.

Bucky O'Neill was one of only 379 Americans killed on the battlefield during the Spanish-American War, but 5,000 died of disease and thousands more fell victim to contaminated food and the noxious conditions in the camps. Achille La Guardia was one of these; when the Eleventh Regiment finally embarked for Cuba, he was too sick to go with them, and Fiorello stayed behind with him. Achille was a casualty of "embalmed beef"—the inspector-general's own term—sold to the army by corrupt contractors. Some of it was preserved with boric acid and nitrate of potash; 500,000 pounds, sent to England the year before and rejected, was so rotten it had begun bursting its tins and spreading its putrescence over all the cases.

Achille would never recover from this poisoning; Fiorello would never forget it. When he was elected to Congress during World War I, the first legislation he introduced was a bill providing the death penalty for "the scavengers of history" who supplied tainted food or defective supplies and equipment in wartime. It died in committee.

Father and son were sent back to Jefferson Barracks, where

the reunited family marked the end of the war on August 12. Cuba was free but the Americans, who had fought to end colonialism in the New World, wound up with quite a colonial empire of their own: the Philippine Islands, Guam and Puerto Rico, all ceded by Spain to the United States. Ten days after the shooting stopped, Achille was discharged from the service for "disease of the stomach and bowels." He was awarded a pension of $8 a month.

The family went first to New York but Achille couldn't find work there. He was now fifty years old, broken in health and low in spirit, and cheerlessly decided he wanted to return to Europe. Before that fateful year of 1898 was over, the La Guardias had sailed for Trieste, where, for the time being, they moved in with Irene's widowed mother, the Fiorina for whom Fiorello had been named.

None of the La Guardia children was enthusiastic about leaving America but kept a loyal silence as their father struggled to rebuild his life. He started a carting business and tried his hand as a ship's provisioner; both proved too taxing for his waning strength. Then things seemed to take a promising turn. Achille leased a neglected seaside hotel at nearby Capodistria and with his close personal attention and the family's help it began to prosper. Around the same time—the end of 1900— Fiorello was offered a job as clerk at the American consulate in Budapest. The pay was less than $9 a month but, as he put it, "It was an opportunity to learn useful things and gain valuable experience," and he took it.

In Capodistria, the hotel was doing so well that, in October 1904, Achille made arrangements to buy it outright. But on the 21st he died suddenly; he was fifty-five years old and as much a casualty of the war as Bucky O'Neill. After the funeral Richard signed on as a ship's interpreter and went off to sea, and Irene and Gemma came to live with Fiorello, who was then posted at Fiume.

When Irene applied for her widow's pension, the War Department put her through two years of bureaucratic torment—prove she had been Achille's legal wife; prove she hadn't remarried since his death; prove she was in financial need. And when she had done all this, when she had provided them with all the documentation they said was required, they finally ruled that her husband's death was not service-connected and she was therefore not entitled to a pension after all. Bitterly, Fiorello added stony, stupid, entrenched bureaucrats to the tinhorns and politicians on his list of those who preyed on a defenseless citizenry.

Fiorello, who was only eighteen and had barely eight years of formal education when he joined the American consular service in Budapest four years before, had been low man on a staff of four or five as ill-trained and badly paid as he was. The difference between them was that he promptly set out to do something about it. He began a systematic study of Italian and German and, with a quick ear, picked up enough Hungarian, Croatian and Yiddish to deal with the growing numbers of Balkan emigrants funneling toward the Adriatic ports at Trieste and Fiume. In this he was encouraged by the consul general, a Boston Brahmin named Frank Dyer Chester, who admired Fiorello's fire and ambition but felt constrained to warn him nonetheless that the lack of a degree from Harvard would keep him from advancing in the foreign service.

This may well have been true in 1900 but it made next to no impression on Fiorello, who only strove harder. He had a surpassing belief in himself and his ability to work his way through or around any obstacle. His consular duties consisted of processing visa and passport applications and gathering information for the consul's periodic reports. Much of his spare time was spent studying the history of the region; he also read every newspaper or magazine he could find with news of home.

Budapest, in those feverish years before war shattered the Austro-Hungarian Empire, was the most vivacious city of eastern Europe, the center of its theatrical and musical life. "One could hear more good music in Budapest in 1902 and 1903 than in Vienna," wrote La Guardia, and eventually every great entertainer of the day played there. It happened that some of them required the help of the American consulate. One such was Loie Fuller, who danced in diaphanous costumes under spectacular lighting and had been toasted at the Chicago World's Fair and by le tout Paris. In Budapest she lost her passport. When

Fiorello appeared at her hotel with a new one, a cocktail party was well under way, the first such ritual he had ever encountered. Would he have a drink? Miss Fuller asked. The teenager declined. Something, then, to show her appreciation, she said, glancing about fretfully, and suddenly decided on a kiss. It must have been a substantial one; "I went away very happy," said the young aide.

Soon after came Isadora Duncan, whose problem was an explosive love affair with a Hungarian actor that left her no time to placate an accompanist who had been wounded by the critics and quit her company. Fiorello never understood why it fell to the consulate, and specifically to him, to persuade the accompanist—whose job it was to recite poetry while Isadora danced—that she could not possibly perform without him. But he did, and the show went on.

Finally there came to Budapest an actress, a bleached blonde of a certain type, against whom Mr. Chester specifically warned Fiorello and his fellow clerks. If he caught them anywhere near her, he said, they could consider their consular employment terminated. "That was enough for us," said Fiorello. That evening he and a cohort called at the actress's hotel and took her to the Folies-Bergère. Unluckily, the consul was waiting there with malice aforethought and fired them on the spot. It took Fiorello's nonstop rationalizations and the backing of the vice-consul to persuade Chester to give them back their jobs.

Fiorello thought highly of the consul but did not understand him. They were of different worlds—Chester the Boston aristocrat with three Harvard degrees, his appointment as consul arranged by Henry Cabot Lodge, the senior senator from Massachusetts. But, as La Guardia was quick to point out, Chester was no politician; he was a scholar, a lover of languages who mastered one after another—but strictly from books. He kept the rabble at arm's length. Fiorello, equally eager to learn, plunged into the mainstream of life in Budapest—and Trieste and Croatia when for brief periods he was stationed there. He reveled in the most tangled consular cases and wound up with the practical equivalent of advanced degrees in sociology, politics, and applied economics, and at least conversational command of seven languages.

What he understood least about Chester was the consul's attitude toward women. Still in his early thirties, Chester was a confirmed misogynist. Mournfully he exhorted the clerks against the devious and dangerous nature of the opposite sex, to which La Guardia, who *liked* a pretty girl and was nothing if not direct, once responded by slamming an old office revolver down on the desk and saying, "Here, take this—what do you have to live for?"

Chester accepted this rebuke silently because, among other reasons, La Guardia was the most valuable man on his staff. But it had no effect. He left the foreign service in 1908 to spend a few years teaching, then devoted the rest of a long bachelorhood to a studious account of the Chester family genealogy.

In 1903, La Guardia's knowledge of Italian and Croatian won him a promotion to the consular agency in Fiume at a salary of $800 a year. A small complication, the fact that he was too young to be a foreign service officer, was resolved by having him serve as acting agent until after his twenty-first birthday some months later; then he was formally commissioned.

That didn't change anything. Despite the fact that Fiume was Hungary's largest seaport and that as many as 1,200 emigrants embarked there for New York on each of the Cunard Line's twice-monthly sailings, the United States consular agency remained a one-man office, and as La Guardia put it, "I acted as boss, clerk and my own messenger." But for the first time he had to make important decisions, and they were more often right than popular—the course he followed all his political life. He became a first-rate consular officer and a headache to every superior from Budapest to Washington. The very first chance he had to get into trouble, he did.

It was Corpus Christi Day, a national holiday in Hungary, and in any case well after hours when a young soldier knocked at the office door. He seemed bewildered by the seedy two-room suite, but grateful to find anyone there at that hour. As it happened, however, only one of the two rooms was the consulate of the United States of America; the other was the bedroom of the consul. The bathroom, shared by other tenants of the building, was down the hall.

The soldier asked to talk with the consul. La Guardia, still hastily buttoning his shirt, assured him he was doing so. The soldier still looked doubtful, but at this point he was clearly bound to tell his story to *somebody*.

His name was Kovacevic. He had been born in Hungary but emigrated to the United States as a youth and found a job in the coal mines. He had become an American citizen. He had saved his money. Then he came back to the old country to see his aged parents and marry his boyhood sweetheart; he meant to take her back to Pennsylvania with him. It was a typical success story except for one thing—he had barely gotten to his parents' home when he was arrested and drafted into the Hungarian Army. Trapped, he had had no hope of escape until that afternoon, when, marching down the street with his regiment, he had seen the American flag outside the consulate.

Could the consul help him?

Fiorello La Guardia's capacity for indignation, which would one day make him famous, may have peaked for the first time that day. Satisfied that the soldier's story was true, he drafted a fiery protest—although this was clearly a diplomatic, not a consular matter—and that very night personally delivered it to the appropriate authority. "In the name of the United States," he declared, "I demand the release of this American citizen."

The discomfited official said he would see what could be done. By morning, Kovacevic had a ten-day leave of absence; by midweek he had been discharged from the Hungarian Army with official expressions of regret, and soon after sailed for New York with his bride.

Meanwhile, La Guardia had filed a jubilant report with Frank Chester in Budapest and haunted the return mails, waiting for the commendation he was sure was coming. What came was an official reprimand for having acted without informing his superiors of the circumstances and without waiting for their instructions. No mention was made of the possibility that if he had, the unhappy Kovacevic could have been lost for years in some remote garrison. Mention *was* made of protocol, channels of command, and the proper conduct of the business of diplomacy. Do not forget them in the future, wrote the consul-general coldly.

La Guardia, white with fury, did not forget them—they just never penetrated his consciousness. That sort of thing never did.

But he remembered Kovacevic, safe in the United States, and the next time he faced a choice between doing something and writing a report about it, he made exactly the same decision.

The Balkans were a tinderbox, barely a decade away from the explosion whose reverberations would come booming down the decades, devastating nations and threatening the world to this day. It was not an accident of history, as young La Guardia quickly perceived. The calculated policy of Hungary's Hapsburg rulers, perhaps the most arrogant and despotic in all Europe, was to divide and conquer, to churn the mutual animosities of the ethnic conglomerate that shared the Balkan Peninsula, lest all draw back and recognize their true tormenters. Wrote La Guardia:

> [The Hapsburg policy] was put into practice every day before my eyes. Antagonisms and hatreds were carefully and systematically engendered. The Croatians were brought up to hate the Serbians and trained and aided by the government in that hatred. All of the South Slavic groups were kept at one another's throats. . . . Dalmatians, Bosnians, Herzegovinians, Montenegrins, Slovenes, all similarly exploited, all kept in the same abject poverty, were stimulated to take their hatreds out on one another instead of on their exploiters.

Those who could, left. Thousands crowded into Fiume before every sailing. The Cunard Line had only recently put four slow-speed steamers into service between Fiume and New York and their principal cargo was immigrants, 90,000 just in the three years La Guardia served as consul. For reasons that had to do with the spiritual sickness of the dying empire, it became a contemporary amusement among the exalted, the aristocracy and high officials—"big shots," La Guardia called them—to watch the boarding. They would stand on the first-class deck, sometimes as many as thirty or forty, and gaily contemplate the spectacle of the passengers, wearing their good clothing and carrying their most valued possessions in carpetbags, filing over the long gangway into the steerage.

No one knew much about immigration procedures, neither the Hungarian port officials nor anyone at the American consulate in Budapest, nearly five hundred miles inland; it was all so new. But it seemed to be going well, so no one worried. Certainly Fiorello La Guardia didn't know anything about it when he arrived. But as was his practice, he began to read what he could find on the subject. That wasn't much, but a certain regulation gave him pause. It said that, as consul, he had to "certify to the health of all passengers and crews and give the ship a certificate that it had cleared from a port free from contagious diseases or illnesses subject to quarantine."

Of course those with obvious sickness were not permitted to sail. But La Guardia knew that every ship that left Fiume came back with passengers, sometimes a dozen, sometimes fifty, who had been turned away by U.S. Immigration doctors, mainly for trachoma, a then-widespread and untreatable affliction that caused blindness. No one came to watch these people debark— alone, often separated from their nearest relatives, usually penniless. How much more logical, how much more humane, La Guardia thought, if all emigrants were medically examined at *this* end, sparing the unlucky at least the long useless voyage and the cost of the passage. He read the regulation again and decided it gave him the power to order exactly that to be done.

Some days later he was invited to tea aboard the S.S. *Aurania*. That was the prevailing etiquette; the consul was then supposed to produce the bill of health required of any foreign vessel entering an American port. La Guardia appeared, but along with the clearance certificate he brought a doctor to examine the passengers. "I cannot describe the consternation of the Cunard officials," he later wrote. "To say that [they] were horrified is putting it mildly." One of them said Cunard had been carrying emigrants to America since before La Guardia was born and not one had ever been examined by a consular officer.

La Guardia shrugged and left the ship, the certificate still in his pocket. When Cunard sent the purser to the consulate to get it, La Guardia turned him away. Soon the captain of the *Aurania* appeared. Was there no way to resolve this dilemma? he asked. He was due to sail in a matter of hours. La Guardia replied that until then the regulations had been interpreted for the financial gain of the company, but from that day on he would clear no ship for the United States until its passengers had been examined and could be reasonably sure they would not be sent back for medical reasons. He had only vague authority for such a pronouncement, and absolutely no idea whether Chester, let alone the State Department, would support him. He just knew he was right.

The captain and La Guardia and the doctor all went back to the *Aurania* together. The emigrants were called up on deck and duly inspected, and then La Guardia passed over the bill of health. Spurred by Cunard, the British consul filed a formal protest with Chester, who wrote to Washington for instructions. The reply—that consular agents were empowered to execute American immigration laws—was loose enough to pass for approval as far as La Guardia was concerned, and he made it stick. He also made the Cunard Line pay the doctor's fees for all subsequent examinations.

There were consequences worth noting. During La Guardia's three years as consular agent, Fiume had far fewer health rejections at Ellis Island than any other port embarking emigrants for the United States, a total of only forty-five for trachoma, for example, against an average twenty-five on *every* ship docking in New York. As La Guardia wrote, both the Public Health and Immigration services became "greatly interested in my innovation." But he also noted that twenty-five more years would pass before the ponderous bureaucracy moved a bill through Congress requiring pre-embarkation physical examinations for *all* emigrants.

Meanwhile, the young consular agent's decisive victory over official inertia had whetted his appetite for power. He knew instinctively that it was a force bound to be exercised by someone and did not see why it should not be he. Not yet twenty-two, he had come to understand these unalterable truths about power: Some people would never have it; most of those who did used it for self-exaltation; those who remained—and La Guardia wanted to be one of these—had a chance to wield power on behalf of the world's weaker and poorer multitudes.

On April 29, 1904, he wrote directly to the State Department urging that the post at Fiume be upgraded to the status of consulate, and that he be promoted to full consul. He made his case forcefully: Emigration was increasing; as most other countries in Fiume were represented by consulates, he was constantly dealing with officials of higher rank, a circumstance that did not go unnoticed in protocol-ridden Hungary, complicating an already vexing job.

Frank Chester loyally supported his subordinate's request. La Guardia was by far his most promising aide and Chester knew he would make a first-rate consul. But unhappily he could not call back earlier complaints: La Guardia exceeding his authority, La Guardia offending the governor-general, La Guardia meddling in embassy matters. And so there was no promotion. But if Washington intended its denial as a warning for La Guardia to mend his ways, it was a waste of time. Fiorello La Guardia was absolutely incapable of being anything but what he was.

One Wednesday morning that spring, he received notice that the S.S. *Panonia*, scheduled to sail the following Saturday, would be boarding steerage passengers that afternoon. Had the sailing date been advanced? inquired La Guardia. No, no, the Cunard envoy airily replied; it was—as the consul must surely have heard—that Her Imperial Highness, the Archduchess Maria-Josepha of Austria was honoring Fiume with her presence this day and, having heard it to be an amusing pastime to watch the proceedings at an embarkation, had set aside the afternoon to visit the *Panonia*. The emigrants, therefore, would be boarded early to accommodate her.

La Guardia's precise reply is not recorded; his feelings can be safely guessed. In any case, the essence of his message to the steamship company was clear beyond misunderstanding: U.S. quarantine regulations required passengers to board ship as close to the sailing time as possible; as a waiting period of three days and three nights could hardly be construed to fit this requirement, he would be unable to issue a bill of health to the *Panonia* if it embarked emigrants before Saturday.

Panic in the highest places! Honeyed words, followed by imprecations and baleful threats as representatives of Cunard, of the director of the port of Fiume, and even of the governor-general all but tripped over one another pounding up the stairway to the American consular office, those dreary little rooms on the Corso which suddenly seemed the most important place in Fiume. Perhaps Mr. La Guardia had not understood: The entire town had labored in preparation for this royal visit; the Archduchess was the wife of Grand Duke Otto; *she was the niece of the Emperor, for God's sake!* And she wanted to see an embarkation *today*. By Saturday she would be gone!

Mr. La Guardia understood. But perhaps the British and Hungarian officials pressing him so hard did not. What they asked was not only contrary to American immigration law—which, they would recall, he was charged with enforcing—but the very idea of herding five hundred souls into the close quarters belowdecks for the amusement of some titled lady and keeping them there while the ship remained tied up at the dock for three full days was repugnant and inhuman. The answer was no.

The pleas grew more anguished: Listen, they were only talking about emigrants—peasants! steerage passengers! Look, maybe it wouldn't be necessary to board all five hundred. Say, two hundred . . .

No.

But the Archduchess was honoring the American consular agent by inviting him to take tea with her aboard the *Panonia*. Afterward, Mr. La Guardia could stand alongside Her Imperial Highness on the bridge to watch the embarkation.

No.

Was he altogether mad, then? To obstruct the Archduchess's expressed wish was grave enough; to refuse her invitation was a direct insult to the Crown! There would be an official protest from His Majesty's Government, serious repercussions; his career . . .

"That's when I got sore," La Guardia liked to say at this point in the story, recounting it decades later. "I told them to tell their precious Archduchess that maybe she could boss *her* people around but she couldn't boss the American consul."

Whereupon he sent a reminder to the ship's master that the penalty for entering New York harbor without proper clearance was a long period of quarantine plus a heavy fine. Then, on the sensible ground that he would find no peace in his office that day, he left it. He simply walked out and disappeared, while the director of the port and an army of his functionaries scoured Fiume in search of him.

"No excuses—find him!" commanded the director of the

port, all the while assuring the governor-general that they would; after all, it was their city, not that young Bolshevik's. But the afternoon passed and they did not find him. And as the Cunard Line could not risk the loss of the *Panonia's* health certificate, the Archduchess was obliged to leave the ship without witnessing an embarkation. Her caustic opinion of the American consular agent did result in a note of protest, but La Guardia heard nothing about it. Though discomfited still again by its most recalcitrant foreign service officer, Washington, for once, could not find it in its bureaucratic heart to reprimand him.

Meanwhile La Guardia appeared as scheduled that evening at the home of the British consul for a dinner party—visibly relishing every detail of the turmoil his disappearance had caused. Where had he hidden? all wanted to know. And the answer was that he hadn't hidden at all. He had simply called at the home of the director of the port, knowing the gentleman to be otherwise occupied, and the gentleman's charming wife had invited him to stay for tea, as La Guardia had hoped she would. Afterward, they passed the afternoon playing the piano for each other.

Though the young American lacked rank and money—he was earning $60 a month at this time—he had become quite popular among the consular officers and military attachés who constituted the diplomatic hierarchy in Fiume. Outspoken and athletic, he was available for a game of soccer, a swim in the Adriatic, or a lively debate over a glass of beer. Women seemed to fancy his wit and trim good looks. He wore a bow tie and the fashionable frock coat of the day, his dark hair parted down the middle, his jaunty dark eyes missing nothing. He used to say that the Turkish consul, "a notorious roué," had once stolen a girl from him, a singer. But he did not lack for female company. And there was the night of the Mardi Gras ball when a young woman's obvious interest precipitated international bedlam.

La Guardia, as he put it, was "rigged out" and feeling silly in white tie and tails. Each lady, elegantly costumed and masked, was privileged by custom to approach the man she found most appealing, and the young consul soon found himself enjoying the companionship of a girl "with a lovely figure and a sweet voice." But trouble lurked outside in the person of a jealous suitor, a reserve army officer of properly hot Hungarian blood.

When La Guardia and his enchanting anonymous companion left the ballroom for a late supper, the aggrieved swain rushed up and tried to tear the girl's mask off. Unsure of local custom in this regard, but feeling "I owed the lady protection, I shot a right hook to the gentleman's chin, which accidentally landed properly and he sprawled in the street."

That episode could have served as a first-act curtain scene, for the affair was thereafter played out like a Strauss operetta, fraught with portents of doom but evolving toward its inevitable happy ending. Within days, seconds of the lovelorn young officer had called on La Guardia and announced that the affront to their principal required satisfaction. He was challenging La Guardia to a duel.

"What's that?" La Guardia asked, bemused.

A duel, they repeated, with swords. Would he kindly name his seconds? And so the preliminaries were solemnized, seemingly inexorably bound for a fatal encounter on the field of honor at five the following morning. La Guardia, who thought it all ridiculous but was constitutionally incapable of turning his back on a fight, named his seconds, one the Turkish rake and the other a scholarly Hungarian civil servant named Radmonovic, who had been coaching him in German. Reluctantly he acceded to Radmonovic's urging that he get some fencing instruction.

Before dawn the following morning, as bidden, he appeared at the Café Grande. His challenger and the four seconds were already waiting. They all stood and bowed to him. He bowed back. Someone handed him a stiff cognac, which he downed manfully, and gave him some papers to sign. Then the offended Hungarian signed. Then the two were told to shake hands. Then all the seconds shook hands, first with the principals, then with each other. La Guardia, unnerved by this apparently mindless ritual, asked where they were supposed to go.

"Home," replied Radmonovic. "It's all over."

La Guardia, more than willing to call the whole thing off, was nonetheless stunned by the abrupt turnabout. He sank into a chair while someone read out the signed documents. They said, in Hungarian and Italian, that the gallantry of the gentlemen in question in electing to resolve their difference by the sword, their exemplary behavior up to this moment in all matters of the code duello, had, of itself, provided full satisfaction. The grievance could be purged from memory; honor had been served. And the surprise ending, yet to come, was eminently suited to this comic libretto. For the fair lady was won by neither of the two principals. Sometime later, having been introduced to the studious Radmonovic by La Guardia, she decided to marry *him.*

La Guardia had now spent three years in Fiume and felt restless. His mother would remind him that he was in an enviable position—he was, after all, an official of the American government and earning a steady $15 a week—but she could see his gathering dissatisfaction. For young La Guardia was taking stock, searching into the future of a consular agent in his situation, and he saw no great promise there. Without a formal education, with neither money nor an influential sponsor, he could not realistically aspire to more than a functionary's job in the foreign service. It was true that he had a gift for language, but that was only a tool, a means to an end. He wanted to be doing important work; he was ready for responsibility, ready to change things. So far, all his worldly experiences had only confirmed the instincts of his boyhood—that life is a struggle in which the odds are stacked against the little people. He had always understood which side he was on, and now he was ready to join up. But he felt himself unprepared. And he recognized the insidious forces tugging him the other way—"the danger of becoming self-satisfied, not too industrious, and of acquiring too much of a taste for idle social life."

In March 1906, with one make-or-break decision, La Guardia took the future into his own two hands. In a characteristically undiplomatic letter to the State Department, he asked to be appointed consul general in Belgrade, then the capital of Serbia: "If knowledge of the language and six years service are not sufficient to counterbalance (my) total lack of political influence, the undersigned begs for a special examination or appointment to a post within the United States. . . . If none of the above can be granted, there is no doubt that this service is not the place for a young man to work up."

Not unexpectedly, none of the above was granted. La Guardia resigned at once and prepared to return to America. His mother begged him to reconsider—where else would he find such a good job? But he had a vision of a grander prize, still undefined but worth every risk. He told Irene that if he stayed he would be no better off at sixty-five than he was now. "I'm going back to become a lawyer, Mother." It was the first time he had ever said those words aloud. They heartened him. "I'm going to make something of myself!"

Early in June he sailed on the Cunard steamer *Ultonia,* paying for his passage by working as a steward and interpreter. A family friend got him a job in a brick factory in southern Ohio, but finding no opportunity to study there, he left after a few weeks. And so it was still summer when he returned to New York, the city of his birth, the city of his destiny. It was stifling hot, as only New York can be in August, and it seemed absolutely indifferent to his fate. But La Guardia would remember the exhilaration of that homecoming until the day he died. He had only a few dollars in his pocket, but "I had a definite plan worked out for my future. I wanted to complete my education, get admitted to the bar and then enter public service."

4 ✱
THE PEOPLE'S LAWYER

La Guardia's first job in New York was with the Society for the Prevention of Cruelty to Children. He was hired on a temporary basis to translate the juveniles section of the French penal code into English—why, no one told him. The salary was only $10 a week but for the time being he was glad to have it. He had returned on the eve of another economic crisis and no one was vying to hire a twenty-four-year-old ex-consular agent with no business skills or commercial experience.

He had also found a place to live, a small room in the home of Mrs. Charles Kohler, a long-ago friend of his mother who was still at the same address, a short stroll from the old La Guardia tenement on Varick Street. Twenty-one years after he'd left as a toddler, La Guardia was back in Greenwich Village.

As it happened, Mrs. Kohler's son Charlie was just beginning a career in politics—not surprisingly in Democratic New York City, with Tammany Hall—and there were some lively arguments between the idealistic newcomer and the worldly young precinct worker. But they remained good friends—"though Charlie became a Tammany leader and I put him out of business," La Guardia later wrote—and Mrs. Kohler was to worry about her boarder working too hard and eating too little for years to come.

When his translating job came to an end, La Guardia found work as a clerk with a steamship company. But he was dissatisfied, a lifelong condition, and quit to invest $7.50 in a shorthand course. After six weeks he was good enough to get a job with Abercrombie & Fitch as a stenographer. The pay was $20 a week, a reasonable wage in those days.

Meanwhile he had taken a civil service test for appointment as an interpreter at Ellis Island, the U.S. immigration center, his knowledge of Italian, German and Croatian giving him a boost on the eligibility list. He was also catching up with his education. For as he learned to his very considerable ire when he applied for admission to law school, the State of New York would not recognize his Arizona school credits. This meant he would have to take special examinations to establish his qualification for law school, and *this* meant he would have to cram a lot of miscellaneous information into his head in a short time. He signed up with a preparatory academy that specialized in just such crises— "They poured the stuff into us as fast as any individual could absorb it," he recalled—and he passed state exams in time to be admitted to the law school of New York University, evening session, for the fall semester. A few weeks later, early in November 1907, he received word that he had won appointment to the Immigration Service as an interpreter at $1,200 a year. He would be able to pursue his studies relatively free of financial pressure.

That year, 1.3 million immigrants came to America, 300,000 from Italy alone—more than the population of the city of Venice. Although the authorities had set 5,000 as the maximum number of people who could be processed at Ellis Island in a single day, there were days that year of 1907 when as many as 15,000 were put ashore. The preponderant number, 80 percent, were under forty-five, young enough for daydreams, old enough to know how easily the vagaries of the bureaucracy could crush their hopes.

They were crowded and jostled into lines in the shadow of the red brick buildings, hearts in their throats. Clutching children and the possessions of the first half of their lives, they were marched up an echoing iron staircase to the massive main hall, where they would learn whether they were to be allowed to bring their aspirations to this shining new world, America.

They began filing past the doctors, trying to suppress a cough, pinching children's cheeks to banish the pallor of the long steerage journey. Some, one out of every five or six, were marked with a chalk letter on the lapel or sleeve—*H* for heart irregularity, *L* for limp, *X* for suspicion of a mental defect—and held for further examination. The others were separated by nationality and questioned by inspectors who might have had no more than a rough knowledge of their language.

Are you a polygamist? Do you have a job? Money? Who is meeting you?

And the immigrants, now so close but filled with fresh terrors of rejection by every interrogation, struggled to understand and frame an acceptable answer. "Yes, yes, I have a job," many instinctively replied, ignorant of the quicksand into which they were venturing: One provision of the immigration law excluded contract laborers, those who had been solicited to come here by offers of work; but another section barred immigrants without prospects of a job on the ground that they were likely to become public charges.

A pregnant woman trailing four small children says her husband has been in America fifteen years, certain this will impress the inspector. She is heedless of the obvious impression, unaware that a charge of moral turpitude is enough to send her back.

Some inspectors are understanding. "Think it over," they say. "Take your time." And the immigrant, bewildered, stuttering with fear, finally utters the right words and is waved through.

It was, according to a contemporary journalist, the nearest thing on earth to Judgment Day, "when we have to prove our fitness to enter Heaven."

Every morning, seven days a week, La Guardia took the subway to the Battery at the southernmost tip of Manhattan, and there caught the 8:40 government ferry to Ellis Island. "It was a constant grind," he said, "from the moment we got into our uniforms in the morning until the last minute before we left on the 5:30 boat in the evening." Then he had to rush home and prepare for his law school classes at night.

Apart from the hard work, La Guardia was sorely tried by the callousness and corruption to which he was routinely exposed. He was no innocent, having seen for himself a dazzling range of depravity in Europe. But that America was no different—that after the sweeping exposures he had read about as a boy, there was still an army of petty officeholders, policemen and judges ready to sell out for a price—saddened and infuriated him. Anna Kross, a law school classmate who was to become a city magistrate, remembered his explosive accounts of transgressions nobody even bothered to hide from him. "But he was always positive that the city *could* be run honestly and well," she said, "and that he would have a hand in making it happen."

Occasionally he was assigned to conduct a couple into Manhattan to be married. Typically, the bride-to-be had crossed the ocean to join her fiancé in America at his urgent entreaty—arriving to learn that the planned wedding had to take place at once, because she could be admitted to the United States only as the wife of a resident.

Enter La Guardia, charged with serving as interpreter, chaperon and custodian until he could certify that matrimonial bonds had been tied. He would lead the couple, and perhaps a straggle of friends or relatives, to City Hall, where a license was issued. In the basement a coterie of city aldermen sprawled in the available chairs, often passing a bottle as they waited. The legislature had given these Tammany ward heelers the legal right to perform marriages and they had turned it into a small sideline worth around $30,000 a year. The official fee for the service was $2; but it was no trick for a bullying official, flaunting the mantle of authority, to extract sometimes ten times that amount from nervous, easily intimidated immigrants.

Not infrequently, the presiding alderman and his cronies made a mockery of the ceremony with raucous, filthy language and lewd references to the bride which sent them all into paroxysms of drunken laughter. La Guardia, who could sometimes protect his charges from the extortion practiced by these "red-faced, cheap, tinhorn politicians," was helpless against their vulgarity; nor was there much he could say to the couple that would redeem this degrading introduction to America.

In April 1910, he wrote to the commissioner of immigration to explain why he deserved a salary increase: "I am the only Italian interpreter speaking and using other languages ... the only interpreter you have who is a stenographer and the only stenographer who is a linguist. ..."

The commissioner, unable to resist this inexorable logic, recommended La Guardia for a promotion and a raise to $1,380 a year. "Mr. La Guardia," he reported, "is energetic, intelligent and familiar with a number of foreign languages. Against him there may be said that he is inclined to be peppery ... argumentative, but he has been spoken to about this and it is not a defect of the first order."

That year, La Guardia was transferred to Magistrate's Night Court, a post that allowed him to do his final year of law school at the regular day session. It also exposed him to another underside of New York life. His job was to act as interpreter for immigrants in trouble with the law—and the only trouble dealt with in Night Court was commercialized vice. It was also his duty to find out from *all* prisoners, thirty or forty a night, mainly pimps and prostitutes, where they had been born and how long they had been in the United States. For the immigration code was explicit: Aliens with fewer than five years' residence who broke the law were to be deported.

He was detailed to the White Slave Division of the Immigration Service, whose chief inspector was a disheveled, cerebral, uncompromising iconoclast named Andrew Tedesco. Right at the outset, Tedesco, who knew where all the bodies were buried, took La Guardia aside for some advice: "You can get experience on this job or you can make a lot of money. I don't think you'll take the money. But remember: The test is if you hesitate. Unless you say 'No!' right off, the first time an offer comes your way, you're lost." La Guardia never forgot that. He turned it into a political maxim and throughout his career pelted everyone who worked for him with it. In public service, he would say, what counts is your first, instinctive reaction to dishonesty.

In the seamy new world he now entered, where huge profits were built on poverty—the exploitation of ignorant, destitute women—where the law was subverted by those sworn to uphold it and you could bribe a policeman for $5 or a judge for $500, nothing was what it seemed. Arrests were made to fill up the police blotter, but nobody went to prison; fines were levied so judges would be perceived as careful guardians of the law, but the penalty was a pittance compared to reapings from the illicit trade. Patrol wagons pulled up to Night Court regularly—on Saturday nights, hourly—and disgorged their haul of gaudily dressed and half-dressed girls. Within the hour, the girls were back on their backs.

One night early in La Guardia's tour, the familiar scene took an unexpected turn. As the girls piled out of the paddy wagon there were urgent, worried whisperings between them and their waiting lawyers. Their studied nonchalance suddenly turned to anger, and the policemen who had brought them in, struck dumb by embarrassment, fell to digging money out of their pockets. Everybody in Night Court knew what was happening, except La Guardia. He had to ask.

"Jailing judge," a more experienced hand told him, and the terse answer explained everything. A last-minute substitution had put a maverick on the bench that night in place of the judge whose reliability had been bought and paid for. The girls were going to do thirty days in the workhouse; the cops were having to pay back their bribes.

By 1910, white slavery—the organized importation and employment of foreign women as prostitutes—was fading. Enactment of the Mann Act that June made it a federal offense to transport women across state lines "for immoral purposes"; there were new teeth in the immigration law, and to most aliens, not even prison was so dire a threat as deportation. So, in the face of last-ditch resistance by some of New York's respected institutions, Tedesco and his White Slave Division had closed up brothels and squeezed out red light districts all over New York City. Of course prostitution of the home-grown variety continued to flourish with the blessings of cops and local courts, as La Guardia saw every day. And that, Tedesco pointed out to him, was just the visible tip of corruption. No illegal enterprise as widespread as prostitution could exist without the complicity of powerful interests in the city—hotels, nightclubs, politicians, lawyers, bail bondsmen—all of whom shared in the substantial returns from systematized vice. But Tedesco and his people were not among them.

La Guardia gave three full years to the Immigration Service and "never became callous to the mental anguish, the disappointments and the despair I witnessed almost daily." Meanwhile, he plodded on toward his law degree, fighting sleep as he tried to study after nine hours of work and three hours of classes. Often his day ended well past midnight when Mrs. Kohler, worrying about his health, marched into his room, turned down the gas lamp, and commanded him to go to sleep.

Given this arduous program, it is hardly surprising that La

Guardia set no new academic records at N.Y.U.; in his three years there, he earned two A's, one B—and just passed his other fourteen courses with grades of C and D. But pass he did, and was awarded his law degree in June 1910. Four months later he was admitted to the bar. On the same day, he quit the Immigration Service and, with his last two weeks' pay in his pocket, rented office space from a law firm on William Street, set a small plaster bust of Napoleon on the desk, and went to work as a lawyer.

Nothing that happened to La Guardia in those fledgling years changed his generally low opinion of lawyers and judges. He quickly saw that it did not, as he put it, "injure any lawyer to know the judge," but he could never bring himself to do the necessary toadying. Once, a judge who had just decided a case against him took time to compliment him on his careful preparation and forceful argument. Stunned, La Guardia said, "Well, if I did so well, why didn't you decide in my favor?"

"Oh, listen, young man," the judge laughed, "I'll give *you* a break some other day."

What a hell of a way to dispense justice, La Guardia all but cried out.

In only a short time he experienced the whole range of judicial incompetence: ignorance of the law, bias against a defendant or his attorney, and plain dishonesty. One judge took such an unmistakable dislike to him that La Guardia felt obliged to tell the jury to ignore His Honor's attitude and remarks. But His Honor browbeat the jury into bringing in a guilty verdict against La Guardia's client and then imposed an unusually harsh sentence.

In another case, La Guardia was representing a woman injured by the negligence of a trolley car motorman. Waiting in the corridor while the jury retired to weigh the evidence, he saw the judge stop on his way to chambers to talk with the trolley line lawyer. "Was it all right, Joe?" the judge asked, completely ignoring La Guardia, who was within easy earshot. Then he went on: "Well, don't worry. If they decide against you, I'll just set the verdict aside."

La Guardia once considered publishing a *Who's Who* of

judges' legal secretaries, since, as everyone knew, they were often
the key to a favorable verdict. They had the political contacts,
made recommendations, and were a real power behind the bench.
And though they were paid around $10,000 a year at a time when
judges themselves drew not much more, they knew little about
the law. What they knew, as La Guardia caustically noted, was
the district leader.

He soon found that most people who consulted a lawyer
either had no real need for one or no case, but he seemed to be the
only lawyer around who ever said that to a client. "Save yourself
some money—try to settle this yourself," was his most frequently
offered advice. He did not regard lawyering as a business. His
job was to help people and if, as not infrequently happened, the
people who came to him with their troubles could not afford to
pay his fee, he lowered it, or represented them for no fee at all.
He was motivated as much by calculation as altruism. The practice of law was never meant to be an end in itself for La Guardia;
it was a tool, like his knowledge of languages, a stepping-stone
toward what he really wanted: a career in public service. And the
friends he made now among housewives, workingmen, poor immigrants—his natural constituency—might become his supporters in the future.

When he found a lawyer who felt as he did, Raimondo Canudo, he opened an office with him on the Lower East Side to
deal only with immigration problems. In 1914 he joined two Jewish lawyers in still another partnership, and was soon consulting
with clients in good idiomatic Yiddish. But there was a more significant consequence to his association with the firm of Weil, La
Guardia & Espen. He was assigned the most junior of the three
secretaries in the office, a slim, blond, eighteen-year-old native
New Yorker named Marie Fisher, who quickly got the hang of
coping with his outbursts and galvanic energy and was thereafter close by for the rest of his life.

By this time La Guardia had moved into his own four-room
apartment at 39 Charles Street, just a few blocks north of the old
neighborhood. But he was not one to sit home alone contemplat-
ing the future; as far as he was concerned, the future was right
now. Through a client, he was invited to join a regular gathering
of lively young people on the fashionable Upper East Side—

writers, artists and professionals who met for a Sunday evening buffet and debated the issues of the moment. Inevitably, La Guardia dominated the conversation and presided at supper. "He let me cut the bread—that's all," said George Baehr, a young doctor who was to become La Guardia's personal physician and adviser in the fields of public health and hospitals.

Another member of the circle was the best-selling novelist-to-be Fannie Hurst, recently arrived from St. Louis. She wrote about meeting La Guardia, "a black-haired, sloe-eyed, fiery little fellow," of whom the hostess said, "Let me introduce you to the next mayor of New York." They became fast friends. La Guardia gave the struggling young writer a good grounding in Italian cooking and street politics, and took her to Ellis Island and Night Court, where there was a whole new world of raw material for her stories.

Through his partner Raimondo Canudo, who also edited a weekly newspaper for Sicilian immigrants, La Guardia came to know a remarkable group of Italian-born intellectuals and idealists, most of them his Greenwich Village neighbors: sculptor Attilio Piccirilli, whose epic monument to the men killed aboard the U.S.S. *Maine* was unveiled in Columbus Circle around that time; Onorio Ruotolo, a twentieth-century renaissance man who sculpted, painted and wrote poetry; the New York Philharmonic Symphony flutist Giovanni Fabrizio; August Bellanca, a crusading labor organizer; and his brother Giuseppe, who—less than ten years after the Wright brothers—built an airplane and taught himself to fly.

This captivated La Guardia at once. When Giuseppe, determined to design and build bigger and better airplanes, organized his own company, La Guardia became a director. The other participants were, as he had it, "about twenty-five cooks and waiters who put in $100 each." La Guardia also did the company's legal work and took his fees in flying lessons. Bellanca had cleared a grassy field outside the shed in Mineola, Long Island, where he was building another plane, and that was his flying school. The summer of 1915, La Guardia was its most persistent novitiate.

The plane on which he learned to fly, Bellanca's first, had room for only the student pilot, who sat in the open, all alone, on a longitudinal brace trying to remember all his instructions.

There was no one to turn to for help if he forgot. Courage was the essential ingredient. The little Anzani engine was rated at 30 horsepower, but had to be wheedled into delivering 15. No one ventured aloft if there was any wind, but who could guarantee one wouldn't spring up between takeoff and landing? Nonetheless, after weeks of ground runs, getting down to turn the plane around, then taxiing back; after more weeks of lifting the craft a tentative twenty or thirty feet in the air and immediately landing, La Guardia was finally allowed to fly enough to circle the field.

"I was not much of a flyer," he said of this new skill, but it would ordain an important turning in his life.

August Bellanca drew him into the struggle of fledgling needle-trade unions and their members for a living wage and a forty-eight-hour week.

By then, New York City was already the world's busiest clothing manufacturing center, its garment trade a big, booming industry employing nearly 250,000 people. "One could never rise so early in the morning nor go to bed so late at night that he would not hear the hum of some sewing machine," wrote Jacob Riis of the factories and tenements of lower Manhattan, which he described as "a big gangway through an endless workroom where vast multitudes are forever laboring."

Nearly all of them were newly arrived immigrants, obliged to take whatever wage was offered and to work ten, sometimes twelve, hours a day in dirty, dangerous sweatshops. There was no one to help them. Employers were interested in profits. The almost all-white, all-male American Federation of Labor, to which 80 percent of unionized Americans belonged, barred foreign-born workers altogether.

Great fortunes were made on this exploitation of labor, and enough of the gains spilled over to satisfy the metropolitan establishment with the status quo. When 20,000 dress and shirtwaist makers, all women, finally organized themselves and went out on strike, in November 1909, Tammany police joined hired thugs in charging their picket lines and beating and arresting any who protested. Before the end of the year, 707 women had been hauled into court, and a judge, sentencing one to the workhouse, solemnly told her, "You are on strike against God."

The women persevered all through that bitter winter but won only the promise of a fifty-two-hour week—not recognition of their union, not a wage increase. Nor did working conditions improve. Barely a year later, on March 25, 1911, a fire swept through the eighth, ninth and tenth floors of the Triangle Shirtwaist Company and 164 workers, mostly women and girls, burned to death or were killed when they threw themselves out of windows to escape the flames. Investigation revealed that firemen's ladders could reach only to the seventh floor, although 500,000 New Yorkers worked at higher levels; that the building had no fire escapes or emergency exits; and that, contrary to law, workroom doors were locked so an employee would have to ask permission to go to the bathroom.

In December 1912, sixty-five thousand men's clothing workers, who labored sixty hours a week for a salary between $5 and $14.50, went out on strike. The employers, who had already had some success pitting the two major ethnic groups in the needle trades, the Jews and the Italians, against each other, now tried to break their strike by launching rumors in both camps that one was selling the other out.

The union needed special help to fight this tactic, someone to explain to the strikers, in their own language, what was happening and what their rights were, a lawyer who wasn't afraid to go up against the establishment to fight picket cases. August Bellanca, head of the Italian section of the germinal groupings that would become the Amalgamated Clothing Workers of America, knew such a man: his friend La Guardia. When asked for his support, La Guardia joined up without hesitating.

It was a cause he could make his own with full feeling, and he went from one storefront or street-corner meeting to another, explaining in ringing, colorfully flawed Italian and Yiddish how important it was for the workers to stand together. The workers listened to this flamboyant young *cowboy* (he had taken to wearing a string bow tie and ten-gallon Stetson to advertise his Arizona origins), this *lawyer* who said he cared about them, this *American* who spoke the language of the old country—and they were captivated.

The leaders perceived him as a natural link between the two groups and used him more and more. He made the first major speech of his career at Cooper Union, where half a century be-

fore, Abraham Lincoln declared the right of the federal government to ban slavery in the territories. It was a freezing cold day,
but a capacity crowd turned out, and when La Guardia exhorted
them—in Italian, Yiddish and English—to forget their prejudices and fight together for their common good, strangers embraced and everyone cheered wildly.

He spent all his nights with the union leadership planning
strategy. By day, when he wasn't making a speech, he was in
court defending pickets. Once he even joined a picket line and
defied the police to arrest him; he would be glad to go into court
with them, he called, to find out under what law they had the
right to interfere with peaceful picketing. But they wouldn't
oblige. They had been told about this La Guardia and didn't necessarily want to tangle with him.

La Guardia loved it. In one of those breathtaking understatements he occasionally unburdened himself of, he said, "I enjoyed the work immensely, for it gave me a greater sense of
accomplishment than routine court work, which might be more
remunerative but was less important."

What was there not to like about it? He had gone into the
strike an absolute unknown and won a reputation as a natural
leader. He gloried in the limelight. He relished taking on the socialist ideologues among his allies; a strong union, he argued,
working within the traditional two-party system, was the workingman's best hope, not some Marxist daydream that ran counter
to man's nature.

When the time came to choose the workers' committee to negotiate a settlement, La Guardia was one of the three men named.
The settlement was not perfect—a fifty-three-hour week and a
raise of $1—but it was regarded as a victory, and La Guardia,
having all but forsaken his clients for four months, gained an
army of supporters.

The next step was predictable. La Guardia, who had taken to
reading *The Congressional Record* the way other men read the
sports pages, decided to run for Congress. He had been an active
member of the Madison Square Republican Club of the 25th
Assembly District since 1907, faithfully appearing at mind-
numbing procedural meetings, neighborhood christenings, bar

mitzvahs, weddings and funerals. He accepted his Election Day poll-watching assignments without complaint; he did the bidding of the district captains like a loyal organization man. He seemed, in fact, to be just another party hack, hard-working and brighter than most, but content to play a minor role in the city's minority party. No one in the 25th A.D. suspected the scope of his aspirations.

Why the ambitious La Guardia, son of a Jewish mother and an Italian father, joined the Republicans, the party of Anglo-Saxon, old-line America, is a game of speculation that anyone can play. Was it, as one journalist put it, his instinct for lost causes and forlorn hopes? Was it a purely political perception— that New York's also-ran Republicans might shrug and let the sons of the new immigrants have a chance, whereas the leadership of that Irish monopoly, the Democratic party, was closed to outsiders? There is likely truth in both suppositions. But La Guardia once made the overriding reason utterly clear: "I joined the Republican party," he wrote in his autobiographical fragment, "because I could not stomach Tammany Hall."

The 25th Assembly District was a mile-square tangle of neighborhoods in the center of lower Manhattan, home base of Tammany leader Charlie Murphy. It encompassed the northwest corner of Greenwich Village; at its heart were thousands of poor and middle-class families, but its image was one part the Bohemian trappings of intellectual revolt, one part Washington Square chic. The Irish ruled the district from their West Side bastion, sent their children to parochial school, and worried about the Italians marrying their daughters. The Jews and Italians, the city's largest ethnic minorities, shared the same tenements and public schools—as well as the scorn of the Nordics —but their fundamental suspicions kept them in separate spiritual ghettos.

By 1914, La Guardia had learned all this, and more. Having covered the district block by block, he knew it as well as anyone in the Madison Square Republican Club. His political education was further advanced by two clubhouse regulars, Louis Espresso and Harry Andrews, neither of whom had any illusions about politics or, for that matter, anything that would pass for a political philosophy; they just knew that the winners got the gravy.

Politics was a game and they prided themselves on playing it well. They saw the promise in La Guardia and became his friends and sponsors. They introduced him to the local leaders, lectured him on which issues mattered in the 25th A.D.—jobs and the rights of minority groups—and escorted him to social gatherings all over the district.

But of course La Guardia was never dependent on others to represent him. Soon he had the ear of the Republican Club boss, Frederick C. Tanner; on September 15, 1911, Tanner was writing the chairman of the New York County Republican Committee to recommend La Guardia for a post on the staff of District Attorney Charles S. Whitman: "I wish to give you information regarding Mr. Fiorello H. La Guardia, who is a bright young lawyer and has done good service in my district. . . ."

That job didn't materialize, but La Guardia worked on and, after he came to prominence in the garment workers' strike, aimed even higher. There is a charming bit of folklore to the effect that he won the 1914 congressional nomination from the 14th District because he "just happened" to be in the clubhouse when the boys were looking for a candidate. But La Guardia rarely "just happened" to do anything. The fact is that he had already written Tanner to give notice that "I am out for the nomination for Congress–14th District. This is my official declaration."

Of course he knew full well that if he did get the nomination, it would only be because it was absolutely without value. The 14th was a Tammany stronghold; never in its history had the Republicans elected a congressman. And so their designation usually went to a contributor or some aging leader who was willing to be bowled over by the Tammany machine in exchange for a few weeks of local celebrity.

But La Guardia looked at the swelling Italian and Jewish population in the 14th and thought he had an advantage the others didn't. Speaking of some election districts overwhelmingly inhabited by new voters, he told Tanner, "Hardly a family down there has not a member, a relative or a friend in the tailoring industry. I am well known in those circles. . . ."

But common sense is not indispensable to the political process and the nomination was given to someone else, a physician who had presented the party with a handsome check. As it happened, the good doctor turned out to be smarter than "the boys"; he declined. And that fateful summer night, when the acting leader came out of the back room and yelled, "Who wants to run for Congress?" La Guardia was ready.

"I do!" he yelled back.

"Okay, put La Guardia down."

It was almost as simple as that. But the man assigned to fill out the nominating petition asked, "What's the first name?" and when La Guardia told him, flung down his pen and groaned, "Oh, hell, let's at least get somebody whose name we can spell."

But La Guardia had come too close to be turned back now. He walked up to the desk and said, "I am going to spell my name for you. Listen: F-I-O-R-E-L-L-O-L-A-capital-G-U-A-R-D-I-A." And the nomination was his.

He had full-time help from Louis Espresso and Harry Andrews, but to the rest of the Republican organization he was the invisible candidate. At the first big election rally all the candidates were introduced and made a speech—except La Guardia. He couldn't believe it. Every time the chairman said, "And now we will hear from a young and promising candidate," he stood up. But it was never his name that was called. Afterward, when he asked why, the leaders had a good laugh. "Because you haven't got a chance of winning," he was told, not unkindly.

"Could I try?"

The smiles faded. "Fiorello, don't be foolish," said one. "You just go out now and help the others, and some day you may get a nomination for an office you can win."

Realizing he was on his own, La Guardia bought himself a secondhand Ford for $100, plastered it with campaign posters, and covered hundreds of miles riding the length and breadth of the 14th Congressional District, which ran from the Hudson to the East River between 3rd Street and 14th Street. His friend Attilio Piccirilli provided the campaign headquarters, the ground floor of a building on Sixth Avenue owned by the Piccirilli family. Plenty of volunteers offered to help, but apart from Espresso and Andrews, enthusiasm was their biggest asset. They were rained on, showered with abuse and overripe vegetables by Tammany toughs, and more than one La Guardia rally ended in a brawl.

None of this discouraged the candidate, who seemed to be making an all-out effort to be everywhere at once. He pounded up and down tenement stairs, knocked on doors, shook hands, spoke on street corners in five languages, stood on the hood of his Ford waving his arms to attract a crowd from among those leaving regularly scheduled meetings. He defended the rights of labor and immigrant groups; he cited his contributions to the workers during the watershed strikes of recent years.

No Republican had ever waged such a campaign in the 14th. No Republican the people had ever seen even looked or sounded like this one—the son of Italian immigrants who could talk all the district's languages and knew about things that mattered: the cost of a chicken or a piece of meat, the exploitation of working people by bosses and landlords who lived in fancy apartments uptown while here there were slums and firetraps for people to live in.

In other circumstances, his energy and intelligence would have overwhelmed his opponent, a lackluster Tammany regular and saloonkeeper named Michael Farley who didn't even bother to campaign. La Guardia handled him so roughly that some Republican leaders warned him against disparaging a sitting congressman. To which the irrepressible La Guardia replied, "I did not disparage him. I merely pointed out that he was not a good congressman and wasn't even a good bartender."

In the end he didn't win. The Tammany machine was too slick; it could call on platoons of hangers-on, some of whom voted more times in a single election than most people vote in a lifetime. But in the face of his own party's stunning indifference to his fate, he cut Farley's plurality from 6,000 to 1,700 and staggered the pros by himself winning more votes than any Republican candidate had ever rung up in the 14th District.

The Republicans were more concerned than the Democrats. How were they going to control this wild man now?

They weren't. La Guardia, thirty-two years old and with the taste of blood still in his mouth, immediately began preparing for the 1916 congressional election.

PART II
WASHINGTON, D.C.

5 ❧
GOING TO CONGRESS

One evening in 1913 the young assemblyman from Greenwich Village, Jimmy Walker, was summoned to the presence of Charles F. Murphy, grand sachem of Tammany Hall, and told he was under consideration for advancement to the state senate. "I am greatly flattered," was his response.

Murphy regarded the slender, dandily attired Walker with world-weary eyes. "I flatter nobody," he said, "and I advise *you* to treat flattery as you would abuse—pay no attention."

Charles Francis Murphy was the best and most enlightened leader Tammany ever had. It is true that he managed to acquire a $2 million estate in the job, which carried no salary, but he also kept more loyal Democrats in office and at work than had any predecessor, and prepared such principled men as Alfred E. Smith and Robert F. Wagner for high public office.

Politics was his sole interest in life, and as the saying went, he didn't bring much to a party. He did not marry until he was forty-four, did not make small talk and, in the belief that an air of mystery enhanced power, rarely said anything at all to underlings except to announce his decisions. Once, at a Tammany Fourth of July celebration, a journalist noted that the leader had not joined in singing "The Star-Spangled Banner" and asked an aide why. The subordinate shrugged and said, "Maybe he doesn't want to commit himself."

But the thing about Murphy was that he was as good as his word, and in the same election in which La Guardia lost so narrowly to Mike Farley, Jimmy Walker, thirty-three, was easily elected to the New York State Senate.

Franklin D. Roosevelt had left it two years before, his rise even less open to question than Walker's. At twenty-nine, a senate freshman, he had led a revolt of reform Democrats against Boss Murphy's selection for the Democratic nomination to the

71

U.S. Senate—and won. He split with Murphy again in 1912, supporting New Jersey Governor Woodrow Wilson for the presidential nomination, while Tammany backed House Speaker Champ Clark. Again Roosevelt won.

All this was called to Wilson's attention after his victory, as was Roosevelt's lofty background, and early in 1913 the New Yorker was summoned to the governor's office in Trenton, New Jersey, for a conference with the President-elect. Patronage matters were discussed, and in time young Roosevelt was offered the post of collector of the Port of New York, a politically powerful vantage point. He declined. "All my life I have loved ships and been a student of the Navy," he told Wilson's emissary, "and the assistant secretaryship is the one place, above all others, I would love to hold."

The offer was duly made and in March the new assistant secretary of the Navy arrived in Washington to take up his duties.

The election of Charles S. Whitman to the governor's mansion in Albany in 1914 was the quid pro quo of the tacit agreement between the parties whereby Tammany rule was only nominally challenged in New York City. Among other, more important considerations, it gave New York County Republican leaders an opportunity to do something for their young rebel La Guardia in hopes of keeping him in tow. He was offered appointment as a New York State deputy attorney general. When he accepted, one could almost hear a collective sigh of relief at the 25th A.D. Republican Club.

It was premature. La Guardia took his new job seriously and went to work at it with full vigor. He was incapable of anything else. He even brought Marie Fisher over from Weil, La Guardia & Espen to continue as his secretary. But he never regarded the attorney general's office as more than a temporary assignment, a hiatus between the election he had just lost and the one he meant to win. Furthermore, though the main work of the state attorney general was in Albany, and the New York City branch—staffed with deputies who usually showed up only to collect their pay—had turned into a dead letter office, La Guardia naïvely began prosecuting cases long insulated by political privilege. One, as we have seen, brought State Senator James J.

Walker into court on behalf of his friends the meat packers; testifying against his own weights and measures law, Walker single-handedly destroyed the state's case. "I already knew how politicians helped their friends," said La Guardia, shaken by the experience. "I just never realized before how far-reaching special privilege and favors really went."

But he was not disheartened and pressed on. With Marie's help, he went through six file cabinets and a couple of trunks filled with studies, reports and unfiled briefs relating to the noxious fumes which were emitted by factories in New Jersey and then drifted across the Hudson to cause stinging eyes and throat irritations up and down Riverside Drive in Manhattan. This had been going on for so long that La Guardia was astonished nothing had been done about it. His research showed that a direct action against the offending companies could be filed in the United States Supreme Court, "so one day I went down to Washington and filed seven complaints in the name of the State of New York against the New Jersey corporations which we charged with maintaining the nuisance."

The roof fell in. Within days La Guardia was called on the carpet for "proceeding so precipitately"—although he had discussed the case with his superior, and the attorney general himself had signed the complaints. He was told to take no further action in the matter.

What had happened? A typical political chain reaction. La Guardia's suit had annoyed the highly influential New Jersey corporations, whose officers contacted some Albany political powers, who gained the ear of Governor Whitman—who gave the attorney general the word to back off. Case closed.

Next La Guardia was sent out to Riverhead, Long Island, a hundred miles from Greenwich Village, to try some fishermen for taking underage scallops, an infringement of the state's conservation law. But the damage the individual fishermen did was petty compared to that of the big oyster companies, whch leased vast tracts of Long Island Sound and Great South Bay and used tugs and mechanized gear to dredge up all the oysters, clams and scallops in their path. La Guardia put aside his pending cases against the fishermen "and went out to try my first big oyster company case."

When the company's attorneys asked for a postponement, he was sure he had them good and worried. When this was followed by four subsequent postponements, *he* began to worry. Finally, though, the case was called to trial and La Guardia stood up to cite the uncomplicated law under which he intended to prosecute: "No scallop under one year of age shall be taken." Whereupon a company lawyer flashed a telegram from Albany; the scallop law had just been materially changed, he announced triumphantly, by the addition of three simple words: "in public waters."

Once more La Guardia had been done in by "the interests"—and so had the little fishermen. Clever lawyers had stalled the case long enough for an obliging legislature to rewrite the law in the companies' favor. Individual fishermen, who had to work in public waters, would still be constrained; but the big companies, which fished in leased—hence *private*—coastal waters, could go on doing as they pleased.

Now La Guardia saw why so many deputy attorneys general simply put in their time. Beaten, broken, they were sucked into the system and learned to live with it. He couldn't. "To raise a howl and kick brands one an insurgent, but it was how I managed to survive," he said. "I left the attorney general's office much wiser and not so innocent as when I entered it."

Early in 1915, Irene La Guardia made the long journey from Budapest, where she now lived with Gemma and her husband, to visit her elder son. They had not seen each other in more than nine years and it may be that Irene, a diabetic, sensed there wasn't much more time. The reunion was filled with joy for both of them. The mother, who stayed at the Charles Street apartment, could not help but realize how far Fiorello had come, and how wide his future had opened; and the son, genuinely proud of having done what he said he was going to do when he sailed from Fiume in 1906, was gratified that his mother could see this for herself. Only a few months after her return to Budapest, Irene La Guardia died at the age of fifty-six.

The past is prologue. That year La Guardia met Thea Almerigotti, a beautiful girl, twenty-one years old, who had been born in Trieste, as had his mother. She worked in the garment district as a dress designer. Years afterward, Fannie Hurst recalled her as "Rossetti-like, porcelainlike, frail, blond and willowy." They were a study in contrasts, La Guardia dark-haired, black-eyed, shorter than Thea, beginning to thicken around the middle. But they fell in love and Louis Espresso was sure they were going to get married "as soon as Fiorello had the time." Thea understood this, too—that no one, nothing, could come before his personal goals and the work he had set himself to do. Preparing for the 1916 campaign, he was often at other people's weddings, neighborhood social events, meetings—functions that were part of the working life of a man in politics. She went when he invited her, and she waited.

Once, when La Guardia was in Washington on business, a congressman gave him a pass to the gallery of the House of Representatives, but he wouldn't go in. He was determined to walk out on the floor of the House as a member and had no interest in being there as a visitor. By then he already understood that he could not count on any help from the district Republicans; as far as they were concerned, the seat from the 14th Congressional District belonged to Tammany Hall. So La Guardia, with the help and encouragement of only a few believers—Andrews, Espresso, Piccirilli, Marie Fisher—spent a year and a half making ready for the 1916 campaign.

His interim strategy was predicated on the obvious, that he could not match the largesse of the Tammany machine. He had at his disposal neither jobs nor a bucket of free coal for anyone who wanted to come get it on a cold winter's day. What he had, and what he dispensed every weekend and after every working day at the attorney general's office, was legal advice and representation. He says his law office became "a regular Legal Aid Society," but it was also a sanctuary and court of human relations for the miserable and sometimes desperate people of his neighborhood: the pushcart peddler whose license had been confiscated by the police; the penniless iceman threatened with prison because his delivery wagon had knocked down a pedestrian; the shopkeeper whose wife wept day and night because she wanted to go back to the old country, where there was nothing for them.

Soon it was known all over the district that any poor man or woman who needed advice or a lawyer to take his case to court

could come to La Guardia and be helped. This was not only excellent politics, the engine that drove what would someday be
called the La Guardia machine, but as natural to La Guardia as
breathing. It seemed to an observer of the time that "the greatest
favor you can do this man is to come to him with a tale of injus-
tice and ask him to fight your battle for nothing."

Which is not to say that anyone was conceding the election
to him—if he ever got to run. For all at once, as he learned with a
stab of dismay when the time came to file nominating petitions,
the organization was preparing to designate someone else for the
congressional seat in the 14th C.D., despite La Guardia's spectacular run for it two years before. In fact, it was his good showing
that suddenly made the nomination worth having, and it appeared to have been promised to a young blueblood named Hamilton Fish, who lived in Putnam County, eighty miles from City
Hall. It seemed that Mr. Fish and his friends had made a substantial contribution to the Republicans' treasury. Furious,
fuming, La Guardia kept hearing the same refrain wherever he
turned for support: that it was for his own good—to be beaten
twice could finish his political career; that his day would come,
and meanwhile, his job was to soldier on.

One can imagine his retort. Finally he went to see his old
sponsor Fred Tanner, who had risen to become Republican state
chairman, and flatly declared that if the nomination he deserved
and had worked so hard to get went to some rich carpetbagger, he
was ready to contest it in the primary election. Tanner tried to
calm him with more platitudes about future considerations and
the virtues of patience—and then made the tactical error of saying that of course La Guardia could be reimbursed for the expense of printing his nominating petitions. La Guardia had
reached the end of his short fuse. He jumped to his feet, told
Tanner to go to hell, and charged for the door.

"Fiorello, hold your horses!" Tanner yelled after him.
"Damn it, if you want to run that badly, go ahead and run, but
don't blame me if you're licked again."

That took care of Hamilton Fish. La Guardia then assured
himself a second line on the ballot—and eliminated a candidate
who would have been courting the same voters—by entering the
primary of the third-party Progressives and winning it. And the
campaign was on.

Outwardly, it was no different from 1914—barnstorming in the Ford, the stump speeches, the gloves-off attacks on the still-impassive Mike Farley. But in fact the war in Europe, going into its third year, had changed everything. For the 14th, with its ethnic neighborhoods, some distinct, others mingled, was Europe in microcosm. And the war, intensifying national feelings, sharpened the conflicts between groups with irreconcilable interests. The Irish wanted Ireland free and prayed for England's defeat; the Italians wanted Trieste back, which could happen only if the Allies won and the Austro-Hungarian Empire was broken up. Jews, Poles, Germans, Hungarians, Rumanians—all had different causes; all were tugged in different directions.

And La Guardia, with his golden gift of language, his consular experience in the Balkans and the years at Ellis Island, navigated these potentially disastrous crosscurrents skillfully and profitably. He was not afraid to take on the incumbent among Farley's own countrymen, who considered the congressman fainthearted for the tepidity of his anti-British speeches. Besides, said La Guardia, "I know more about the history of Ireland than Mike Farley ever did."

But it was on the East Side, a turbulent slum where the castoffs of eastern and southern Europe had crowded into sunless, garbage-strewn, tenement-lined streets, that La Guardia had his most fervent supporters. There he "dismembered the Hapsburg Empire and liberated all the subjugated countries almost every night," as he recalled it. The Italians were told that any just peace must return Trieste to Italy, the Jews that the anti-Semitic tyranny of the Czars would end, and that they "and the whole of the Russian people" were to be free.

One constant was his conviction that new Americans had every right to a concern for what happened in their native lands. Elsewhere, the war had made this an unpopular stance and the loyalty of unassimilated immigrants had been publicly called into question. For this was the era when the United States thought of itself as the great melting pot; newcomers were expected to purge themselves of ethnic identity and emerge as 100 percent Americans. But in the 14th, where nearly everyone came from somewhere else, the need for a contact with the past was deeply felt, and La Guardia, who considered himself as American as any Anglo-Saxon son of a first family, understood this sensibility and spoke out for the people's right to express it.

Marie Fisher was established in his storefront headquarters as first lieutenant; Andrews and Espresso served as shock troops, advance men, organizers, string-pullers and bodyguards. And La Guardia, storming through the district like a whirlwind, carried the fight from river to river, assailing his opponent in a high-pitched voice that, in the heat of the fray, sometimes ran away from him altogether. "I covered every corner of that district, I think," he later wrote. "We would start early in the evening, on the West Side, and keep going east [until] one o'clock in the morning. Then to some coffee house for another hour or two of campaigning."

By contrast, Farley was rarely seen. He seemed to have hunkered down behind his bar, waiting for La Guardia's barrage to lift. It never did. La Guardia once parked in front of the saloon and loudly dared Farley to come out and debate. When nothing happened, La Guardia angrily told the crowd it was because his opponent didn't know anything about the issues and was so dumb he couldn't read a speech if it was written out for him. Finally goaded into doing *something,* Farley issued a ten-point platform—and La Guardia fell on it with glee. Eight of the proposals had already been dealt with in one legislature or another, and when the other two were brought up in Congress, Farley was back home tending bar.

Obviously La Guardia was not immune to attack. The stump speakers who substituted for Farley regularly assailed him as a dago and a greenhorn wop, unfit to represent real Americans. Nor did Tammany seem in the least concerned about the outcome. After all, the 14th was Charlie Murphy's home district; it was inconceivable that anyone could seriously undermine the machine-made Democratic majority there. Also, there were Republican leaders on the West Side, their bread buttered by Tammany, who had no interest in seeing La Guardia win. And, as a last resort, there were ways—and Tammany men knew them all—of "adjusting" the vote after the polls closed, should that prove necessary.

But the Democratic faithful had underestimated their opposition this time. There was a momentum for La Guardia, a response to the reforms he preached and to his involvement in the ambitions and fears of the people. There was a Republican victory in the air—La Guardia sensed it. All he had to do was keep them from stealing it from him.

He had been at one meeting or another until 2:00 A.M. the night before the election, but was up at 5:00 to lead a band of supporters, laden with rolls and pots of coffee, to the flophouses along the Bowery where Tammany traditionally fattened the Democratic vote. This time, though, it was La Guardia who gave "the boys" breakfast and walked them right up to the voting booths, so that by the time the Tammany delegation arrived, it was too late; the bums had already voted—Republican.

When the polls closed, La Guardia men were dispatched to the polling places to watch the counting, La Guardia himself taking on a tough waterfront district where the Democrats usually rolled up a five-to-one advantage. Charlie Culkin, the local boss, astounded to see him, said everything was fine; he should go home. To which La Guardia replied, "You better sit here and help me watch, Charlie, because if it's not an honest count, someone is going to jail. And I mean you."

The final tabulation was not released until 4:00 A.M.: La Guardia 7,272; Farley 6,915. He had won by 357 votes. The inconceivable had happened. A Republican had been elected to Congress from the 14th District. He would be the first American of Italian descent ever to sit in the House of Representatives.

His reception at the East Side Republican Club was tumultuous. He was one of them—and he was going to Washington! But at the 25th A.D. clubhouse on West 14th Street, his own home base, all was gloom. Through the open door of the back office, La Guardia heard one of the hangers-on telephoning the Democratic leader of the 14th. "No, Joe, we didn't double-cross you," he was insisting. "We didn't do anything for this fellow. You just can't control him."

That winter, Americans saw that the thundercloud across the sea loomed larger; the war in Europe, once remote from the daily concerns of all but a few, was now a worry for all. Not even the presidential election had pushed it off the front pages, for Wilson, the pundits were saying, had been sent back to the

White House because the people believed the Democratic slogan: "He kept us out of war."

But two weeks into the new year, 1917, an intercepted telegram exposed a German plot to lure Mexico into war against the United States by promising the return of "the lost territories"— Texas, New Mexico and Arizona. On January 31, the German ambassador in Washington notified Secretary of State Robert Lansing that beginning the next day, German submarines would be waging unrestricted warfare against all merchant shipping, neutral as well as belligerent, on the high seas. By mid-March, four unarmed American freighters had been torpedoed and sent to the bottom. On the 21st, President Wilson, having already broken off diplomatic relations with Germany, called on Congress to convene in special session April 2; the speculation was that he meant to ask for a declaration of war.

Meanwhile, La Guardia, whose stunning upset of the Tammany machine had attracted national notice, found himself something of a celebrity, star player in the newest reenactment of that eternal favorite, the David and Goliath story. In Washington, which he visited frequently between the election and the convening of the special session, he found himself assiduously courted; the new House of Representatives was split between Democrats and Republicans, 215 members each, and the matter of who would organize it appeared to rest with five independents, of whom La Guardia, having been elected with Progressive party support, was considered one. Invited onto the floor although not yet sworn in, flattered by the leaders of both parties, La Guardia, whose dream had come true, declared exuberantly, "I liked Congress from the first day."

The 65th Congress convened at noon, April 2; its first order of business the election of a speaker and other officers. La Guardia, in one of his infrequent spasms of party loyalty, voted with the Republicans, but the Democrats prevailed and he went into the minority, there to remain most—and temperamentally, all— of his political life.

The organization of the House was finished barely forty-five minutes before the arrival of the President. He came riding through a hard spring rain, escorted by a troop of cavalry to ward off pacifist demonstrators massed on Capitol Hill. At 8:30

P.M. he mounted to the speaker's platform and looked out at the grave assembly, the joint session of the Senate and House; the justices of the Supreme Court in front-row chairs, and behind them the Cabinet and members of the diplomatic corps; and the galleries filled with people who well understood the gravity of this moment. Not since Lincoln was confronted with the Confederate attack on Fort Sumter had America come to such a crucial crossroad.

President Wilson began to speak, and his speech, magnificently delivered, filled with phrases that would live on in history, was of an order that few even in that distinguished gathering— and certainly not La Guardia—had ever heard.

> I have called the Congress into extraordinary session because American ships have been sunk, American lives taken ... the ships of other nations have been sunk in the same way. The challenge is to all mankind. . . .
> We fight for the ultimate peace of the world and for the liberation of its peoples, the German people included. . . . *The world must be made safe for democracy. . . .*
> It is a fearful thing to lead this great peaceful people into war. . . . But the right is more precious than peace. . . . America is privileged to [fight] for the principles that gave her birth. . . . God helping her, she can do no other.

The subsequent debate lasted three days and most of three nights. It was heartfelt and sometimes bitter, as when Senator George Norris, the Republican progressive, angrily mocked "all this high-flown talk about a duty to humanity." The war fever had been whipped up by arms merchants and stockbrokers, he declared, who would make enormous profits by American intervention. "We are about to put the dollar sign on the American flag." In the House, William La Follette spoke for the progressives, then moved that munitions manufacturers, pro-war editors "and the J. Pierpont Morgans" should offer themselves or their sons as soldiers, or should give half of all their worldly goods to justify "their patriotic desire for our entering the European war."

The roll call began at 3:00 A.M. on April 6, 1917—Good Friday. For La Guardia, its most unforgettable moment came when the clerk called the name of Jeannette Rankin, just elected, the first woman ever to sit in either house of Congress, for it best expressed the emotional wrench of the decision for so many. At first Miss Rankin did not reply; then she stood to speak, breaking a House rule of 140 years expressly forbidding any comment or explanation during a roll call. "I want to stand by my country," said the congresswoman from Montana, "but I cannot vote for war. I vote 'No.' "*

Afterward, La Guardia was asked if it was true that the dignified Miss Rankin was crying as she spoke, and he didn't know. "I could not see because of the tears in my own eyes."

It had not been an easy decision for him, either. On most issues he stood with the progressives, and men like Norris and Senator Robert La Follette would become his close friends. He knew there was strong anti-war sentiment back home in New York's 14th Congressional District, among the Irish and Germans, obviously, but also among those new Americans who had most energetically supported his candidacy and wanted to be finished with the turmoil of Europe's endless conflicts.

He would have been less than human if he did not, at the least, feel it a sorry twist of fate that he should have to put his political career at risk with his very first vote. But he never hesitated. He cared about opinions in his district, but he was guided by his conscience. He once said the best thing he could give those who elected him was "total ingratitude." They had the option of turning him out of office; but if he voted contrary to his conviction of what was right, he would be no use to them and no use to himself. Now he was convinced that the higher morality called for the United States to fight for its principles, and for the liberation of the millions dominated by Europe's autocracies, and when the roll call for war reached the name La Guardia, the answer was a firm "Yes."

He would soon have a spectacular chance to regain his popularity in the 14th, but meanwhile there was the hard, slogging work of mobilizing a nation with an innate suspicion of the military establishment. In April 1917, the United States went to war with a standing army of 128,000—fewer than the French lost at

* On December 8, 1941, when Congress declared war against Japan after the attack on Pearl Harbor, Congresswoman Rankin again cast a negative vote—the only one.

Verdun. The Navy had been resting on its Spanish-American War laurels, and there was nothing that could pass for an air service, not a single plane capable of fulfilling a combat mission.

Wilson, who knew the urgency with which England and France awaited an American expeditionary force, asked for a draft of all able-bodied men. Even before the bill was introduced in Congress, La Guardia was conducting a postcard referendum among his constituents—and in an accompanying letter, lecturing them on how they ought to choose:

> This country is at war and needs every available man. I think conscription is needed and I am trying to educate the people up to it. There have been attempts to introduce bills into Congress which would exempt the farmer from service, or the cotton grower, or the tobacco grower. If New York does not watch out she will be having to supply as large a proportion of the Army as she now does of the taxes, which is one-third. The only way to avoid this is to institute compulsory service. It is up to you to respond; don't blame me if you don't like the way I vote.

They didn't. Although the majority of his respondents expressed disapproval of a draft, La Guardia voted for it anyway. And though minorities and immigrant groups had no better friend in the House of Representatives, neither were there many there with La Guardia's patriotic zeal. He told his constituents straight out that in wartime the United States demanded their absolute allegiance. In May he went back to address a labor rally of one thousand Italian-Americans, and again laid it on the line:

> I want to drive it home and impress it upon you, if I can, that we are in the midst of the most cruel war in the history of the world . . . and those who prefer Italy to America should return to Italy. I know there are some of you in my district who won't sacrifice themselves for *any* country, and if I thought I owed my election to that sort I would resign.

An unwritten law of the House that freshmen members should be seen and not heard went absolutely unheeded by La Guardia. He was into everything. With his father's fate in mind, he introduced the bill mandating the death penalty for "the fraudulent sale" of food or arms to the government in wartime. It was referred to the Judiciary Committee, and was not heard of again. He introduced an amendment to the draft law that would have nullified all exemptions: Conscientious objectors were to be given noncombat duties, and the physically unfit less strenuous work. It was defeated. When a foreign loan bill was introduced providing for an unprecedented $3 billion in loans to our allies, La Guardia was all for it. But when a parade of so-called experts testified that the loans would cost Americans nothing, as they would be repaid in full and with interest, the first-term congressman from New York's 14th District took the floor and, with an intuition denied to most of his more experienced fellow members, set the record straight:

> I do not share the belief of some of my colleagues in the complete restitution of these $3 billion . . . a good portion will be in due time returned, but much will have to be placed in the loss column of Uncle Sam's books. Let us understand that clearly now and not be surprised later. Even so, if this brings about a speedy termination of the European war and permanent peace, it is a good investment at that.

This excellent advice was largely ignored, and all through the 1920s, wrangling about the loans was the acrimonious keynote of transatlantic relations. Years afterward, following defaults and lengthy refunding negotiations, the former allies made an offer; but a hardening sentiment developed in the House against any terms but the return of the full principal plus interest. Once more Congressman La Guardia rose to address the issue, saying simply, "Take it. Be lucky if you get it all. I doubt that you will get even this much." He was right again.

Although La Guardia supported the war effort unequivocally, he was constantly on guard lest the interests of the poor people he represented, and millions like them across the country, be trampled in the rush to profit from the emergency by those better positioned to do so. When a revenue bill to meet the war's enormous cost was being debated, he proposed two amendments: one, to exempt from taxation married men earning less than $2,000, and the other, a levy on bank checks instead of an increase in the postal rate. Neither was adopted. Hammering away against profiteering, insisting that the war must not be fought to make the rich richer, he urged government controls on the price and distribution of food, clothing and shelter. His plan was buried in committee; prices soared and shortages became a condition of wartime life.

In May, Congress took up a bill to insure security against espionage, and La Guardia saw in it the evils nations sometimes embrace in a good cause—the abuse of individual liberties, the curtailment of free speech. He pointed out to the House that if an army unit were to be incapacitated by reason of being improperly supplied, under the proposed act no newspaper or individual could bring out that fact because it related to "national defense." This section was stricken from the bill as passed, but La Guardia voted against it anyway. Some of his darkest predictions came true: Eight hundred people were jailed under the Espionage Act, not one for an act of espionage.

His aggressiveness, his egalitarian harping on the needs of the poor and the rights of ordinary citizens, did not endear him either to Old Guard Republicans or old-line Democrats. Congress had never seen his like before and some congressmen did not like what they saw. A few wondered aloud whether "that little wop radical" could even be considered American.

During the debate on the Selective Service Act, a member in opposition had asked sarcastically which of his worthy colleagues, so anxious to send American boys off to a foreign war, would go themselves. La Guardia jumped right to his feet. This didn't enhance his popularity, either—only four others joined him. But in July 1917, with most of the needed mobilization laws on the books, he went down to the Southern Railway Building in Washington and signed up with the Aviation Section of the Signal Corps.

6

GOING TO WAR

That had always been his intention. When the draft bill first came up for debate, he had let it be known that if he voted to send men overseas, he would be going with them. He was thirty-four, in good health, and knew how to fly an airplane. He was also a United States congressman who spoke several European languages, and on all these grounds the fledgling air service was glad to have him. He was commissioned a first lieutenant and assigned to the Italian Royal Flying School near Foggia, where his father had been born and earlier generations of La Guardias were buried, and where American aviation cadets would now be taught to fly.

In the weeks before his departure, La Guardia, who had attained prominence as a political curiosity, was suddenly transformed into a national folk hero. Newspapers hailed America's first flying congressman; he was named to prestigious committees and invited to receptions for visiting dignitaries. New York's Little Italy exploded with pride and patriotism when he appeared in uniform to address a war rally. Even the Republican regulars of the 14th were captivated, if only for the moment, and organized a dinner in his honor attended by one hundred local notables.

It is said that he asked Thea to marry him before he sailed, and that this time she was the one who held back; she wanted to wait until the world was at peace. What an unlikely scenario! If La Guardia had wanted to get married then, he almost certainly would have—talking nonstop, fighting down arguments, defenses and all resistance until Thea was exhausted and yielded. It is far more likely that *he* wanted to wait, that having achieved his political goal, there remained this unexpected last item on his agenda: the war. When he had gotten *that* out of the way, he would think about himself and marriage.

In September 1917 he was promoted to captain and assembled 150 cadets at Mineola in preparation for embarkation. They were a decidedly upper-class contingent, every one a college student or graduate. Among the few enlisted men in the outfit were Albert Spalding and Frank Giordano. Spalding, already famous as a concert violinist, had been in too much of a rush to wait for a commission, but came to camp in a hand-tailored uniform nonetheless. And Giordano, who owned a small barbershop in Greenwich Village, had been shaving La Guardia and cutting his hair for more than ten years.

"From the day war was declared I just could not get rid of Frank," said La Guardia. "He wanted to enlist, but he was married, over-age, had three children and flat feet."

What good was it to have a congressman for a friend, Giordano demanded, if the friend couldn't even get him into the army during a war?

When it turned out that the cadets had to organize their own mess and would need a cook, the "friend" went to work on the necessary waivers and got Giordano assigned to his outfit. "He was a mighty fine barber," La Guardia later noted, "but not much of a cook."

The night before they sailed, September 17, Spalding played a benefit concert at Carnegie Hall and according to La Guardia, who was there, received a tremendous ovation. Later, in Italy, the student pilots would groan in mock dismay when he took out his violin, but La Guardia, from whom music and musicians called forth near-reverence, became his patron. Spalding was detached in Paris for a time, but at the first opportunity La Guardia had him transferred to Foggia, saw that he got a lieutenant's commission and made him his adjutant. The one benevolence he refused was the thing Spalding most wanted—to be trained as a flyer. Every request was turned back with some variation on the theme that Spalding was too useful where he was and too old to fly—he was twenty-nine; La Guardia, about to go north as a combat pilot, was thirty-five. But Spalding soon divined the truth: "His real preoccupation was with a fiddler's fingers, which must be kept safe against the return of peace."

La Guardia reached the Eighth Aviation Instruction Center in southern Italy—quickly shortened to Camp Foggia by the Americans—in mid-October. The field lay in a long valley and

was divided into West Camp, commanded by La Guardia, and
South Camp, under Major William Ord Ryan, a West Point cavalry officer who was the overall American commander. Their responsibilities were only administrative; by agreement with
Washington, the Italians were to provide housing, planes and
instructors.

All were wanting. J. S. (Sandy) Hand, who arrived during
a February snowstorm, still shudders recalling the stinging cold
inside the old unheated sheep sheds with dirt floors that served
as barracks. "We were given two blankets each and woke up blue
with cold. All the brass talked about it, but nobody did anything
until one day Captain La Guardia took some people and got on a
train and came back with three dozen oil heaters, nobody knows
how."

Or how he paid for them. His style was forthright—he went
out and got what his boys needed—but his accounting methods
were arcane. He just figured that someone—the Quartermaster
General, the State Department, the good Lord—would pay.

For example, he didn't see how his boys could stay healthy
on the ration of an Italian enlisted man: daily helpings of macaroni paste, a ladle of melted lard, "and once a week a diminutive
piece of boiled meat." So he contracted with a private caterer to
feed the men "big, well-balanced, typical American" meals.
Major Ryan had his doubts about all this, but La Guardia told
him not to worry. When the bills reached the chief quartermaster's office in Tours, provoking cries of outrage, he was summoned to account and threatened with a court-martial by the
Judge Advocate General. He duly identified himself as a congressman—he was never shy about that—and said that if War
Department regulations made it impossible for him to feed his
men properly, he would, by God, personally see that the regulations were changed. Chastened, the general quit talking about
courts-martial, but insisted the quartermaster had no basis for
approving payment of a private caterer's bills. So La Guardia
went to Paris to see Charles G. Dawes, then chairman of the
Interallied Finance Commission (and later Vice-President of the
United States) and talked *him* into paying them.

At Christmastime, the cadets had accumulated leave, back
pay—and nothing to do. Even training was at a standstill for

lack of equipment. As Major Ryan was away, La Guardia author-ized leave for his men in Rome. And well aware "that single men in barracks don't grow into plaster saints," as he put it, he lectured them on venereal diseases and the means of prevention, and told them he was sending the unit medics to man a mobile prophylactic station in Rome's red light district. But he had calculated without the senior medical officer, who denounced the plan on the ground that army regulations nowhere authorized the use of men or equipment to encourage immorality; he refused to carry out La Guardia's orders. La Guardia, a fair man, gave him an opportunity to change his mind. Then he put him under arrest and, as acting camp commander, issued the orders himself.

The results of his experiment were entirely salutary. It is true that following a formal complaint by the medical officer, he was called upon by the Surgeon General's office to explain. But when he did, the Surgeon General was absolutely intrigued with La Guardia's tactic and began planning to apply it throughout the European theater.

Washington had contracted with an Italian aircraft company, S.I.A., for a large number of reconnaissance planes, but when the Americans reached Foggia none had been delivered. Soon La Guardia found out why: The plane, a new design, had a tendency to tear apart in midair. S.I.A. was holding back on deliveries in a frantic effort to rectify the flaws, but at length the company realized that was not possible. The craft was inherently unsound. Rather than absorb the loss, it began shipping the "flying coffins," as La Guardia characterized them, to the Americans. A marine lieutenant at Foggia took the first one up. It had barely attained altitude when the wings tore off and what was left came down with a crash that killed the pilot instantly.

La Guardia went personally to the S.I.A. factory and canceled the order. There were the usual repercussions—La Guardia, the Air Service captain, ordered to Paris by the Interallied Purchasing Commission to explain on what authority he had canceled a $5 million contract; and La Guardia, the congressman, replying, "By the authority vested in me to safeguard the lives of American airmen." The planes already delivered were kept, to be used in ground training. The rest of the order stayed canceled.

With all these self-assigned responsibilities, La Guardia still had to qualify as a combat pilot. He thought the Italian instructors "splendid," but none of them spoke English and the cadets weren't so enthusiastic. Sandy Hand said some of the men got off the ground with little more than an encouraging smile from their instructors. Everyone was handicapped by the shortage of training planes. A cadet was lucky to get fifteen minutes a day of dual instruction in the air; after two hours, he was considered ready to solo.

La Guardia remembers his solo flight as "the thrill that comes once in a lifetime . . . a great feeling . . . exciting. The only one who suffered was the instructor, anxiously awaiting [my] safe return."

Sandy Hand's recollection is a little different: "With only one man aboard, the Farman trainer tended to climb, and you really had to throttle down for a landing. I guess La Guardia forgot that, because he kept hitting the ground like a rock, with full flying speed, and going straight up again. Those of us watching were deliberating whether we should let him run out of gas or shoot him down to keep him from starving to death. Finally it got through to him that he couldn't stay up forever. But still he didn't throttle down—he just cut the switch and made a dead stick landing; the thump would have broken the bones of a skinnier man."

La Guardia never claimed any dazzling gifts as a pilot. He said he had trouble with landings and takeoffs, but that in between, "I can fly the son-of-a-gun okay." He was certified on December 12; three months later he came to grief.

He had been scheduled to fly a cross-country test on a day that dawned blustery with rain. A more prudent man would have acknowledged nature's message and gone back to sleep, but La Guardia badgered the flying officer into letting him take off. On the last leg of the triangular course he ran into headwinds stronger than the forward speed of the plane. Soon he had been blown clear off the limits of the map on his knees and dropped to within a few hundred feet of the ground to get his bearings. Suddenly a violent gust flipped the plane completely over. He lost control and crashed. Only the fact that his safety belt broke on impact, throwing him clear, kept him from being crushed under the motor. He was pulled out with severe hip contusions and a bruise of the spine that bothered him all his life.

The accident came at an inopportune moment. Hospitalized, La Guardia was unable to attend the regular monthly meeting of the Air Service Command in Paris. For, incredibly, he was also deeply involved with the military and political bureaucracy of Rome and Paris. He had made himself a direct link between America and her allies. He bulled his way through regulations and red tape to get things done. And both the American high command and the Italian government acceded, for he was a United States congressman in Italy who spoke Italian and knew how to make the most of it. As one observer noted, confining a dynamo like La Guardia to the duties of a flying officer would have been as wasteful as using a locomotive to pull a hay cart.

In January 1918 he became a member of the Joint Army-Navy Aircraft Committee; within a few months he was chief in all but name of American aviation in Italy. He shuttled between capitals and wrote reports on the Italian military situation based on private talks with cabinet members and staff officers, who would not have been so frank with an interpreter present. When General Armando Diaz, chief of the Italian General Staff, wanted to convey the gravity of the Italian position to the commander of the American Expeditionary Force, General John J. Pershing, he entrusted the highly sensitive message to La Guardia—who delivered it personally.

The Italian situation was indeed desperate. There were Allied observers who believed Italy would be knocked out of the war in weeks—and many Italians who believed this would be a good thing. In October, the Austrian army, reinforced by seven German divisions, had torn open the Italian front at Caporetto, an Alpine village fifty miles north of Trieste. In the catastrophic retreat that followed, Italy lost 305,000 soldiers, of whom 275,000 surrendered. The remnants of an army fled headlong down out of the mountains, not stopping until they had reached the far side of the Piave River north of Venice, one hundred miles away.

Caporetto unnerved the high command. It came at the very moment when the Bolsheviks had seized power in Russia and Lenin was calling for peace at any price. The further loss of Italy could be fatal to the Allied cause. King Victor Emmanuel III strove to rally his people: "Citizens and soldiers, be a single army! All cowardice, all discord, is treachery!" British and French divisions were rushed into the breach. An Allied Supreme War Council was formed to cope with the most pressing problems.

And Captain Fiorello H. La Guardia was called to Rome and shown into the United States Embassy office of Ambassador Thomas Nelson Page.

The peace crusaders were strong and growing, Page told him. Now the Americans were being blamed for prolonging the war but failing to provide the troops to win it, and the Germans were busily stoking the anti-American fires. La Guardia had to help him reach the Italian people, said Page, a scholarly novelist with iron in his backbone, because there was no one else. "There wasn't standing room in hell" for the American community in Rome, he added scornfully. He wanted La Guardia to address a mass meeting in Genoa, to deliver America's message "in short, simple words . . . which can be understood by everybody." If it worked, the embassy would arrange a whole series of such meetings up and down the Italian boot.

And if it didn't?

La Guardia would have to be repudiated, was the forthright answer. Page would have to say that "you were not talking for the American government and deny that [the embassy] had anything to do with the meeting."

It was exactly the sort of challenge La Guardia could not resist. Facing a crowd of more people than he had ever seen in one place (one estimate was 300,000), he told them in his colloquial Italian—which provoked titters but soon caught them with its fire—that the Americans were here. He was one of them! And millions more were coming, but there was no fairy godmother; Italy's fate was in her own hands. The Italians, accustomed to orotund phrases and predictable themes, were electrified by the slashing La Guardia campaign style. They cheered themselves hoarse. "Luckily for me," he wrote later, in another of those striking understatements, "they were enthusiastic . . . and the Ambassador never had to repudiate me."

For the next six months, with Albert Spalding as his aide, he maintained a herculean schedule, traveling by night—Rome,

Naples, Milan, Bologna, Turin, Florence, Bari—to address huge audiences, which came to see America's flying congressman, and returning the following night so he wouldn't miss more than one day of training or, later, of combat flying. In time, he said, "My service at the front seemed my most peaceful activity since I had landed in Italy."

But he went wherever they sent him and the results were spectacular. The Americans had not joined in the war to prolong it, he told the Italians, but to finish it. A moment later, he was lashing out at the "financial slackers" and those among them who drank too much and didn't work hard enough. In Bologna he said, "If we lend you money, it is for the war, not to be stolen or to serve for building private factories." Said the New York *Globe:* "Captain La Guardia received great applause."

He appealed to the people to support Italian war loans and reminded them that President Wilson's war aims included recovery of Italian populations that had come under Austrian rule: Trent, Istria, Trieste. He promised them a better world and a better life, and they believed him because he so obviously believed it himself. In Rome they broke into cheers of "Viva Wilson!" "Viva America!" An enthralled cabinet minister declared that La Guardia was more popular than an Italian deputy. "I love him like a brother!" And *The New York Times,* reporting on his triumphal tour, wrote, "President Wilson and the United States could not have chosen a better representative in Italy than this brave soldier."

After the accident, they kept him in the hospital as long as they could: two weeks. One doctor suggested some surgery, but La Guardia wouldn't hear of it. By April 4, 1918, he was in Paris, laying plans for a cloak and dagger operation that would have been a coup for a fulltime intelligence agent. La Guardia says the assignment was handed to him at headquarters. Albert Spalding, who was with him, says he thought the whole thing up himself. No one disagrees about the mission or its difficulty: how to get several thousand tons of steel from Spain, then under the oppressive influence of the Germans, to Italy, where it was badly needed for the manufacture of airplanes, trucks and motors. Spain, though neutral, had yielded to Germany's pressure and virtually embargoed the shipment of critical materials to the Allies.

But "smuggling," La Guardia mused aloud, "is an ancient art." And when Spalding's eyes widened in astonishment, he smiled mischievously and said, "I can see by your expression, Al, that you are all for it."

"Fiorello La Guardia," said Spalding, "was perhaps the only person who has ever called me 'Al.' " But that was not surprising; Spalding had been present at a private dinner with Victor Emmanuel III at which, once the formalities were dispensed with, La Guardia fell to calling the king "Manny." What sent Spalding's eyebrows up was the very idea that the high command would condone a *smuggling* operation.

That didn't bother La Guardia in the least. As soon as his proposal had been forwarded for consideration to General Pershing's headquarters in Chaumont—he was promised an answer in ten days—he told Spalding to go out and get them some civilian clothes and tickets on the next night's sleeper to Barcelona.

"But . . . but . . ."

"But what?"

It was the matter of the orders, said the aide weakly. They couldn't get across the border without orders. They couldn't even get their transportation countersigned by the provost marshal without them. And, as they had just been told, there would be no orders for at least ten days, if at all.

"We leave tomorrow night," La Guardia snapped. "Tickets, clothes, orders—those are your affair. Use your imagination; any kind of orders will do—I won't ask any questions."

So Spalding found himself a typewriter and faked two sets of orders. Then he went out and bought tickets and clothing. La Guardia had been busy too. Somehow he had gotten them passports and two letters of credit, together worth $5 million. And the next night they were on their way.

On the train La Guardia "turned off his galvanic energy and relaxed." He showed Spalding a picture of Thea and said he was going to marry her when the war was over. But when they arrived in Barcelona's blinding spring sunshine, he was again all business. First they made a search of the newspaper files of the past three years, and learned that the Taja Steamship Company

had lost more tonnage to German torpedoes than all other Spanish lines together. Then La Guardia made an appointment to see
Señor Taja, the owner.

"His uncanny instinct," Spalding later wrote, "had led us to
the one man who could help us most in our mission." For Taja
had lost not only ships to Germany's ruthless submarine warfare, but also his only son, who was aboard one of them; "and his
hatred of the Hun was an unquenchable flame." He listened to
La Guardia's proposal and willingly became not just his agent
but his accomplice. He told the two Americans whom to see and
whom to trust. He outlined a program that left little to chance,
and himself volunteered to arrange the necessary port clearances
or evasions, whichever seemed appropriate. Before the war
ended, 1.5 million dollars' worth of Spanish steel reached Italy in
Taja's ships.

Meanwhile, La Guardia and Spalding reported to the
United States Embassy in Madrid, where they wrote out an ac-
count of their mission and sent it to Paris in the diplomatic
pouch. They also cast off their self-imposed anonymity, and La
Guardia gave a newspaper interview in which he bluntly told the
Spanish people that they had their money on the wrong horse.
Their friendship with Germany was bringing them nothing but
grief, he said, citing statistics freshly in mind: seventy-eight
Spanish merchant ships sent to the bottom; dozens of Spanish
factories idle for want of raw materials. SHUN KAISER, SPAIN IS
TOLD BY LAGUARDIA was the next day's headline.

Finally, about to return to Italy, La Guardia was handed a
dispatch from American Expeditionary Forces (A.E.F.) headquarters in Chaumont. The orders from General Pershing had
arrived.

He could have had a staff job in Paris, or put in all his time
as a propagandist for the war effort, as his friends in the Italian
government urged him to do. But there was never any question
of that; his heart was set on flying, and on July 20, 1918, he was
assigned to an Italian squadron based in the Veneto, near Padua,
and went into action at once. He flew in the left-hand seat of a
Caproni biplane, a lumbering three-motor bomber that couldn't
exceed 110 miles an hour loaded, and his co-pilot was either

Major Cambiaso Negrotto, a member of the Italian parliament, or Captain Federico Zapelloni, an ace. Their objectives were principally enemy airfields and munitions depots, but "since the Austrians were well within Italian territory, we had to be careful not to bomb our own people." The fact is that the Italian population in the Piave war zone was far from enthusiastic about the raids, for the very practical reason that if their flyers didn't bomb the Austrians, the Austrians wouldn't come back and bomb them.

"On the whole," La Guardia wrote, "our missions were rather tame jobs [but] seemed exciting enough at the time."

They must have. Once, while strafing enemy trenches, he and Negrotto became separated from their escort and were attacked by two Austrian fighters. Only the chance arrival of a squadron of English planes saved them. Another time, returning from a raid in the dark, their Caproni was caught in a cone of searchlights and pounded by antiaircraft fire "for at least four minutes." When they got back, another pilot counted two hundred holes in the plane they had dubbed "The Congressional Limited," and found a piece of shrapnel in the magazine of La Guardia's machine gun.

But his zest for flying remained undiminished and he sometimes marched into the operations office after a mission and asked to go right out on another. As always, his main strength as a pilot was determination. The judgment of a loyal comrade at the front was, "You couldn't say he was an artistic flyer—but how he loved it!" On one raid, having just returned to active duty after one of his propaganda speeches, he took off with Zapelloni to attack an enemy airfield. Releasing his bomb, he pulled the plane into a precipitous turn and, unable to see the field, yelled over to Zapelloni, "How did I do?"

"Best damned speech you ever made," the Italian called back.

That summer the flow of American men and equipment finally began to make itself felt, and the tide of the war turned in favor of the Allies. By autumn the Austrian armies were in full flight. The end was clearly near.

Back in Rome, Albert Spalding got someone to approve his application for flight training at last and, as the distance between them seemed safe, wrote to tell La Guardia. Back came a letter "affectionately and passionately profane about what he termed my insanity—a characteristic document."

La Guardia, who was also commander of all American combat pilots in Italy, had been promoted to the rank of major on August 5. But while he was becoming an authentic American hero and his press back home was nothing short of sensational, an alliance of pacifists and suffragettes in New York was petitioning Congress to vacate his seat so the 14th District could be "represented." The election campaign of 1918 had clearly begun.

Even outsiders rallied to his support, the Philadelphia *Record* commenting, "Congressman La Guardia, absent to fight for his country, is absent little more than some congressmen during the baseball season. Why raise a fuss over him?"

And when a *New York Times* correspondent showed La Guardia a copy of the removal petition and asked for a comment, he made the most of a golden opportunity: "You might say that if any signers of the petition will take my seat in a Caproni biplane, I shall be glad to resume my upholstered seat in the House."

But on October 28, with the Armistice two weeks away and election day closer still, having been ordered home on some War Department pretext, he arrived in New York to fight for his "upholstered seat."

7

THE BEST OF TIMES, THE WORST OF TIMES

Major La Guardia came down the gangplank in a freshly pressed uniform, wearing silver wings and three decorations for bravery, but everyone waiting on the Cunard pier was meeting someone else. The press and a crowd of his friends and supporters were blocks away, somehow expecting him on a French liner docking at the same time. Not knowing what else to do, he went to the Hotel Brevoort in the Village and Louis Espresso found him there several frantic telephone calls later. With a crush of reporters only minutes behind, Espresso shouldered La Guardia into the men's room and briefed him on what had been happening in Washington and New York.

His congressional seat was being protected by Speaker of the House Champ Clark, that most loyal of Democrats. The removal petition had been filed in a desk drawer. Meanwhile, though, the Socialists had nominated a young and appealing candidate to run against him in the 14th District: Scott Nearing, an economics professor whose radical politics had cost him posts at two universities. Now he was campaigning vigorously, exhorting the people to declare their independence of big business, "as Americans in 1776 declared their independence of British royalty." He hammered at La Guardia for going off to fight an imperialist war and leaving the 14th unrepresented in Congress.

But the absent congressman's friends had not been asleep. Marie Fisher, manning the district office in Washington and turning into a very clever operative, struck just the right note of innocent conviction when she wrote the newspapers:

> From the various letters which Mr. La Guardia has written, I feel free to state that he considers his present military service as an important part of his duties as a Congressman. He was many times distressed at the lack of experience and first-hand information in the House on important military matters. . . .

98

La Guardia's congressional colleagues spoke up in his support, too. In New York City, Republican leader Samuel S. Koenig railed against the spirit of Bolshevism sweeping Greenwich Village; Harry Andrews and Louis Espresso warned that radicals were out to punish La Guardia for serving his country. Perturbed by the strong Socialist showing in the municipal election of 1917, Republicans and Democrats agreed to run fusion candidates in four vulnerable congressional districts; one was the 14th. Proclaimed Tammany's Charlie Murphy to his minions: "Sink all partisanship! Name only 100 percent Americans to Congress. Elect them to help win the war and a victorious peace."

With bipartisan support, there was no real danger of La Guardia losing his seat. But the people and the politicians were watching to see how he handled Nearing, Espresso now warned, and what they saw could be central to his future.

There was no need for concern. Moments after coming out of that men's room at the Brevoort, La Guardia had all but annihilated Scott Nearing. Surrounded by reporters firing salvos of questions at him, he chose to respond to one asking his opinion of Scott Nearing. "Who is Scott Nearing?" he inquired with the barest trace of a smile.

The reporters were entranced. "Who is Scott Nearing?" would be the gist of all the next day's headlines. When La Guardia wondered aloud what regiment Nearing came from, the newsmen fell right in with his game and told him what he already knew: that Nearing came from no regiment, that he was a Socialist, a pacifist and—what La Guardia had *not* known—that he was under indictment for writing an anti-war leaflet, *The Great Madness,* that ran afoul of the Espionage Act.

La Guardia, whose opposition to the Espionage Act was so intensely felt that he would spend ten years trying to have it repealed, interrupted to offer a little homily: "The question of patriotism must not be introduced into this campaign. Scott Nearing must have a fighting chance. I did not know that he was under indictment, but remember this—under the laws of this country, a man is innocent until he is proven guilty." And *that* made the papers too.

By evening he was campaigning full tilt, bringing a packed

Democratic clubhouse on the West Side to its feet with a rousing appeal to patriotism. At a Republican meeting on Second Street next night, his entry interrupted the speech of Governor Whitman, the crowd springing up at the sight of the khaki-clad La Guardia and cheering him for fifteen tumultuous minutes. He spoke briefly, then moved on. A cluster of people that grew to a mob of two thousand before the evening ended followed him from place to place, applauding adoringly and threatening to overwhelm him with their enthusiasm. At one open-air meeting he told the audience, "Scott Nearing is a man without a country unless he stands for what the American flag stands for." He derided his opponent's socialism and called him "a silk stocking university professor who condescends to come here and attempt to foist Bolshevism on America."

Nobody ever accused La Guardia of pulling punches in a political fight. And in 1918, he felt a special obligation to deflate Nearing's passionate paean to socialism as the highway to utopia. He cared about the people he represented, poor and longing for a better life, and had to convince them that no Marxist miracle was going to ennoble and enrich them all.

In the frenetic seven days that led up to the election, he charged through the district igniting the overflow crowds that materialized wherever he was billed to speak. On November 1, the two candidates met in a stormy debate at Cooper Union, and according to one writer, "The solemn and didactic Nearing took such a verbal beating around the head from the bruising professional politician that it would be surprising if he knew which way was Union Square." La Guardia cited the "miserable failure of socialism in Russia" and the acquiescence of the German Socialist party in the Kaiser's "orgy of butchery." He, too, was against war, he cried: "I went to war to fight against war. I don't think we can end war by merely talking about it on East Side street corners."

Scott Nearing, blond, boyish, in way over his head, tried to pump himself up to La Guardia's level of indignation. He hailed the Soviet Revolution with eloquence, condemned Wall Street, and attacked the profiteers. In rebuttal, La Guardia cited his congressional bill providing the severest punishment for wartime profiteering. Then, uncharacteristically—no doubt he felt the contest was already over—he took some of the sting out of his assault. Smiling at Nearing, he said, "I can't debate this man. I understood he was a professor of economics. That's a mistake—he's a poet." The two shook hands and the debate was over.

In effect, so was the election. La Guardia, burying Nearing under an avalanche of votes, winning by a better than two-to-one margin, had never before received such organizational support, and never would again. The other coalition candidates defeated their Socialist opposition as well. A week later all parties had cause to celebrate: The Germans asked for an armistice, which was signed on November 11. On the 12th, La Guardia resigned his commission, "got the old suit out of camphor and returned to the House."

When the final session of the 65th Congress ended, La Guardia, now thirty-six years old, asked Thea Almerigotti to marry him and she said yes. She had waited through a world war and two election campaigns—which, in the La Guardia manner, proved almost as hectic. They were married—Thea a Catholic, La Guardia a sometime Episcopalian—in the rectory of New York's Saint Patrick's Cathedral on the morning of March 8, 1919. The bride carried a spray of orchids and looked lovely in a smart, fur-trimmed suit; the groom wore his uniform for the last time. Louis Espresso was best man. There was a short honeymoon; then the La Guardias took up residence in his Charles Street apartment. The next year and a half may have been the happiest time in both their lives.

In Europe, that same bright springtime of 1919, an era lay dead but not buried. The once-dazzling empires of the Hapsburgs and the Hohenzollerns were in ruin, and the Romanovs, slain by revolutionaries, bleakly symbolized the old order's stunning disintegration. The League of Nations, conceived as the instrument of a new design for peace among nations and self-determination for all peoples, was on the verge of being rendered permanently impotent. Though La Guardia had his quarrels with President Wilson, godfather of the League, and though the Senate, not the House, would decide its effective fate, he spoke ardently in its defense:

Mr. Speaker . . . We told our boys before they went across that we were fighting for an ideal. . . . Now we have a right to de-

mand that out of all this gigantic struggle and the millions of lives
sacrificed we shall come to an understanding among the nations. . . .

Four months later the Senate voted down the Treaty of Versailles, of which the League was an integral part.

During the war, 96 percent of American chambers of commerce had voted for the United States to "take the lead in forming a league of nations." But now a great disenchantment was
sweeping the country. More than 100,000 American soldiers had
died in a bloody struggle which many felt was none of our affair,
and still the Europeans wrangled over obscure territories whose
names Americans could not pronounce and whose importance
eluded them altogether. Problems at home seemed much more
pressing. The war had created seventeen thousand new millionaires, but prices soared and most people could barely afford food
and shelter, a poor reward for twenty months of wartime sacri-
fice. Veterans were having trouble finding work and even the
government was turning down men who had left its service to
join up.

These were the issues on which La Guardia took his stand,
his natural battleground; he had no time to brood about the
League. He noted "the profiteers buzzing around the capital
[who] were being better cared for than the men who fought the
war." His speeches were full of his concern for the small busi-
nessman, the wage earner, "the hungry people of the cities," and
jobless veterans who deserved better of their country. Early in
1919 he introduced an amendment to an appropriations bill providing that federal civil-service employees who had been drafted
or enlisted be reinstated in their former jobs. It was sidetracked
by a parliamentary tactic and died.

He waged a ceaseless, slashing battle against profiteering,
underscoring his keynote—that the vast majority of the population had had no share in the riches harvested from the war by big
business—with reams of statistics to show how corporate profits
had fattened. And still an indulgent government beamed on the
"interests," he protested, disposing of surplus airplanes, copper
and food, for which it had paid top dollar, at a fraction of their
value so that artificially high prices could be propped up.

When the director of the Bureau of Surplus Supplies came up to Capitol Hill to testify in favor of a $1 million salary appropriation—of which his share was $25,000 a year—La Guardia let him have it right between the eyes. What did the gentleman intend to do with the millions of pounds of bacon and the millions of tins of corned beef and roast beef stored in army warehouses? he began.

Well, the gentleman replied, the meat packers had advised him that it was not suitable for Americans; the bacon needed to be recured and "no family in the country could use a six-pound can of corned beef or roast beef at a time." It would just have to be shipped off to Rumania or some place.

There were a few more seemingly innocent questions—La Guardia lining the bureaucratic target up in his sights—with a tart comment to the effect that he had eaten army bacon overseas regularly and found it "excellent," and another about lush government salaries. Then he fired. Even his political foes had to chortle at the devastating effect of his scorn:

> Now let us see what this $25,000 beauty says about meat and foodstuffs. He said he might find a market in Rumania . . . or some other country like that. The gentleman does not know that those countries never use canned beef. You could not find a can opener in all of Rumania. And yet we are paying [him] $25,000 a year for expert advice. . . . It surprises me he did not offer this bacon to some Jewish synagogue. . . .
>
> If he will put that stuff on the market in New York City or Philadelphia or Boston he will find hungry people willing to buy it and eat it. They will be able to digest army bacon. It may interfere with the profits of the packers, but I am not interested in that.

That summer, he joined the losing battle against the Volstead Act, the law to enforce the Prohibition amendment adopted during the war and ratified in January 1919. For La Guardia it was another crusade; and long after the bill passed, he fought on. He resented the time Congress was giving to a problem that was not, in his judgment, within the jurisdiction of government. He predicted with deadly accuracy that the law would be impossible to enforce, "and if this law fails to be enforced . . . it will create contempt and disregard for law all over the country."

But what provoked his bitter anger was the argument that Prohibition was needed to control "foreigners" in the cities whose dissolute habits were undermining the nation's Anglo-Saxon standards of morality. He took the floor to say that "this so-called foreign element was not the consumer of hard liquor—they can't afford it." But, as often happened, his point was most vividly made with antic wit. In an exchange with Congressman Upshaw of Georgia, a vaudeville image of the country bumpkin, he teased, "The gentleman knows that the moonshiners of the South are very anxious to get this bill through, because their business will increase."

> UPSHAW: I will answer the gentleman by saying that as long as New York and Baltimore and virtuous Chicago . . .
> LA GUARDIA: I will say to the gentleman that if the people traveling from other states would keep out of New York City, we would have no drunks in the streets.
> UPSHAW: Does the gentleman intend to suggest that he does not want the financial patronage of the glorious "Dry South" in the cities?
> LA GUARDIA: Absolutely not. It keeps our courts congested.

He didn't lose every battle—some say because he fought so many that the law of averages caught up with him. He was instrumental in the passage of a bill to feed postwar Europe. To a chorus of opposition from xenophobes and isolationists, he fired back, "We did not liberate them from Hapsburg or Hohenzollern oppression to stand idly by and permit them to starve. . . . You cannot preach self-government and liberty to people in a starving land." Anti-Semitic riots in Poland spurred him to introduce a resolution of protest. Adopted by the American delegation to the Peace Conference, it led to full religious and civil rights for Jews in newly created European states. When the bill chartering the American Legion reached the floor of the House, he added an amendment opening it without discrimination to everyone who had served in the war. Some Southern congressmen objected, but La Guardia was adamant: "The Negro soldiers fought alongside us, did they not?"

There was one victory he came to regret. In the postwar surge of anti-militarism, he led the fight against a million-man army, half to be conscripted, pruning it back to 200,000 men, all volunteers. In August 1919 he told the House, "I think the best thing I ever did in my short legislative life was in opposition to the appropriation bill in which we cut down the Army." A second world war later, in April 1947, he was to confess that it was probably the worst. In a *Reader's Digest* article, "Why I Now Believe in Universal Military Training," he was unsparing of himself in tracing America's military weakness from that August day and linking it to the outbreak of World War II. He concluded: "In a frightfully realistic lesson, I have learned that to advocate preparedness is not at all incompatible with a consuming desire for peace."

La Guardia's absolute honesty was in one part the source of his abrasiveness—he simply had to say what he thought. The other part was the sheer dramatic core of him, the delight he took in confounding and startling an antagonist. Nothing could change him. He had no such thing as a "best behavior"; he was always the same. So it is hardly surprising that in the small, cloistered Southern city that was Washington in 1919, where indirection was a virtue and candor in a social setting was only slightly less reprehensible than sex in a public place, La Guardia was the best-known loner in town. He did not mesh with any of the clubby, cohesive social groups and did not accept invitations to the wall-to-wall parties on the cocktail and dinner circuit, although as a congressman and an away-from-home bachelor, he had been frequently on the lists sold by professional party planners and traded by ambitious hostesses. He was busy; his capacity for work—evenings, Sundays—was stupefying. But he must also have been ridden, as he was in all-American Arizona, by his sense of being the outsider. Sensitive, thin-skinned, a world away from his New York milieu, he protected himself by making it abundantly clear that he didn't want or need Washington's social acceptance.

He tells of making an exception when New York's Senator William M. Calder, who had befriended him when he first came to Washington and who still called him Sonny, invited him to a dinner party that friends were giving at a restaurant. It was an unqualified disaster. During cocktails, he fell to talking with someone about Serbia. La Guardia didn't like the man's attitude.

"What do you know about it?" he demanded. "I've lived in that part of the world for three years and I know what I'm talking about."

"I'm the Serbian ambassador," replied the man.

Dinner was called. La Guardia started talking to the woman on his left about General Motors' Liberty airplane motor, which he had been attacking on the House floor as an engineering disaster and a financial scandal. All this he related with relish, continuing relentlessly in his condemnation of General Motors' economic tyranny. Eventually someone told him the lady was the wife of a GM vice-president.

He went to the men's room. One of the group at dinner came in and asked how he liked the party. "Why I never saw such a bunch of nuts before," La Guardia burst out. "I'm going. Want to come?"

"I can't," said the gentleman. "I'm the host."

In 1918, Al Smith, a Democrat with a future, defeated Governor Charles S. Whitman and gave up his position as president of the New York City Board of Aldermen to go to Albany. Manhattan Republican leader Samuel S. Koenig looked at the upcoming special election to fill the vacancy and saw a chance to break Tammany's hold on the city's second highest office. The Democrats were in trouble with immigrants and first-generation New Yorkers, who blamed President Wilson for every postwar affront to their native lands—the Italians because he failed to secure Fiume for Italy, the Irish because he didn't press for Irish independence, the Germans because of the *Vaterland*'s harsh treatment at Versailles. Koenig thought the Italians especially could be won over—and become the key to a G.O.P. victory in New York State in the 1920 presidential election. It was true that no Republican had ever taken a municipal election citywide, but with the right candidate, this time it was at least imaginable. In Koenig's view Fiorello La Guardia was not only the right candidate but the right man for president of the Board of Aldermen.

That summer of 1919, when he had persuaded the other four county leaders, he put it to La Guardia. The offer did not sweep the congressman off his feet; he liked the job he had. But Thea was intrigued by the possibility of having him in New York all the time instead of in Washington most of the time. He thought about it; there were more talks. The determining factor seems to have been La Guardia's understanding of a promise by both Koenig and the national chairman of the party, Will Hays, that if he won this one, he was to have the nomination for mayor in 1921. He agreed, and from then on the dream of being mayor of New York possessed him.

The Republicans, with their eyes on 1920, were extremely interested in La Guardia's campaign. Even if he didn't win— and only a few unseasoned optimists expected him to—the ethnic vote he rallied might be decisive in carrying New York for the presidential candidate the following year. So they provided him with a campaign manager, Paul Windels, and, after some foot-dragging, $35,000 in campaign funds.

Windels was tall, elegantly dressed, sedate beyond his thirty-four years, and a thorough-going conservative—in short, all the things La Guardia was not. And yet the two trusted each other from the first and became friends. Windels noted that "La Guardia was a very unusual type . . . a mercurial temperament which went off in every direction. For some curious reason I seemed to have a quieting influence on him. . . . The campaign workers always wanted me to go around with him to the evening meetings."

He was awed by the candidate's stamina. Immune to fatigue, La Guardia roamed the five boroughs of the city from early morning, stumping in favor of the five-cent transit fare—about which he so far knew little—and denouncing skyrocketing food prices and firetrap school buildings, speaking wherever he could collect anything that passed for an audience. In the evening he was back at campaign headquarters in midtown Manhattan, where Thea would shove a sandwich at him; Marie, up from Washington, briefed him on the evening schedule, and Frank Giordano tried to corner him long enough to give him a shave and "get him in presentable shape" for the ten or more meetings to be covered that night. Said Windels: "He was a man of inexhaustible mental and nervous energy and physical strength."

The Democratic candidate was a florist from the Bronx named Robert L. Moran, and it is a mark of Tammany's confidence that its nominee, hastily installed as interim aldermanic president to give him a record, was a lackluster party drudge, so sickly that he did almost no campaigning. La Guardia further benefited from endorsements by the Citizens Union, an influential civic-betterment group, the Hearst press and *The New York Times,* which called him "that gallant aviator, that ardent American patriot ... Put him on guard to protect the people's money in the Board of Estimate."

In his mercurial way, La Guardia could go from a cocksure certainty that he was going to win to the most profound despair, and it took only one discouraging turnout, or a meeting that seemed unmoved by his exhortations, to cast him down. Toward the end, Windels would steer him to some Italian neighborhood, where the response was invariably fervent, for a windup speech and a nightcap. "That kept our courage up and the campaign was carried through to the last minute on a note of intense activity and drive."

On Election Day, November 4, 1919, La Guardia and Thea voted early at their polling place in the Village, then posed for the press photographers. In one picture he is seen about to cast a paper ballot, fingers hooked into his talismanic broad-brimmed hat; Thea looks radiant—she had just learned she was going to have a baby. For the rest of the day the candidate scurried between campaign headquarters and polling places where he suspected "monkey business." When the polls closed, he and Thea installed themselves at the Hotel Brevoort. Returns were telephoned to him there.

It was a long and nerve-racking night, neither candidate able to pull away to a convincing lead. Not until 4:00 A.M. did Sam Koenig, watching over the final count at police headquarters, call the Brevoort. "F.H.," he said succinctly, "you're in."

Barely. La Guardia had lost the Bronx, Queens and Staten Island, but it was a record turnout for an off-year election and the Italian districts in Brooklyn and Manhattan had pulled him through by fewer than 2,000 votes out of the nearly 1 million cast. But he had done it: He was the first candidate running on a straight Republican ticket to win city-wide office since the five boroughs joined together to become Greater New York City.

Tammany held its aching head. The more perceptive of the Irish leaders now knew they had better make room for the Italians. "Show me another La Guardia," said one, "and I'll run him."

*   *   *

Paul Windels gave him a copy of the city charter which, according to Marie Fisher, he thereafter "went around with under his arm, day and night. He just made a study of it." He took office on January 1, 1920, and one observer says that when he walked into City Hall he paused in the graceful Colonial rotunda for a long moment to look toward the office of Mayor John F. Hylan.

That was where his heart was and no one who had business at City Hall could fail to see it. "Do you know what a good mayor could do for this town?" he once asked Thea. It was hardly a rhetorical question; he spent the next twenty minutes detailing the answer. But he was not the mayor. He was president of the Board of Aldermen, an anachronistic and largely ceremonial council, and his only real power came from his seat on the Board of Estimate, the city's executive committee, and from his standing as New York's second-ranking official.

But as he climbed the curving marble stairway to the aldermanic chamber on the second floor that January day, he was beginning the two years that would fix the La Guardia image on the whole of New York City, his ultimate constituency. As a congressman, he had been only one of twenty-three from the city, and far away; now he was one of a kind, the Number 2 official of the nation's Number 1 city.

It was also America's news, radio and magazine headquarters, and La Guardia presented the press with the most engaging, theatrical, and always potentially explosive, political personality around. They didn't all love him. He was far too prickly and didn't curry favor. Once, when he was trying to get the pay of police and firemen raised, publisher Frank Munsey wrote him a letter of praise and offered to help. The best help Munsey could give, La Guardia shot back, would be to set an example by raising the salaries of his own underpaid employees. In this period, when the newspapers began referring to him as the Little Flower, which is the meaning of Fiorello in Italian, one reporter suggested he would have been more aptly named Sacro Terrore.

It was the best of times. La Guardia battened on the controversies at City Hall and luxuriated in his happiness at home. Thea grew even more beautiful during her pregnancy, and the father-to-be, who loved children and had a wonderful way with them, now counted the days until he would at last have one of his own. He slowed his furious pace. There were evenings at the opera and the couple frequently entertained a small circle of close friends, almost none of whom had anything to do with politics, in the apartment on Charles Street; the Bellancas, Piccirilli, the sculptor Ruotolo, Windels, Albert Spalding, and the most famous Italian in the world, Enrico Caruso.

Caruso, who hated crowds and was almost never seen in a public place, loved to be with his friends Piccirilli and La Guardia. The peerless tenor and his American wife, Dorothy Benjamin, had solemnized their earlier civil marriage in a Roman Catholic service at Saint Patrick's Cathedral on the same day the La Guardias were married in the rectory around the corner. Nobody dreamed that death would soon link them again. They surrounded themselves with such gaiety: Caruso singing "Mamma Mia," making them laugh with his highly personalized English idiom; La Guardia enfolding himself in an oversize apron and cooking mussel soup and spaghetti. No one thought of death. Life had been so good to them. They had all come into their own and the future was golden with promise.

Even at his more reasonable tempo, La Guardia worked ten, sometimes twelve hours a day. He ate lunch at his desk, studied the proposed city budget, reports and ordinances, probed the activities of municipal departments and the performances of its employees, and slowly learned what it took to run a city of 5.6 million. Soon the man who had campaigned for high civic office with nothing more than an emotional faith in the five-cent fare was an expert on New York City's transit system and its problems.

The thing he learned most rapidly, as had the handful of other capable people who served on the Board of Aldermen, was that its members' salaries, a total of $200,000 a year, was mostly money thrown away.* As a member once put it, "The Board is utterly extravagant, entirely subservient to political leaders and does no constructive work." Once they were known as the Forty Thieves. Tammany's notorious Boss Tweed, who finally went to prison in 1876 for enriching himself at the city's expense, used to

* La Guardia took this lesson to heart; when he became mayor, he abolished the Board of Aldermen altogether.

say, "There never was a time when you couldn't buy the Board of Aldermen." It was also no trick to confuse them. A newspaperman with a sense of humor once got an oblivious Irish alderman to introduce a resolution commemorating Queen Victoria's birthday. When his furious constituents stormed the aldermanic chamber with murder in mind, the worthy rose to his feet to plead innocent: "Does anyone here think I would introduce such a resolution if I knew what was in it?"

The Board's wings had since been clipped. La Guardia presided over a sixty-seven-member body—thirty-seven Democrats, twenty-six Republicans and four Socialists who were being rewarded for faithful political service—whose record of achievement, individual and collective, was notoriously undistinguished, and whose chief function was to debate ordinances and resolutions of less than great gravity. La Guardia could vote only to break a tie, but the rules did permit him to speak—a good rule, observed a reporter, "like the one which permits Niagara Falls to fall." Meanwhile the affairs of the city were largely directed by an executive committee, the Board of Estimate, whose eight members had sixteen apportioned votes, of which three were allotted to the president of the Board of Aldermen.

He also served as acting mayor in the absence of The Honorable John F. Hylan. Honest John, as his friends in Brooklyn liked to call him, a beefy, big-boned Irishman with a red moustache, was a tribute to the American dream. He had risen past any number of men with more brains, personality and qualifications to become chief executive of the nation's greatest city, no one was sure exactly how. Al Smith once said of him, "If Mayor Hylan has helped the Albany situation to the slightest degree, he has helped it by going to Palm Beach for a month every winter."

Paradoxically, incredibly, this man who came when Tammany called and danced when Tammany whistled took a liking to Fiorello La Guardia. He may never have known another honest politician before, and though he was incapable of ever grasping the goals or motivations of a man like La Guardia, it must have been a relief for him to know there was someone in the city government he could trust. For his part, La Guardia perceived in Hylan a certain muddled integrity. They also shared an antipathy to the city's third-ranking officer, Comptroller Charles L.

Craig, a fat and pompous Tammany martinet with a nasty racist streak. And so they sealed an unlikely alliance—the mayor, a plodding organization Democrat, and La Guardia, the fast-moving, incisive, nominal Republican—at an official reception one night at the 69th Regiment Armory.

Honest John broke the ice. "La Guardia," he said solemnly, "any time you think there's anything wrong, you come to me first, and if you find that I'll not cooperate with you, or that I will stand for anything not right, you may go the limit."

La Guardia asked him if he meant that. He said he did and they shook hands. It was a union that soon bore fruit, although, as the mayor ruefully recalled, "In many instances it caused me to incur the displeasure of the Tammany organization."

The level of debate in the aldermanic chamber was not high. The heat of ordinary exchanges rose rapidly and was apt to call forth such epithets as "Liar!" and "Anti-Semite!" Once, when La Guardia ruled a Republican alderman out of order, he shouted back, "You are a disgrace to your party!"

La Guardia primly replied, "Every member present must behave as a gentleman, and those who are not must try to."

But when humor could not prevail, nor even the enormous command of facts that made him such a dangerous opponent in a stand-up fight, La Guardia was perfectly capable of climbing down into the arena, where he contributed to and usually escalated the rhetoric of mayhem. He had early provoked Comptroller Craig's fury by joining with Hylan to kill such dubious Craig proposals as increasing the salaries of already overpaid political appointees and exempting some hundred positions in the comptroller's department from civil service examination—which La Guardia charged was "a brazen attempt to discharge employees who have been in the service of the city for a good many years, and to appoint the riffraff who could not pass the test."

Craig, who was not without verbal resources, coined the term "Blackguardia" to characterize such La Guardia broadsides. Soon the two were hurling headline-making taunts and sensational charges back and forth. At one public meeting, goaded beyond control, Craig cried out to the presiding officer, "Will you please hit that little wop over the head with the gavel!" It took several men to keep the charging La Guardia from swarming all over him.

During another splenetic argument, when a Craig ally slipped behind La Guardia's chair, he whirled and yelled, "If you try to start anything with me, you'll go out of that window, you bootlicking valet!"

"I'm no wop," was the profound reply.

"What's that you say?" La Guardia screamed. "What's that you say?" And again he had to be forcibly restrained.

The invective from the other side may have stung more deeply, but there is no question about who inflicted the lasting damage. La Guardia's most famous success was in exposing a scandal in a courthouse construction project close to Craig's heart. The Little Flower had opposed it from the first, but not until after the contracts were let did he find proof of the bid-padding he always suspected. Then he went directly to Hylan.

"Mr. Mayor, you remember what you told me that night at the 69th Regiment Armory? Well this courthouse business stinks." Voice in crescendo: "It's rotten." At its screeching apex: *"The city's being robbed!"* When Hylan asked what he should do, La Guardia told him to delegate someone to look into it. "If I am wrong," he rushed on, "I will publicly state that I have been wrong. But, on the other hand, if you find that I am right, for goodness sake, protect the city!"

He wasn't wrong. Starting with La Guardia's discoveries— inflated prices for limestone, and more limestone than could ever be utilized in the building—investigators uncovered a tangle of looting and corruption that, as La Guardia put it, "out-Tweeded Tweed." Over Craig's bitter objections, Hylan bravely canceled the contracts, saving the city around $3 million, and sixty-nine indictments later, some of the comptroller's best friends went to prison. Craig himself was apparently innocent of actual fraud and stunned by the outcry; helping one's friends was no more than Tammany had always done.

La Guardia was criticized too. In the high levels of the state Republican party, it was being suggested that he had fired too soon. Had he restrained himself until election time, the wasted city funds would have given the G.O.P. a sensational campaign issue. When he heard this, La Guardia called it "the doctrine of the old school of politics. I consider that it is my duty to serve the city first and look for campaign issues afterward."

When he wasn't tilting with Craig, he was evolving a whole

range of constructive, forward-looking proposals for the betterment of New York: reorganization of the police department to
military standards; expansion of docking and warehousing facilities at the port; unification of the rapid transit system under
municipal jurisdiction; taxation of idle property to force speculators to sell, or build badly needed housing; modernization of
the charter, which, he pointed out, was so out-of-date it was still
concerned with prohibitions against driving hogs through the
city's streets.

And even that didn't cover the sweep of his interests. In little more than one year in office, he had gone to the firing line in
favor of the women's suffrage amendment, the direct primary, a
four-year course of study at West Point, a plan to launder
street-cleaners' uniforms at the city's penal institutions and another to require police ranks from lieutenant to inspector to walk
ten miles a day for three consecutive days each year. Concurrently, he was vigorously opposing daylight savings time and a
certain fountain in Crotona Park in the Bronx, and mediating
threatened strikes by the children's shoe workers and the housewreckers' union.

On April 8, 1920, in time for the upcoming baseball season,
the New York Yankees sent him a season pass. They had it back
before opening day:

> I beg to acknowledge with thanks receipt of season pass No. 507,
> and desire to thank you for your thoughtfulness in sending it to
> me. Inasmuch as I have made it an ironclad rule not to accept any
> passes, or favors of any kind, while in public office, I am com
> pelled to return it to you.

By the end of 1920 there were in place all the elements for
classical Greek tragedy: La Guardia, the doomed hero, having
aspired too high and attained too much, blinded by his gifts and
flawed by self-confidence, is about to be brought down by apprehensive gods.

Throughout the year, he had in the main been a loyal party
man, the exceptions forgivable. Soon after taking office he denounced the state legislature for expelling five legally elected Socialist members, but so had Charles Evans Hughes, Senator

Warren Harding and other conservative Republicans. In March he went up to Albany to testify at a legislative hearing on rent controls and announced, "I come not to praise the landlord, but to bury him!" The six hundred landlords present to lobby against the bill turned red with rage, but the party leadership was willing to make allowance for their Little Flower's idiosyncratic feelings about wages, prices and rents.

In September 1920 he was elected national chairman of the Italian-American Republican League. He campaigned hard for Harding, the candidate of the Ohio bosses, who had somehow come away with the Republican presidential nomination, and for Nathan L. Miller, the party nominee for governor of New York. Neither would have been his own choice. The ticket of Harding and Coolidge won in a landslide—carrying even New York City—defeating Democrat James L. Cox and his handsome young running mate, Franklin D. Roosevelt. Miller was swept in with the Republican tide; and Will Hays and Sam Koenig, who had gone after the Italian vote with La Guardia as their magnet, had reason to congratulate themselves.

But the trouble began right after Miller moved into the Executive Mansion in Albany, for La Guardia and the new governor shared almost nothing but membership in the Republican party and the human race. Miller was a shrewd, unbending upstate corporation lawyer whose political ambition was to resurrect the nineteenth century. He was opposed to the direct primary, public housing, the five-cent fare, even the League of Women Voters; he favored Prohibition, movie censorship and immigration restrictions. In his view, New York City, full of foreigners and their radical ideas, was all that was wrong with New York State. Conflict was inevitable, and when it came, La Guardia for once would be outgunned.

In addition, he had just been dealt a stunning personal blow. His baby girl, Fioretta, born in June 1920, was not healthy; she did not grow and flourish as an infant should. And Thea, who had gone through her pregnancy without a complaint, suddenly began coughing alarmingly and her lovely face turned wan and haggard. Before the year was out, the doctors told La Guardia that both his wife and child had tuberculosis.

At first he raged against the fates to his friends Piccirilli

and Giordano, but remained certain that Thea and the baby
would get well—*he* was going to see to it. He bought a stucco
house in a then-rural area of the Bronx, going into debt to do it,
sure the fresh country air would restore mother and child to
health. But they continued to waste away before his eyes. He
built a sun porch on the back; it didn't help. He rented another
house, far out on Long Island, and rode the train back and forth
every day, until an understanding of the inevitable outcome
began riding with him. Desperate, he settled Fioretta in a hospital and moved Thea to a tuberculosis sanatorium at Saranac
Lake in the Adirondacks. But Thea must have sensed the end,
too, for she asked to come home to be with her baby and her husband. When Fioretta died of tuberculous meningitis on May 8,
1921, not even one year old, Thea was too ill to attend the funeral
and La Guardia went alone to bury his child.

Meanwhile, a second hammerblow was about to fall.

The state legislature, dominated by Governor Miller, had
undertaken repeal of the direct primary law, which gave registered voters the right to choose their party's candidates for elec-
tive office. In its place, the Republican majority proposed to
restore this power to the party conventions. Next came a bill for
the reorganization of New York's transit system; it vested effective control over the city's subway and trolley lines in the state
legislature and, ominously, offered no guarantee of a continued
five-cent fare.

Even with the grief he had at home, and knowing he was
flying in the face of men with power over his destiny, La Guardia
counterattacked with all his old fury, bitterly telling a Brooklyn
audience that the state senator who wrote the transit bill came
from a little upstate town that hadn't even a single streetcar,
"yet he proposes to tell us what we should do."

He tried to convince the city's Republican leaders that
Miller's program was a prescription for their political undoing,
but the pressure from Albany was relentless. One by one, the
county leaders fell into line. Years later, Sam Koenig would
write of 1921, a black year for all Republicans in New York,

... the Legislature created several laws which were very unpopular in the city of New York. One was the Transit Commission ...

the act for the enforcement of prohibition . . . movie censorship . . .
I don't wish to criticize Governor Miller or the Legislature, but it
just so happened that they dealt almost a death blow to the
chances of the Republican Party that year.

What he does not say is that La Guardia warned him that this
was precisely what would happen, but that a more persuasive argument was the governor's exquisitely timed appointment of
Koenig's brother to the state bench.

La Guardia took his fight to the clubhouses, but the word
had been passed that Miller had had enough of the Manhattan
maverick, and he faced increasingly hostile audiences. Angered,
plagued by his public anxieties and private anguish, he lashed
back with ever shriller attacks on the governor and his "trained
legislature." Brawls broke out. One night, when he came to address the Junior Republican League, no one spoke to him or offered him a seat, and when the group's business was finished, the
chairs were removed and the meeting declared closed. Thereafter
the clubhouses locked him out altogether. "They will be sorry,"
he promised bitterly.

In March his old friend Senator William Calder said, "If the
Republican party does not make this little wop mayor next fall,
New York is going to hell." But by summer, Calder, too, had
abandoned him. On August 2, 1921, with Miller cracking the
whip, the Republican machine put together a fusion slate that
had Manhattan Borough President Henry Curran at the top as
nominee for mayor. When La Guardia, wild with rage, demanded
to know what of the promises made to him, no one remembered
any promises.

A clever politician, even a principled one, would have swal-
lowed this bitter pill and bowed to the decision. To do otherwise
was to commit political suicide. Winning without any party support was all but impossible; losing would leave his public career
in ruins. But La Guardia never gave any other option a thought,
some say because he was distracted by his trouble at home and
not thinking clearly. But the fact is that La Guardia was not a
man who could sidestep, let alone retreat. He moved in only one
direction, forward, and he immediately announced that he would
challenge Curran in the Republican primary.

Koenig took him out to lunch and tried to talk him out of it. "Don't do it, Fiorello," he said earnestly. "This town isn't ready for an Italian mayor. You'll lose and you won't be able to make a living."

"Sam, I'm going to run," La Guardia answered. "So long as I have five dollars in my pocket, I'm all right."

But he wasn't all right. Even his most devoted supporters— Paul Windels, Espresso, Andrews—were forced to desert him, unwilling to buck the Republican machine. *The New York Times,* which had praised him to the sky only months before, now called him "picturesque, amusing, and impossible." Publisher Frank Munsey took his revenge, his Republican newspapers reading La Guardia out of the party with daily denunciations of his "loud, ignorant, demagogic disloyalty—La Guardia, the petty and pitiful."

Almost alone, with no campaign fund, he stumped the city from end to end in a hopeless battle, railing against the "Albany dictatorship," but also offering a reasoned and intelligent platform worked out during his nearly two years at the heart of the city's government and based on home rule and sound municipal management. Each night, late, he returned to the stucco house on University Avenue in the Bronx for a few whispered words with Thea and a few hours of sleep. Then he started again.

None of it helped. He got only 37,000 votes to Curran's 103,000 and failed to carry a single borough, losing as badly as a serious candidate ever had in a New York primary election. Crushed, heartsick, he tried to carry on, mending fences, even making a few campaign speeches on Curran's behalf. But the hammerblows kept falling.

Thea grew worse. In October, La Guardia himself fell ill, suffering excruciating pain from an abscess that had formed at the base of his spine, a result of the wartime injury. Finally he had to undergo surgery.

And in Naples, his friend Caruso had died of pleurisy, at the age of forty-eight. On the afternoon of November 27, 1921, La Guardia represented the widow at a memorial service at the Metropolitan Opera House, where Caruso had reigned as king for nearly two decades. The great stage was somber, dark with the presence of death, and La Guardia's voice broke as he presented

Onorio Ruotolo's heroic bust of "the greatest tenor of all times" and spoke of the light that had gone out of all their lives.

He returned to Thea's bedside then and didn't leave it for the next two days. He clenched her thin white hand as if that alone could somehow keep her with him. But it couldn't. At 10:00 P.M. on the 29th, when they were alone in the house, she slipped away from him. She was twenty-six years old.

La Guardia could not resign himself to this loss. Frank Giordano, who moved in to look after his old friend and idol, saw him stand at the open coffin in the dining room, then drop to his knees to kiss the dead and once-beautiful face, breaking into tormented sobs. One morning, when Giordano returned with the newspapers and breakfast rolls, La Guardia turned on him savagely and cried out in Italian, "What devil sent you? Go away!"

Mayor Hylan, who had crushed Curran to win reelection, came with some others of the city administration to pay his respects, bringing some whiskey to lighten the gloom. But when the visitors fell to drinking and political talk, La Guardia lost control and raged at them, "What do you think this is, a German wedding?" He smashed glasses and bottles and shoved them out the door.

After Thea was buried beside her daughter in Woodlawn Cemetery, he returned to City Hall, but he was not the same man. Some said he was drinking, heavily, seeking in a bottle the solace he found nowhere else. Years later, when this was reported in an early biography, an enraged La Guardia threatened a libel suit unless the offending pages were cut out of the book, and this was done. But it was a characteristic overreaction, an inability to concede weakness. Suppose it were true—as it almost surely was? Who except his bitterest political enemies would fail to understand and have compassion for the hero, suddenly dragged down to the depths from his high perch?

With his aldermanic term almost over, La Guardia issued a farewell statement: "New York is the richest city in the world. But until every child is fed and every home has air and light and every man and woman a chance for happiness, it is not the city it ought to be."

Charles Craig, who had also been reelected in the Tammany sweep, and whose norms of conduct sometimes shamed even

Tammany, crowed, "The trouble with La Guardia is that he
wanted to be Mayor and the people gave him their answer. Now
he is sore. He's the 'late lamented La Guardia!' "

For once La Guardia hadn't the resources to fight back. He
sat there and took it. No one who was there that day doubted that
he was finished, his political career over. The Westchester *Globe*
wrote his epitaph:

> The prestige of La Guardia in office has gone and will not return.
> A political party ... has little use for a man who denounces the
> party which gives him office. ... The Republican Party will live
> on, while individuals drop out of sight.

And so it seemed to be. No one in his party came forward
with a word of praise or comfort for this troublesome but once-
valued colleague who in a sudden, shattering upheaval had lost
his family and his career. No one spoke of him anymore. Only
John Hylan remembered. Fumbling, foolish Tammany hack that
he may have been, only Hylan perceived La Guardia's loss as a
public misfortune, and on the last day of the year sent him this
moving letter:

> I could not let this, your last day at City Hall, pass without
> writing you how sorry I am that you are leaving, and particularly
> that the people of this city are losing your services. I want to take
> this opportunity to express to you my appreciation and grati-
> tude. . . .
> There is no office in the gift of the people that is too good
> for you.

A lone reporter, a feature writer for the New York *Evening
Mail,* having seen La Guardia's farewell statement, came out to
the house on University Avenue to ask whether he could take the
million-dollar daily budget of New York City and use it to turn
the city into something better than it was. The old passions were
not dead, and his answer poured out in the flood of feeling he had
been choking on all these weeks:

> Could I! *Could I!* Say—first I would tear out about five square
> miles of filthy tenements, so that fewer would be infected with
> tuberculosis like that beautiful girl of mine, my wife, who died—
> and my baby. . . . I would keep every child in school to the

eighth grade at least, well-fed and in health. We could support enough schools for every child in New York on what we saved from penal institutions.... I would provide more music and beauty for the people, more parks and more light and air and all the things the framers of the Constitution meant when they put in that phrase, "life, liberty, and the pursuit of happiness."

On December 17, gentle, soft-spoken Attilio Piccirilli took him away on a trip to Cuba. They didn't come back until January 1922, La Guardia still wearing a black necktie and a black armband.

The new year dawned bleakly for Franklin Roosevelt, too. In August, he had been stricken with polio and now sat limp-legged in a wheelchair. Of the three New Yorkers born so close in time, whose political futures had glittered with such promise, only Jimmy Walker, already being eyed by Al Smith as a replacement for Hylan, was riding high.

8

THE SUMMONING OF DESTINY

Friends came. August Bellanca moved in for a while. But few men had ever been more alone than was Fiorello La Guardia in those first aching weeks after Thea died, alone in the presence of devoted companions who tried to distract him from his paralyzing grief, alone through the long days when they were gone and the empty house on University Avenue kept telling him what he'd lost—the winter sun flooding the sun porch, uselessly; the second bedroom that had been a nursery for such a heartbreakingly brief time, now shuttered and dark.

And then one day—no one, not even La Guardia, remembered when—he must have taken a deep breath and decided that he had to get back to work. In the hard, slogging, day-to-day tasks he was born to do—not in a bottle, not in sterile memories and useless might-have-beens—he would find deliverance from the desperate hours and the empty house. Anyway, he told Bellanca ruefully, he needed to earn a living.

A new law firm, La Guardia, Sapinsky & Amster, had been organized as of January 1, 1922, with little more than his assent. Now he began to participate actively, and though still operating with something less than his onetime exuberance, he was more than a match for either colleagues or adversaries. Fittingly, his first retainer came from the Free State of Fiume, which appointed him special counsel, as did a newly formed Italian movie company. Then, at Mayor Hylan's bidding, the City of New York hired him to try a condemnation proceeding against a Queens water supply company. La Guardia did his homework, laid the facts on the table—and persuaded the company to reduce its claim by nearly two thirds. The city saved $7.5 million.

The legal fee was a substantial $27,700, and noting it, a newspaper charged that Mayor Hylan had cut his old aldermanic ally a fat slice of pork; in passing, it called La Guardia a hobo plutocrat. The Little Flower fired right back with a libel suit. Someone told him he had done the right thing, that for a newspaper to call a former congressman a hobo was a rank insult. La Guardia's reply demonstrated how soundly his spirit was healing. "You have me wrong, brother," he said. "I'm suing because they called me a plutocrat."

Around the same time, he was solicited for membership on the steering committee of an association fighting the Prohibition amendment. He was inclined to join up except, as he wrote back, "for the suggestion you make in your letter that there will be no obligation 'in any way for active work.' I am not accustomed to inactivity, and hence cannot accept your invitation."

The offending newspaper apologized; the anti-Prohibitionists hastened to assure him he could be a whirlwind of activity on their behalf if he chose to; and Fiorello La Guardia, pasting together the broken pieces of a life, was again in command of his special destiny.

He could not have stayed away from politics if he had wanted to, which he did not. In a way, he was involved even before the dark time ended. Two officers who had served under him in Italy, now patients in an army hospital, wrote asking his support for legislation that would provide retirement pay for disabled veterans, and he sent letters to former colleagues on their behalf. An old friend offered him a chance to teach a class in local government at the Columbia Grammar School; he accepted. He also began addressing groups of immigrants on civic responsibility and American history. When it was proposed that New York build a grand arch to commemorate the war dead, La Guardia countered with a plan for a "memorial school [which] would teach the brightest youths of all nations the futility of warfare." All this, to him, was politics, or public service as he preferred to call it—a concern for people, an involvement in their needs.

But having been active on the larger stage, understanding its power to change things, he wanted to go back to Congress. So it happened that those who cherished the notion that they had disposed of La Guardia for good and all were disconcerted by spring and unhinged by summer to see him emerge as the inspiration and effective leader of the League of Italian-American Republican Clubs, a potent constituency, and to be faced with

his name again every time they picked up a newspaper—La
Guardia attacking war, Prohibition, jazz; La Guardia heading
the Salvation Army drive, arguing for a soldier's bonus, cham-
pioning the League of Women Voters, writing a series of articles
in William Randolph Hearst's New York *Evening Journal,*
which carried his message on the new politics across the city.

Then, suddenly, Hearst was booming La Guardia for governor, and—making even strong men in the Old Guard want to
weep—La Guardia seemed to be taking it seriously. On June 29,
1922, he electrified the leaders of both parties by issuing his own
version of a Republican state platform: forty-two planks calling
for such basic social reform as equal rights for women, old-age
pensions, workmen's compensation, a minimum wage, an eight-
hour day, and the abolition of child labor. If his program was rejected and Governor Miller renominated, La Guardia solemnly
announced, he would feel bound to organize an independent
ticket and enter the gubernatorial race himself.

His platform did not generate dancing in the streets. The
Times wondered why he had left out free municipal ice cream.
But William Randolph Hearst applauded it vigorously. "Major
La Guardia," he said in his ponderous way, "is the logical candi-
date on the Republican side."

He didn't mean it for a minute. He knew, as did La Guardia,
that Miller had the Republican nomination sewn up. But, as only
a perceptive handful realized, Hearst had a plan: He meant to
use La Guardia as his stalking horse. Long a stormy petrel of
Democratic politics in New York—he had once served in the
House of Representatives—the millionaire publisher now
thought he saw his way to the White House and that it led
through the Governor's Mansion in Albany. And how better to
achieve that point of departure than by being the Democratic
nominee for governor while Fiorello La Guardia sundered the
opposition for him with an independent candidacy.

In another place, against lesser competition, Hearst might
have prevailed. But he was playing in a very tough league and
was badly outclassed. Al Smith, the Democrats' new star, easily
took the gubernatorial nomination, then shut the door on any
other post for the erratic Hearst. As for La Guardia, the so-called
stalking horse, it turned out that the hoof was on the other foot.

The Little Flower had no real interest in running for governor, but given the backing of the most powerful newspaper chain in the state, he certainly did have the means to wreck Miller's chances. As he well knew, the Republicans were going to have to do something about that. And so Hearst, who was sure La Guardia was his ticket to Albany, turned out to be La Guardia's ticket to Washington. Which is just about the way La Guardia planned it.

Sam Koenig came to see him one August day and, in exchange for an end to all the talk about his running for governor, offered him the Republican nomination for Congress from the 20th District, East Harlem. His old district, the 14th, had again slipped under the sway of Tammany Hall and it would take more than a two-month campaign to win it back. Holding the high cards, La Guardia accepted on condition that it be understood he would be campaigning on *his* platform, not Miller's. But after August 30, 1922, when the announcement was made—"The New York County Committee is proud to nominate the distinguished former President of the Board of Aldermen for Congress from East Harlem"—he quit publicly attacking Miller, now officially his party's choice for governor and his own fellow nominee. Still, no one in East Harlem would ever mistake them for political soul mates, and loud were the lamentations among the county committeemen when the Little Flower started campaigning:

> I am a Republican [he said at the outset and emphasized in different ways throughout the campaign] but I am not running on the Republican platform. I stand for the republicanism of Abraham Lincoln, and let me tell you that the average Republican leader east of the Mississippi doesn't know any more about Abraham Lincoln than Henry Ford knows about the Talmud.
> I may as well tell you now, for it wouldn't be fair to put it off until after I am elected, that I don't fit in at all with the average so-called "Republican" in the East. I am a Progressive.

New York's 20th Congressional District, which ran from the East River to Fifth Avenue and from 99th Street to 120th Street, was a single square mile of humanity, as many as five thousand people in one block, mainly Jews and Italians but also with little enclaves sheltering twenty-five other nationalities. The one thing they had in common was poverty; next to Manhattan's Lower East Side, this was the most congested slum in the United States. To an outsider, East Harlem was a dangerous, crime-ridden jungle which had nothing in common with the real America. To the 250,000 people who lived there, it *was* America.

Fiorello La Guardia, who understood this and its implications, set up his headquarters in a rented store on Madison Avenue near East 109th Street, with Marie Fisher again in charge. A handful of volunteers fanned out to ring doorbells and distribute campaign flyers. The candidate himself, working the neighborhoods from the back of a truck, saw every corner as a chance to take a stand on some issue close to the hearts of these people he wanted to represent in Congress: compensation when they were hurt on the job, a soldiers' bonus, liberalized immigration laws, the repeal of Prohibition or at least its modification to permit the sale of beer and wine.

The Republicans had given him their nomination but nobody was guaranteeing that he would be elected. He was not well known in the 20th District and open to the charge of carpetbagging, although his home in the Bronx was little more than a brisk thirty-minute walk from the district border. In addition, he faced two strong opponents: William Karlin, a Socialist endorsed by important trade unions and running on a something-for-everybody platform, and the Democrat Henry Frank, who was a pedestrian and politically untested lawyer but had the advantage of Tammany Hall's very considerable support.

The campaign, which was to end in a savage confrontation, began as a civilized discourse between gentlemen, each of whom credited the others' competence and sincerity, reserving for himself only some special leverage—party connections, commitment, experience—that would enable him to do more for the district. La Guardia was downright friendly; when Karlin sent him a starchy challenge to debate, the Little Flower responded with a "My dear Bill" letter: "While it is true that we are both candidates for Congress, I hardly see the necessity for making your letter so cold and formal. Why, bless your heart, of course I'll debate with you."

The encounter, before a good-natured crowd of three thousand at the Star Casino, was thoroughly amicable. La Guardia called himself a radical running on a conservative ticket and said

Karlin was a conservative on a radical ticket. "As a man, Mr. Karlin is very capable. As a Socialist congressman, he would be alone, powerless." Karlin insisted that no Republican, not even La Guardia, could adequately represent labor in Congress. They were both cheered and shook hands warmly at the end.

Meanwhile, Henry Frank and his Tammany advisers, looking around at the support building for La Guardia, decided this gentlemanly campaign could well snatch away a victory they'd assumed was locked up. Republican Senator Hiram Johnson, the Progressive hero who had been Teddy Roosevelt's running mate in 1912, sent a telegram from California that made all the newspapers: "I KNOW LA GUARDIA AND IF I HAD A THOUSAND VOTES IN HIS DISTRICT I WOULD CAST THEM ALL FOR HIM." New York's Democratic mayor, John Hylan, broke ranks to come uptown and declare, "Now that [La Guardia] is running for Congress, I hope that all my friends in Harlem, regardless of party, will vote for him."

The Hearst papers and the *Evening Mail* had already endorsed him, and the *Times,* the *World* and *Daily News* found something good to say about him every day. He seemed to be winning over the Socialists and, according to an important Italian daily, *Bollettino della Sera,* already had the Italians in his hip pocket: "For the Italians, Major La Guardia has no need of an expressed program. His name is the program."

The glum Democratic strategists saw only one way to salvage the situation: They made up their minds to go all-out for the Jewish vote. They were going to try for a knockout, no holds barred. It was not a wise decision. As they would remorsefully learn, they were up against the best counterpuncher in the business.

On October 30, 1922, eight days before the election, Jewish voters by the thousands in the 20th District received a postcard in the mail:

> The most important office in this country for Judaism is the Congressman. Our flesh and blood are . . . on the other side of the ocean. Only through our Congressman can we go to their rescue.
> There are three candidates, who are seeking your vote: One is Karlin, the atheist. The second is the Italian La Guardia, who is a pronounced anti-Semite and Jew-hater.
> Be careful how you vote.

Our candidate is Henry Frank, who is a Jew with a Jewish heart, and who does good for us. Therefore it is up to you and your friends to vote for our friend and beloved one, Henry Frank, for Congressman.

The card was signed "The Jewish Committee" but it had Tammany paw prints all over it.

When someone brought one into the storefront on Madison Avenue, La Guardia allowed himself the momentary luxury of a fine and furious rage. Then he got down to business. First he sent his volunteers out with a typewritten sheet of "Instruction for Speakers: 'Friends, a last-moment campaign trick has been pulled by a defeated candidate.... You will notice that this is an anonymous communication. [Otherwise] Major La Guardia would have had the person responsible arrested for criminal libel!'"

Then he himself went charging out into the Jewish neighborhoods, mainly clustered in the side streets off Fifth Avenue, nailing the lie at one corner after another and denouncing Frank and his Tammany manipulators for their shameful attempt to stir up racial prejudice against him. An aide advised him to make a speech about his mother, revealing that she was Jewish, but he did not want to resort to that; he had always considered himself Italian and to imply otherwise now would be too transparently self-serving. But sensing that they had come to a turning point in the election, concerned that he would be unable to reach enough Jewish voters in the remaining time to reassure the ghetto, he tried to think of something else. And soon his antic imagination, running free, told him what he had to do. Racing back to headquarters, he burst in yelling, "Ma-RIE!"

Miss Fisher came running, pencil poised, for that tone carried its own message.

"An open letter to Henry Frank," he began, loping nervously around the store, running his fingers through his already rumpled black hair. Then he rattled off the letter with barely a pause for reflection:

At the beginning of the campaign I announced that I would not indulge in personalities nor in abuse of my opponents. I have kept that pledge....

You have seen fit, however, to resort to the kind of campaigning which was discredited in American politics over twenty years

The son of the bandleader at Whipple Barracks graduates
from grade school in Prescott, Arizona Territory. (Wide
World Photos)

BELOW: Major La Guardia with Maggiore Negrotto, Capitano Zapelloni, and Mitragliere Firmani (seated). (Photo courtesy of J. A. Hand and A. A. Zapelloni)

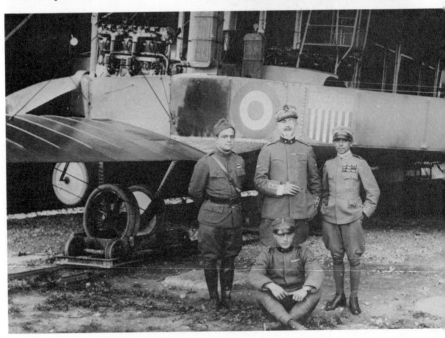

Representative La Guardia of New York making his debut
over WJZ in the early days of radio. (UPI)

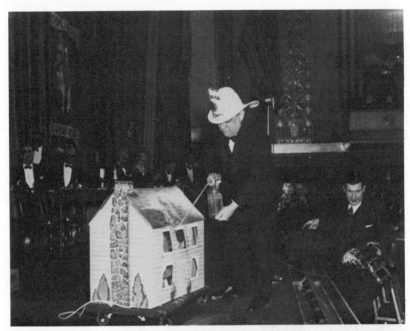

ABOVE: Mayor La Guardia in action during the entertainment by the Circus Saints and Sinners Club for the President's Birthday Ball at the Waldorf-Astoria. (Wide World Photos)
BELOW: As guest conductor of the National Symphony Orchestra. (Wide World Photos)

ABOVE: Reelected for the third time as Mayor, La Guardia reflects on the job that lies ahead. (Wide World Photos)
BELOW: Taking the oath of office on January 1, 1942, at the home of Justice Samuel Seabury, with his wife and children, and Justice Philip McCook (far right). (UPI)

ABOVE: With Mrs. La Guardia at the voting booth on November 2, 1943. (UPI)
BELOW: The official welcome at City Hall for General Eisenhower on June 19, 1945. (Wide World Photos)

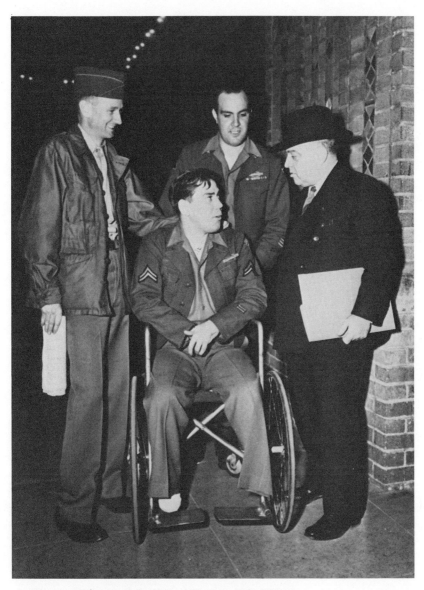

As Director General of the United Nations Rehabilitation
and Relief Association talking with veterans in Atlantic
City, New Jersey, March 28, 1946. (Wide World Photos)

La Guardia with his son, Eric, returning from a European
UNRRA trip on September 5, 1946. (UPI)

ago. You ... are making a racial-religious appeal for sympathy votes [and] I regret exceedingly that this has happened. However I have always met a fight on any issue openly. ...

Very well, then ... I hereby challenge you to publicly and openly debate the issues of the campaign, the debate to be conducted by you and me *entirely in the Yiddish language.*

We will suit your convenience in every respect.

Miss Fisher, who had finished writing before she realized what she had written, looked up with blue-eyed innocence. "But, Major," she said, "Mr. Frank doesn't speak Yiddish."

"I know," beamed La Guardia. "Isn't it wonderful! Type that thing up right away."

When it was ready, he himself translated it into Yiddish. By the next afternoon thousands of copies, in both languages, had been run off and distributed throughout the district.

Henry Frank must have felt as though he had been hit by a subway train; he didn't know what to do. Eventually someone let out the word that he was "indisposed, sick in bed," but then he was seen rushing into what must have been a desperate strategy session at his headquarters. La Guardia, meanwhile, virtually camped in the Jewish quarter. "I'm waiting," he kept saying, and while waiting he stumped the neighborhood and made three ringing speeches—in Yiddish, of course. He flayed his opponent for resorting to racist slurs and then refusing to answer for them in open debate. He reminded the preponderantly Jewish crowds of his official protests against the Polish pogroms when he was in Congress and reiterated his support for the Jews and their aspirations. The people were enthralled. They were still waiting for Henry Frank to say one word of Yiddish to them—what kind of Jew was *that?*—yet here was this *Italiener,* this *goy,* speaking just like one of them. Said one journalist, "The rabbis themselves led the applause."

Frank, seeing the election slipping away from him, stung to recklessness, made yet another mistake, and this one was fatal. Forty-eight hours before the polls opened on Tuesday, November 5, 1922, he finally responded to La Guardia's challenge in a letter released to the press:

A challenge from you, with your well-known anti-Semitic tendencies to debate in Yiddish is an insult and an affront to the

Jewish electives [*sic*] in our community. You are certainly not
qualified to represent the people, and you will know it on the day
when the people send you back, bag and baggage, to your little
cottage and sun-parlor on University Avenue in the Bronx.

La Guardia, who could turn on an imposing burst of rage
when it suited his purpose, did not have to embellish this time.
The cruelty of the reference to the sun porch, scraping still-raw
wounds, made him want to commit mayhem. Instead, he took his
fury back to the street corners off Fifth Avenue, crying out, "A
man who would write a letter of that kind has sunk to the lowest
possible level.... He *knows* I was compelled to move out of my
district and purchase that house with the sun-parlor in order to
try to save the life of my poor wife."

His anger was genuine and the emotion it fed honest; newsmen reported tears in his eyes as he spoke. But La Guardia was a
political animal to the essence of his being now. Sensing that the
crowd was with him—provoked, Jews and Italians could shriek
"Dago!" and "Kike!" at one another, but they shared a deep feeling for family—he derided the notion that only a Jew could represent the Jews of the 20th District in Congress. Then he turned
back to Frank and got off a line that is remembered whenever La
Guardia stories are told. "After all," he asked in his best mocking
falsetto, "is he looking for a job as a *shammes* [caretaker of a syn-
agogue] or does he want to be elected congressman?"

There was a moment's electric silence. This was cutting very
close to the bone. But so cleanly had he caught the word's disparaging flavor—a *shammes* is every Jew's low man on the totem
pole—that juxtaposed with the ghetto's exalted concept of a
United States congressman, it touched off a storm of laughter
that went echoing through the district and left Frank with his
credibility seriously impaired among thoughtful voters.

The next day, a Jewish newspaper came out for La Guardia
as "one who speaks Yiddish like a true Jew" and who, over the
years, had been a good friend to the Jewish people.

On Election Day, for as long as the polls were open, La
Guardia nervously toured the district with two policemen, for it
was clear that there was now only one way Tammany could win.
There were several clashes that more than once almost came to
blows. But he couldn't be everywhere and no one could say how

many La Guardia votes were thrown in the river or stuffed down some handy sewer. He knew there would not be an early decision, and when the last ballot box was sealed he went home to the house on University Avenue with no more than a reasonable chance of finishing on top.

The Jewish assembly districts, which reported first, gave Frank an early lead. But it was not the commanding lead the Democrats counted on; La Guardia's late forays into the ghetto had won him a lot of support. Now the only question was whether there would be enough votes from the predominantly Italian areas to carry the day. So close was the outcome that not until November 7, two days after the election, was it made public: La Guardia 8,492; Frank 8,324; Karlin 5,260. On the strength of a 168-vote margin, the Little Flower was going back to Congress.

Frank filed suit for a recount on the grounds of fraud by Republican election officials, which came to nothing. But the astonishing paradox—*Tammany* crying fraud—was gleefully noted in all parts of the city.

By the time La Guardia took his seat in the 68th Congress, which did not convene until December 3, 1923, the political landscape was dramatically changed. Al Smith had won back the governorship of New York so convincingly that even the deposed Miller conceded his policies might be at fault. Meanwhile, sociable, pliable Warren Harding had died—fortuitously, said some; helped along by his wife, said others—just as a shattering series of scandals involving his administration and personal life was about to be exposed. It was so gross that for fifty years, until Watergate, it stood as the metaphor for presidential malefaction. The new president, Calvin Coolidge, was a dour New Englander of whom Will Rogers said, "He didn't do anything, but that's what the people wanted done."

So it seemed. The United States was busy celebrating the Roaring Twenties, and big industry, free of wartime government restrictions, was off on an apparently endless spree of production and profit-making. The business of the country was business, the heralds of the new order were saying, and the least government was the best government. Businessmen, engaged in an orgy of speculation and self-congratulation, could only agree.

The stock market climbed giddily; wages rose to new heights. Everybody seemed to be making money. Everybody was buying radios, refrigerators, automobiles.

Not everybody. In fact, most Americans knew little of this widely proclaimed prosperity beyond what they read in the newspapers. Less than 1 percent of the population invested in the stock market; a third of the homes were without electricity. Farmers in the South and West were in distress and agriculture across the country was slipping into a depression from which it would not fully recover until World War II. Though craft union members and other skilled workers were indeed faring well, the larger part of the American work force—miners, textile workers, manual laborers—unorganized and untrained, was having a hard time making ends meet. The official figure for unemployment was low but did not take into account the millions who were laid off for a month or two every year, or those idled by the long and bitter strikes that marked the twenties. In families like these the loss of the breadwinner's wage, even for a few weeks, brought privation.

So La Guardia looked around and saw plenty of causes to engage his attention. He did not wait for the congressional session to start before picking up his fight against the greed, indifference and villainy on which he blamed America's ills. Only days after his election he was asked for help in the matter of a young Italian immigrant girl, barred from entry to the United States because of illness but refused a requested delay in her deportation so her mother could return with her. La Guardia's wrath fairly leaps from the telegram he shot off to the relevant authority, Secretary of Labor James J. Davis:

> We may as well understand each other at once. You and your department cruel, inhuman, narrow-minded, prejudiced. Attitude towards immigrants and unwarranted interpretation law been rebuked all over country. . . . This attitude must change at once. I will not tolerate any more this hardhearted treatment of immigrants. I insist upon this stay being granted.

It was not. But Davis, flintily replying that he was simply obeying the law, had not heard the last of La Guardia. A few weeks later, when three hundred Jewish immigrants were about to be deported because their national quotas had been filled while they were on their way to the United States, the irrepressible congressman-elect went to the very top. Tracking the vacationing President Harding to a houseboat in Florida, La Guardia sent him a telegram appealing "for the sake of humanity and charity" that the deportations be delayed until the quotas opened up again. This time he won out.

In April, 1923, he organized a consumers' strike against inflationary meat prices in Harlem; it spread across the city and resulted in cuts up to 10 cents a pound, a not inconsiderable saving for working-class housewives who had to make pennies count. In Buffalo he joined the fight of the Amalgamated Clothing Workers for recognition. In New York City he agitated for a better transit law, rent controls, and public parks for the islands in the East River. By the time the 68th Congress was called to order, he had earned his place as a leader of the corporal's guard of insurgent Republicans who banded together under the Progressive banner. Their dean was Senator Robert M. La Follette of Wisconsin, now nearly seventy years old, his wild wiry hair gone white but his eyes still smoldering with conviction. To those who believed with him that the first issue of the time was "the encroachment of the powerful few upon the rights of the many," Fighting Bob remained the Progressives' idol, inspiration and guiding spirit.

La Guardia was assigned Room 150 in the House Office Building, a marble and wood-paneled edifice of hushed voices and endless corridors through which the nation's legislators sauntered to and from committee hearings and roll call votes on the House floor. The offices were sanctums of calm, droning, slow-motion activity, each one, even those of the Democratic members, hung with a studio portrait of Calvin Coolidge wearing his wintry smile. The only exception was Room 150, whose wall featured a big photo of Rudolph Valentino; and when the door was opened snatches of sound and fury leapt out. A contemporary journalist, Duff Gilfond, spent some time inside and drew an intriguing word picture of the principal occupant. We see La Guardia

gesticulating wildly as he argues in Italian with a constituent, dictating a letter urging a Cabinet officer to be sensible, feeding the newspapermen with another rum-running revelation, mimick-

ing the secretary of the treasury, listening to the sob story of a
rabbi told in Yiddish—his own Yiddish, and his Italian and
English, are repeatedly interpolated with the same adjective—
lousy . . . and all this more or less at the same time.

The office was not his natural habitat. He raced through
chores and appointments and, except for letters from constituents, which were separately and carefully handled, flipped
through his mail with such terse dismissal notices as "Bunk!,"
"We appreciate his respect," and, in response to a financial appeal from a religious group, "Something for Jesus? Nice boy,
Jesus," meanwhile all but vanishing in a cloud of smoke from the
two-for-a-nickel cigars he had taken up. He is waiting for the bell
signaling the convening of the House, skittish, keyed up, a prize-
fighter anticipating the start of the next round. When the bell
sounds, he will go barreling down the corridors—"like a student
late for class," says Miss Gilfond—and once on the chamber
floor, will stay there or within earshot until adjournment, eating
peanuts instead of lunch lest he miss something to object to.

He earned, observers said, no worse than a tie for first place
among the members for loquacity. Colleagues sometimes groaned
when he rose to speak—no one condemns speechifying more than
politicians, or does more of it—but few of them left the floor, and
without the La Guardia entries, *The Congressional Record* for
the years 1923–1932 would have been a far duller document.

Nothing was outside the realm of his interest. When the rifle
lobby proposed public shooting grounds next to migratory bird
refuges for better "management" of the flocks, La Guardia
bounded to his feet:

I am for the conservation of bird life; but when I want advice on
the subject, I refuse to take it from the paid agent of ammunition
and gun makers! If this bill is to pass, gentlemen, let there be no
hypocrisy about it. Let it be known as "The Bird Slaughter Bill."

He seemed so vulnerable in debate—a short, fat, Italian
from New York City who spoke in a squeaky voice and was often
in a minority of one against the sense of the whole House—that it

took a while before those who sought to make a reputation as wits at his expense realized he was leaving them for dead. Otis T. Wingo, who didn't object to being known as the Adonis of Arkansas, once tangled with him over an appropriation for the federal assay building in New York.

WINGO: If the gentleman does not know that is a pork barrel bill, he has not enough sense to get in out of the rain.

LA GUARDIA: If the gentleman designated that as a "pork barrel" bill he is *still* out in the rain.

WINGO: That may be; but I have enough sense to keep out of the rain, and I know something about my own country.

LA GUARDIA: But, apparently, you know nothing about the bill.

WINGO: Yes, I know about that bill. . . . They came in here and wanted $385,000 for the adornment of the façade. Does the gentleman from New York know what a façade is?

LA GUARDIA: Of course he does. Does the gentleman from Arkansas?

WINGO: (*Preening as he prepares to demolish the little wop from New York*) Yes. That is the same thing to a building that a snout is to a hog. It is the front part of it. And a porkeater ought to know what the façade is.

LA GUARDIA: (*Sighing as he sinks the final barb where it hurts most*) If the gentleman from Arkansas were less interested in his own façade and more in the inside of his head, he would be a better legislator.

This last was expunged from the *Record*, but no one who was on the floor or in the galleries that day would ever forget it—or could keep from laughing at Wingo's red-faced rage.

It was a time when jingoistic fantasies about America's Nordic origins and virtues opened into a decade of genteel discrimination and vicious bigotry: cross-burnings, floggings, lynchings. The Ku Klux Klan, in white-sheeted anonymity, could parade by day and assail blacks, Jews and Catholics by night without generating even a word of censure from the President of the United States; during the election campaign of 1924, when it seemed prudent to cover his flank, Coolidge assigned the matter of the Klan to Vice-President Charles Dawes, who, La Guardia noted, "praised it with faint damn."

Jesus Christ, wrote one momentary savant, was an Anglo-Saxon. So were Dante, Michelangelo and Columbus. While La

Guardia was deriding this arrant nonsense and reminding the House that the Romans brought civilization to Nordic England, then barbarian, Congressman John W. Summers of Washington interrupted to ask, "Has it not been a question whether Christopher Columbus came from your country or not?"

La Guardia bolted out of his seat. "My country? My country is the United States," he cried out, and later added with passion, "I was raised out in the big State of Arizona, and anyone who seeks to question that Americanism, I do not care how big he is, will do so at his peril."

At the height of the Nordic supremacy claptrap, a magazine article charged that New York's congressional representatives weren't even "real Americans," whereupon the *World* took it upon itself to report on the ancestry of each member of the city's delegation. La Guardia could not resist the opportunity; he responded to the questionnaire by saying that he himself had no family tree, but that his dog Yank did, "a distinguished one, to be sure. But he's still only a son of a bitch."

For a long time La Guardia's antics and sizzling repartee gave him a reputation as a comic and obscured his important legislative contributions. Consciously or otherwise, he had to bide his time. Denied a place on any meaningful committee because of his insurgency, his proposals ignored or derided, he was forced to operate from the sidelines, and his only weapons, as historian Arthur Mann notes in his study of La Guardia's pre-mayoral years, were ridicule, exposure and dissent. And yet the fact is that he knew more about pending legislation than most House members, and affected more bills than any of them. With a fanatic attention to detail, he saw things they missed and was ready with objections, amendments and riders. With his omnivorous interest in every branch of the government, there was scarcely one he didn't try to reform.

La Guardia spent twelve years in the House of Representatives, but it is little understood that his service there, consummated by his final term, probably surpassed his three terms as mayor of New York in lasting achievement. He once said, "As long as a person talks about great American standards he is applauded; when he asks to put them into practice he is a radical."

But when the bubble of endless prosperity burst, when the Depression breadline replaced the ticker tape as the symbol of the American economy, La Guardia's radical ideas no longer seemed so radical. They had nothing in common with the panaceas of either the extreme right or the extreme left. His faith in the American system ran deep and did not waver, and as his concerns had always been for the very people most beset by the crisis—the poor city-dweller and the marginal farmer, immigrants, blacks, migrant workers—the raillery long aimed at him from both sides of the House aisle suddenly stopped. Colleagues began listening to what for a decade had been a voice in the wilderness. And in the next years, when La Guardia was no longer in Washington but in New York, every important proposal he had made and that had been scorned, ridiculed and shouted down—minimum wages, old-age pensions, a child-labor law, workmen's compensation, social security, the repeal of Prohibition, government regulation of utilities and the stock market—every one became the law of the land.

9
1929

In the House restaurant one morning, some tourists testily wondered why the rumpled little man at the next table had been served before they were. "Oh, I work here," Fiorello La Guardia told them cheerfully. "They know I have to get to work."

Everyone, friend and foe, was awed by his capacity for work. Late in the day, every day, following adjournment, when some members unwound with a drink in a few privileged, out-of-the-way offices, and the rest fled Capitol Hill, La Guardia walked back to Room 150 with a stack of bills for study under his arm. When the bills came to the floor of the House days or weeks later, he knew them inside out and was ready to answer the questions of his less-prepared colleagues—the abominated but essential boy in the class who does his homework.

He was particularly relentless in his scrutiny of the Wednesday consent calendar, a traditional House device for speeding courtesies and minor district appropriation bills through the legislative process by unanimous consent, without the embarrassment of debate or a roll call vote. It was considered an infraction of the unwritten rules for a congressman actually to study the consent calendar, let alone raise an objection, which would require the bill in question to be withdrawn. But La Guardia, who paid little attention to any rules, written or otherwise, ignored this one completely. Miss Fisher, whose job it was "to get the calendar up for him, and anything\connected with every bill on it," recalled that he "took such an interest in it that he more or less had charge on Wednesdays . . . he was just the best objector."

"Mr. Speaker, reserving the right to object, I call the attention of the House to this bridge bill that is coming up," he began on an otherwise cheery Wednesday morning, ruining the day for at least one legislator and provoking mournful sighs throughout the chamber. That was a memorable occasion. Having blocked the granting of a bridge franchise to a man who had sold a previous franchise for a hefty profit, La Guardia stayed on the floor munching peanuts through the lunch hour so he would be on hand to object to the sale of some public property by private arrangement, and later still to bar a plan to lease out a 12.7-million-dollar naval base for no other return to the government than a promise to "upkeep the premises."

"The function of a progressive," he once said, "is to keep on protesting until things get so bad that a reactionary demands reform." He persisted in introducing bills that could not pass— "They serve an educational purpose"—and in attending every congressional session and all his committee meetings. But the diversity of his activities and interests did not reduce his effectiveness on the big issues of the 1920s. The first of these, the administration's tax policy, involved him in a ten-year running battle with Secretary of the Treasury Andrew W. Mellon.

To a dispassionate observer it might have seemed an unfair fight—the tough-talking, street-wise congressman from a New York tenement district against a frail wisp of a man, silver-haired, seventy years old in 1925, who, said a Philadelphia editor, "looks like a tired bookkeeper afraid of losing his job"— except that Andrew Mellon was one of the richest men in the world. In order to serve as Treasury Secretary, he had to resign from the boards of sixty corporations with an aggregate capital of $60 billion.

"Logically and conscientiously," wrote Samuel Hopkins Adams, "Mr. Mellon conceived his official duty to be the conservation and protection of wealth." When, early on, La Guardia wrote him asking how much tax revenue would be required to pay a soldiers' bonus, the Secretary replied peevishly, "I regret that unless you can present some comprehensive plan by which you propose to raise the necessary money . . . I am unable to give you specific figures." When La Guardia did come up with such a plan, it was flatly rejected.

Mellon's program called for the repeal of the excess profits tax and sharp reductions in inheritance and income surtaxes, all of which were of keen interest to millionaires but to few others; there were no comparable reductions in the lower brackets. Mellon also kept busy disbursing federal funds to the larger cor-

porations, including several of his own, in the form of cash re-
bates, credits and tax abatements. He was a dauntless believer in
business as the fountainhead of the national well-being, and felt
that business would prosper in proportion to the easing of its tax
burden. By 1930 the Treasury had paid out $3.5 billion under
this unpublicized program—adding that much more fuel to a
speculative fire already out of control.

That the business interests did not always get everything
they wanted was due only to the rearguard actions fought by the
Progressives. "Something is wrong with the economic system of a
country," said La Guardia, "when the Chief Executive asks for
charity for dependent widows and orphans and the Secretary of
the Treasury asks for a bill to repeal taxes on incomes of $5 mil-
lion a year."

To a stenographer, a member of the Women's National Republican Club, who wrote that she was joined by others in asking
him to withdraw his objections to the Mellon tax plan, he replied
with rankled irony:

> I can readily understand your anxiety and that of your co-work-
> ers on the taxes over $200,000 a year. I was a stenographer once
> and I remember how much I had to worry about my income over
> $200,000 a year.

In March 1929, when Calvin Coolidge retired to Vermont, a
man who made $1 million a year was benefiting from Mellon's tax
reductions to the extent of a 31 percent gain in income after
taxes; a man earning $5,000 gained 1 percent. And the wispy lit-
tle billionaire from Pittsburgh was being hailed as the greatest
Secretary of the Treasury since Alexander Hamilton.

La Guardia took on Henry Ford with better success. Ford
was bidding for two nitrate plants and a half-finished dam
at Muscle Shoals, Alabama, on the Tennessee River; they had
been built by the federal government for the production of ex-
plosives during the war. Ford expressed interest in developing
the site "for the manufacture of low-priced fertilizer for the benefit of the American farmer," and though he offered to buy it at
a fraction of its cost, farmers cheered and Secretary of Commerce Herbert H. Hoover praised the auto magnate for "real

business courage." President Coolidge, only too eager to re-
move the government from any semblance of competition with
private enterprise, urged Congress to accept the offer. The
price, he said, was secondary.

Today it is conceded that the Tennessee Valley would be a
poorer region if Ford's bid had been accepted. But in 1924, when
Henry Ford's esteem in the eyes of his countrymen was so high
that many of them were booming him for President, when business was regarded as the national calling and businessmen as the
nation's true patriots, it took a certain reckless gallantry to
stand up in the Congress of the United States and say that Ford
was out to fleece the public. But a lionhearted handful did it, and
their leaders were Nebraska's Senator George W. Norris and
East Harlem's Fiorello La Guardia.

Norris, a Progressive supporter of both Theodore Roosevelt
and Robert La Follette in their independent campaigns for the
presidency, and hence not much more popular with the Republican hierarchy than La Guardia, had caught a vision of how inex-
pensive electricity could "lighten the drudgery of farms and
urban homes, while revolutionizing the factories." So inspired,
he was ready to fight every attempt to hand over the power resources of America's river valleys for private exploitation.

La Guardia understood Norris's dream, and shared it. But
his most basic feeling about Muscle Shoals was generated by his
antipathy for Henry Ford. Millions might see Ford as the Lone
Ranger of American industry—the foe of Wall Street, the manu-
facturer of the poor man's car, the trailblazer of the five-dollar
day—but to La Guardia he was just a profiteer, and an anti-Semite at that,* with "hatred in his heart . . . ignorant of history, literature and religion."

"Why, Gentlemen, this proposition makes the Teapot Dome
look like petty larceny," he said during the debate, and called it
"a bill to make Henry Ford the industrial king of the United
States." He tied up the required legislation with endless parliamentary maneuvers, at which he was expert, as did Norris in the

---

* For years, Ford's *Dearborn Independent* printed scurrilous attacks on the Jews, blaming
them for almost every American affliction, from the war to high rents and short skirts. In 1927
he was forced to retract these statements and apologize for them; by 1942 he was speaking out
forcefully against anti-Semitism.

Senate. Seeing clearly that the manufacture of fertilizer was
only a smoke screen for the true allure of Muscle Shoals, he made
sure the world knew it, and eventually introduced his own bill
for government development of the site.

> LA GUARDIA: Let's be perfectly frank about it, Mr. Chairman.
> Muscle Shoals is the greatest power plant in the country and *that*
> is what makes it so attractive. All this talk about a keen desire to
> help the farmer is simply window-dressing. If you offer Muscle
> Shoals to anyone and tell them that you will give them all the
> help, all the *power* they need to make *fertilizer* and limit them to
> that alone, they will not give you five cents for it! That being so,
> why should the Government part with this priceless pos-
> session? . . . I am not afraid of this talk of the Government going
> into business. . . . I remember the time, and you do, too, when it
> was considered Socialistic for a municipality to own its own water
> supply. . . . Gentlemen, times are changing.
> CONGRESSMAN BOYLAN: You think then that it is their underly-
> ing purpose to get this development for power purposes only?
> LA GUARDIA: Certainly, because while good sound business men
> may try to kid this committee and Congress . . . we must face this
> proposition, and face it truthfully. My resolution would provide
> for the Government to keep that plant and it would be a model
> power plant for the whole United States and would start a new era
> in this country.

By then, Ford had given up and withdrawn his bid. "We
have lost our interest in Muscle Shoals. Productive business cannot wait on politics," he said loftily.

The rest of the battle was not so easily won. Electricity
would be the most saleable source of energy for the rest of the
twentieth century, and though support for a public power bill
grew, it was up against the relentless lobby of the private utilities: fifteen holding and operating companies which controlled 80
percent of all the gas and electricity produced in the United
States. Twice, Norris and La Guardia arduously assembled the
votes and shepherded joint resolutions for federal development
of Muscle Shoals through both houses of Congress, and twice
they were undone by presidential vetoes.

But Norris persevered. Under a new President, a month
after La Guardia had left Washington, the enabling legislation
passed and Muscle Shoals was saved for the people. And Muscle

Shoals was the starting point for the integrated development of a seven-state region, administered by the Tennessee Valley Authority (TVA), which brought electricity into a million candlelit homes, restored badly eroded farmlands, and stirred a moribund economy back to life.

All through the 1920s, *The New York Times* devoted more space to La Guardia's activities and attitudes with regard to Prohibition than to his views on any of the infinitely more significant issues of the day. Yet taxes, labor relations and rising prices, to name just three of his concerns, each claimed more of his time and energy than his well-publicized forays against the drys. But of course Prohibition was the flashiest ongoing story of the decade and it is perfectly true that the gentleman from East Harlem contributed his fair share of the pyrotechnics.

Everyone who opposed the Prohibition laws recognized their foolishness and ultimate futility. But to La Guardia it was more than that; it was another "them against us" issue, and this is what engaged his ardor. As Professor Mann has pointed out, the Eighteenth Amendment sprang from the same impulse that led to restrictive immigration laws: the longing of Protestant, small-town America to keep the orderly and compatible society it had inherited. It was, in essence, a struggle between the cities and the rural areas, between new arrivals and proud, old-stock Americans—between two worlds. It was no secret where La Guardia's love lay and he mocked and taunted his bluenose puritan opponents mercilessly.

In 1919 he had warned the House that the effort to enforce Prohibition would "create contempt and disregard for the law." By 1925 he was more than justified, but took no satisfaction from it. The Volstead Act had bred wholesale corruption involving big money, organized crime, and the government itself. Sadly summing it all up on the floor of the House, La Guardia said, "Politicians are ducking, candidates are hedging, the Anti-Saloon League prospering, people are being poisoned, bootleggers enriched, and government officials corrupted."

Gentlemen [he told the House in February that year], what is the use of closing our eyes to the existing conditions? The im-

portation of liquor into this country is of such magnitude, it
comes in such enormous quantities, involving use of a fleet of
steamers, involving enormous banking operations, involving hundreds of millions of dollars, that it could not carry on without the
knowledge if not the connivance of the authorities entrusted with
the enforcement of the law.

To dramatize the futility of policing a law regularly broken
by otherwise respectable millions, he once proposed increasing
the Prohibition Bureau's enforcement staff from 2,000 to 250,000
and raising its annual appropriation from $12 million to $300
million. There were no takers. Someone said that if the Bureau
had La Guardia's sources of information—mainly leads sent him
by sympathizers and doggedly researched—it could *cut* its staff.
He once told a stunned House that 350 cases of confiscated whiskey had been "removed" from the office of the United States
Marshal in Indianapolis and bootlegged. Scornfully, federal
agents went to investigate; it was true. The Department of Justice liked to boast of Franklin L. Dodge, a crack investigator,
who had broken up an Ohio whiskey ring and sent its leader,
George Remus, to prison. One day in 1926, La Guardia rose in
the House and charged that with Remus out of the way, Dodge
had moved in with Mrs. Remus and helped himself to 200,000
dollars' worth of the bootleg whiskey.

LA GUARDIA: What do you intend to do about your "ace" now
that he is violating both the Mann Act and the Volstead Act?
CONGRESSMAN BLANTON: Ought we not hold the infamous liquor
traffic responsible for seducing this Government agent and leading him astray?
LA GUARDIA: What do you want to do—give him a Congressional
Medal? I would put him in jail.

Dodge denied the charge and was never prosecuted. But as
soon as George Remus got out of prison, he went looking for his
wife and shot her dead.
     Almost as enduring a legend as La Guardia reading *Dick
Tracy* to New York's children during a newspaper strike was
what happened after he announced, in the very precincts of the
torpid House Committee on Alcoholic Liquor Traffic—of which
he had unaccountably been made a member, the only wet one—

that he was going to brew beer. It all began when he forced a meeting of the committee, the first meeting in four years, by producing a witness who gave evidence on the link between bankers and bootleggers. The chairman, Congressman Grant M. Hudson of Michigan, infuriated by the Little Flower's smirking delight in the testimony, ordered him to behave.

LA GUARDIA: The chairman is sore because I have shown how his sacred Prohibition law is being violated.
HUDSON: I am not irritated. Good God, if you want to go get drunk every day, go and do it. I do not know personally that the dry laws are being violated.
LA GUARDIA: (*Shouting*) Then go and learn something! You are probably the only man in the United States who would make such a statement.

Afterward, brooding, he turned that madcap imagination of his loose and came up with a splendid plan for exemplifying the absurdity of the Volstead Act. The "moneyed class" could buy the best liquor and drink it undisturbed; now he was going to do something for "the little guy," he told the startled committee— and later the newspapers. Tomorrow he was going to show them how to brew beer "right in this room!" On the afternoon of June 19, 1926, he duly appeared, accompanied by a former brewer. The few members on hand ran off in alarm, but La Guardia had an audience of nearly fifty elated reporters and photographers and he did not disappoint them.

"Follow me, gentlemen," he commanded in his best military manner, and marched them off to Room 150. There he produced several bottles of cold 0.5 percent beer, which was legal, and a malt extract, sold for medicinal purposes, containing nearly 4 percent alcohol. These he proceeded to mix in a suitably dramatic manner, stirring the contents with a pencil from his pocket until a thick, tantalizing foam overflowed the glass and ran all over his carpet. As the photographers fired away and the reporters pressed close, La Guardia's piping voice exulted, "You needn't feel anxious, gentlemen. There will be at least a little for all of us."

The brewer sipped. "It tastes delightful," he said.

"Now I'll make Pilsener," said La Guardia.

Predictably, the Anti-Saloon League denounced him and demanded his arrest. La Guardia would have loved that, but La Guardia in court was the last thing the harried Prohibition administrator, Brigadier General Lincoln C. Andrews, wanted. "It is not good beer," he said lamely. "The public won't like it."

But the comedy was only half over. In Albany, New York's Prohibition enforcement headquarters announced that anyone in the state caught making beer "with the La Guardia formula" would be jailed. La Guardia immediately accepted the challenge; he could hardly wait for Congress to adjourn so he could take his show on the road. On July 17, 1926, *The New York Times* carried this breezy report:

> Representative Fiorello H. La Guardia will walk into a drug store at 95 Lenox Avenue, near 115th Street, at nine o'clock this morning and there purchase a bottle of malt extract, 3.5 percent alcohol, and a bottle near-beer. He will mix the two at the soda fountain and drink the concoction. Then he will stand by and wait to be arrested.

The Little Flower appeared at the stroke of nine. He was immediately surrounded by a great throng and enough newsmen to cover a declaration of war. Merrily he brewed beer and the crowd drank and the photographers took pictures—but no one representing the Prohibition enforcement unit of the State of New York appeared. When a lone policeman strolled by, La Guardia called out hopefully, "I'm mixing beer. Won't you arrest me?"

"Oh, that's a job for a Prohibition agent," the canny patrolman replied, and kept strolling.

Newspapers all over the country carried the story. There was a nationwide run on malt extract. And although La Guardia had been unable to break into jail, he had done more to discredit the Volstead Act than all the denunciations in *The Congressional Record.*

He had time for everything, especially lost causes. In 1925 he testified at the court-martial of General Billy Mitchell, who had ruffled the brass by evangelizing for a unified and expanded air force, and whose views La Guardia shared. Mitchell warned that some day Japan would find an easy target in Hawaii unless the plans for its defense included adequate air power. He was found guilty of insubordination.

In 1926, La Guardia flew to Boston in a last effort to help Nicola Sacco and Bartolomeo Vanzetti, two poor, Italian-born anarchists waiting to be executed for the murder of a guard and a paymaster during a shoe-factory holdup in South Braintree, Massachusetts. Sacco and Vanzetti may or may not have been guilty as charged, but the fact is that they were tried by a biased and vindictive court and convicted, not on the evidence, but because of their origins and political beliefs. La Guardia's efforts were in vain and the two were put to death in August 1927.

On December 17, 1927, the submarine *S-4* sank after being rammed by a Coast Guard destroyer a mile outside Provincetown harbor. The next day, an exchange of Morse code messages tapped out on its steel hull revealed that at least six men of a crew of forty were still alive. "How long will you be?" was their poignant question to the navy diver, and already-desperate efforts to raise the crippled vessel were intensified. But submarine rescue was then an untested art, and as an appalled nation hung on every bulletin, the hours and the days passed without result.

In Washington, La Guardia, still in his pacifist phase and particularly opposed to the continued construction and deployment of submarines, had prepared a blistering attack on the navy, then impetuously decided to find out for himself exactly what was happening. On New Year's Day, 1928, when perhaps no other official of his rank was at work anywhere in the United States, he gained the navy's permission to observe the rescue operations and hurried to New London, Connecticut, to be taken aboard a sister sub of the *S-4*. For the next thirty-six hours, most of which were spent on the bottom of the sea, he watched and, uncharacteristically, listened, and when he returned to Washington he tore up his speech. Instead, he told Congress that the navy was doing its valiant best, and that the submarine service, full of danger, tension and discomfort, deserved special consideration:

> I believe that both officers and crews should receive additional pay such as we are now allowing for flying service. . . . Insurance should be provided by the Government for the dependents of men who lose their lives in the line of duty. Now, let the House of Representatives send word down to Provincetown that we have con-

fidence and faith in these men who are working night and day and
we know that they are doing everything which is humanly possible under the circumstances. (*Applause*).

It was not enough; the *S-4* became the tomb of its crew. But
La Guardia's spirited speech, as he immodestly declared, "ended
the hysteria throughout the country and in Congress against the
submarine." Twenty years later, Admiral Ernest J. King, who
had been a young officer involved in the rescue operation and
later became commander in chief of the U.S. Navy in World War
II, confirmed that this was so:

> [La Guardia] was largely instrumental in quelling the hue-and-
> cry of an aroused public opinion, premised on incomplete and in-
> correct information. . . . His forthright defense of the Navy in
> connection with the loss of the S4 had an important influence on
> the future of submarines.

None of which is to say the Little Flower was mellowing.
When Martin J. Insull made a radio speech denying there was
such a thing as a "Power Trust," La Guardia rode roughshod
over him, calling him an apologist for his brother, utilities tycoon
Samuel Insull, mastermind of the biggest power trust of all, "a
greedy, vicious association of various power and electric companies." When the Insulls said that only on the floor of the
House of Representatives, where he was immune to the laws of
libel, would he dare make such an outrageous statement, La
Guardia practically ran outside to the Capitol steps and repeated it. No one sued anybody.

Nothing escaped his attention. Once he was struck by an
army enlistment poster featuring a snappy cadet and the caption
"Do You Want to Go to West Point? Ask a Recruiting Officer."
La Guardia asked—and learned that perhaps one man in
twenty-five thousand could ever hope to be appointed to West
Point from the ranks. By his rigorous standards, this made the
enlistment appeal misleading, if not downright fraudulent, and
he badgered the Secretary of War until the posters, 300,000 dollars' worth, were recalled and destroyed.

On April 9, 1929, he "noticed in the press agitation among
some members against" the assignment of office space near theirs

to newly elected Congressman Oscar De Priest, a black from Chicago. On the 10th he wired Speaker Nicholas Longworth, "I shall be glad to have him next to my office." De Priest thanked him but said he would keep his assigned office. "Those who do not like to be near me can move. I have no objection to any member making a fool of himself." No one moved.

But the matters closest to La Guardia's heart were those directly affecting the people he represented, and he never forgot them. Nor could anyone more tellingly dramatize them. Arraigning William B. Ward and his bread trust, whose assets were nearing $1 billion and who had driven thousands of small, independent bakers out of business, he brought a loaf of bread into the House, squeezed it down by half and then opened his hands to let it puff up to the original shape. "Pneumatic bread," he said, daring anyone not to believe it. "They're selling us air!" On the strength of his resolution demanding an investigation of Ward and his allies, the Department of Justice charged them with conspiracy in restraint of trade and broke up the monopoly.

He also went after the meat-packing barons. When beef prices jumped 10 cents a pound in New York City during the summer of 1925, he telegraphed his colleagues from the cattle-raising states to verify a suspicion that cattlemen were gaining nothing from the price boosts. One congressman sent him a bill of sale for three cows that went for 1.5 cents a pound; another wrote that beef on the hoof was bringing so little that ranchers were going broke on the cost of feed. La Guardia passed this information to the press, then wrote the Department of Agriculture asking for an investigation of the packers. Back came a letter from Secretary William J. Jardine to the effect that such a study would entail too much time and expense; instead he enclosed a department bulletin on the economical use of meat in the home. La Guardia, furious, let fly with one of his fulminating letters, adding, as he often did now when blasting inept officialdom, "Nothing in this letter is in any way confidential."

I asked for your help and you send me a bulletin. The people of New York City cannot feed their children on bulletins. They may be very interesting to amateur parlor reformers and to society cooking clases ... but the housewives of New York have been trained by hard experience on the economical use of meat. What

we want is the help of your department ... to bring pressure on
the meat profiteers who are keeping the hard-working people of
this city from obtaining proper nourishment.

Three months later, during the debate over an Agriculture
Department appropriations bill, he told the House of his fruit-
less exchange with Jardine. Waving a copy of the pamphlet,
"Lamb and Mutton and Their Uses in the Diet," he lamented,

> *This* is the help I got.... Why, 90 percent of the people of New
> York City cannot afford to eat lamb chops. I have right here with
> me now—where is it? Oh, yes, here it is in my vest pocket—30
> cents' worth of lamb. (*Holds up spindly lamb chop. Laughter.
> From another pocket, produces a steak.*) Here is $1.75 worth of
> steak. (*Then a roast.*) Three dollars' worth of roast. What working
> man's family can afford to pay three dollars for a roast of this
> size?
>
> Now, gentlemen, we simply have to eat. We have formed the
> habit.

Thus La Guardia—the impassioned advocate, the relentless
gadfly, the eternal showman.

He would never become chairman of a congressional committee. His seniority and his party rank seemed to be marching
in opposite directions: Elected seven times, he lost ground in the
Republican hierarchy every time he defied the leadership, which
was often, and at the end he had not much more influence in
party councils than a first-term regular. On the other hand, he
was the nearest thing to a congressman-at-large the United
States ever had. Whenever he made an important speech, people
all over the country wrote him letters, people who would never
think of writing to their own congressman. Obviously not all of
them agreed with him; there were typewritten letters from bankers and brokers decrying his destructive radicalism, and elegantly written ones on engraved stationery calling him a dirty
communist or a dago bastard, or both. But mostly the letters
came on ruled paper torn from five-cent notebooks and were hard
to read and, in one way or another, said, "Go to it!"

"It was like he owned the United States," Marie Fisher said
long afterward. "Nobody should do anything to it."

When Mussolini came to power in 1922, many Italian-
Americans, shamed by the forlorn aspect of so many previous

Italian governments, were taken with the dash and vigor of the
Fascists and altogether swept away by Il Duce's unabashed na-
tionalism. La Guardia was not one of them. He did not see how
lasting good could come from a regime that silenced its opponents by cracking their skulls. But he did not make any anti-
Mussolini speeches; he said he did not want to split New York's
Italian community over an external matter. Obviously he also
did not want to have to run against Mussolini in the 20th District.

But allied with other concerned local leaders, he fought for
the minds of the more than 1 million New Yorkers of Italian descent over this explosive issue, and one of his weapons was a new
magazine. In 1925 he launched *L'Americolo,* The Little America,
an Italian-language illustrated weekly that, claimed the proud
La Guardia, had "pep, life and punch." The editorial office was
in New York, but the publisher, who wrote the editorials—anti-
Mussolini, pro-La Guardia—and went over every article, picture
and cartoon, ran the show from Washington.

L'Americolo, aiming for a circulation of 40,000, never came
close. It lost money steadily, draining La Guardia's limited resources; he had to mortgage his house again and borrow on a personal note. Then, with the magazine on the verge of bankruptcy,
the day suddenly seemed saved by a lush advertising contract for
a patent medicine. "A full page in every issue for the next year!"
the business manager wrote ecstatically. "How's that?"

Not so good, La Guardia replied. "If your wife would give
the medicine to your own child, sign the contract. Otherwise, reject it." Knowing the answer, he added, "It is not right and, if it
is not right, we should not do it."

That was it. In October 1926, *L'Americolo* failed. La Guardia assumed the corporate debt—which he was not obliged to
do—and ultimately lost $15,000. The mortgage on the University
Avenue house was foreclosed, and, broke again, he moved to East
Harlem, renting a four-room apartment on East 109th Street
near Madison Avenue. When Miss Fisher offered a word of sympathy, he let her have an all-is-not-lost grin and said, "Listen,
they can't call me a carpetbagger anymore!"

In Washington, he shared rooms for a while at the residen-
tial Continental Hotel with a Minnesota congressman, Ole J.
Kvale, a Lutheran minister who had won his seat from Andrew

J. Volstead in 1922. Later he took an apartment on Q Street. He was only rarely at either place, working away with an extravagance that would have felled a lesser man. He still shunned the Washington social circuit, sending White House invitations to children in his district as souvenirs, but occasionally unwound at the movies, which he loved, or a baseball game when the Yankees were in town. Sometimes he invited a few friends for a Sunday evening spaghetti dinner: journalists Duff Gilfond and Ray Tucker, and House colleagues whose political views were sometimes at wide variance with his own but with whom he shared warm personal relations, such as Kvale, who had campaigned on the slogan "Drier Than Volstead," and the Pennsylvania conservative John M. Morin.

But his one sure and consistent ally was Marie Fisher. Once, she had been his entire Washington staff—secretary, researcher, press attaché. Now, having been with him fifteen years and, "having grown up with the work," as she put it, she probably knew as much about the 20th District and pending legislation as he did.

One night, so the story goes, during the Christmas recess of 1928 when, typically, they were working late at the office—La Guardia railing about some missing papers, Miss Fisher smoothly extracting them from the heap on his desk—the congressman asked her if she had eaten yet. She said she had had a sandwich. He said it was almost midnight and sent her home, then chased her into the corridor and asked her to marry him. In *Fiorello!*, the hit musical of 1959, the dialogue went this way:

> FIORELLO: Wait a minute—come here. You're fired!
> MARIE: Fired?
> FIORELLO: As of now . . . I can't court a girl who's working for me.
> MARIE: Mr. La Guardia!
> FIORELLO: Will you marry me? (*Music starts softly.*)

However it happened—these days, Mrs. Marie La Guardia, prizing all versions, smiles tolerantly and contradicts none—La Guardia, a widower for seven years and lonely for all his apparent flamboyance, must have known for a long time how much he cared for the devoted Miss Fisher, how much he depended on her loyalty and judgment. He had always been a closet romantic and might have silently nurtured the idea of marrying her for a long time. Then—perhaps it *was* that December night—it came over him in a burst of pragmatism that it was "a good idea." Miss Fisher thought it was a good idea, too—she had thought so for years—and said yes.

They were married on the morning of February 28, 1929, in the Q Street apartment, the Reverend Congressman Kvale presiding. La Guardia was forty-six, the bride thirty-three. There was a wedding breakfast attended by a few close friends and then—to them it seemed the most natural thing in the world— the newlyweds turned up on Capitol Hill and went to work. Felicitations and good wishes were offered on the floor of the House and, declared Speaker Longworth, carried unanimously. Afterward, when a crowd of secretaries rushed up to offer congratulations, La Guardia waved breezily and said, "Sorry I can't marry all of you." On March 4, when the congressional session ended, not before, they went off on a wedding trip to Panama.

La Guardia returned to the beginnings of a boom by some Italian Republican clubs in Brooklyn and Manhattan to win him the nomination for mayor—which he did nothing to discourage. Ever since 1919, when he was promised and then denied the chance to run, he had been obsessed with being the mayor of New York.

In 1929, however, his prospects of winning were not the brightest. Jimmy Walker, mayor since 1926, had captivated the city with his wit and dazzling charm. He didn't work hard at the job—"He would arrive [at City Hall] around 3 P.M. a couple of days a week," reporter Warren Moscow recalled, "and other days not at all"—but no one cared. No one wanted anything to change in that palmy spring of 1929 when stocks climbed every day and every investment turned a profit and everyone had money in his pocket. "We in America today," said Herbert Hoover accepting the presidential nomination of the Republican party, "are nearer to the final triumph over poverty than ever before in the history of any land."

Walker's picture was always in the newspapers. There seemed to be a ticker tape parade up Broadway every few weeks—Lindbergh, Gertrude Ederle, Admiral Byrd—and there at the steps of City Hall, waiting to greet the latest hero, was the

abiding hero of sophisticated New Yorkers, His Honor the
Mayor, James J. Walker. That didn't hurt when it came to election time, and neither did the sheer numbers: 1.3 million registered Democrats and only half as many registered Republicans.

La Guardia didn't worry about any of that. He never
thought about losing an election; he never expected to lose. And
in any case, his first problem was getting nominated. It was the
same old story: La Guardia was anathema to the Old Guard,
which went about desperately trying to find a conservative alter-
native with enough nerve to tackle Walker. But after La Guardia
announced his candidacy and, as usual, threatened a primary
fight, Sam Koenig gave him his blessing. La Guardia, he reminded the unhappy party regulars, had already beaten Tammany six times and was the only candidate with even a remote
chance of winning against Walker. So, finally, reluctantly, the
Republicans gave the Little Flower their nomination, but
Koenig recalls being "roundly abused . . . and one important individual said we were disgracing the party." Wrote *The New
Yorker:*

> On the night of August 1, the party assembled in the ornate
> Mecca Temple and bowed to the inevitable. With fixed smiles and
> synthetic cheers the delegates told this maverick of the herd that
> he might go forth against Tammany Hall. In their hearts there
> can have been little cheer, however. . . . They had applauded a
> suggestion that Walker be branded as "Jimmy the Jester" for
> campaign purposes, but the respectables of Republicanism then
> asked themselves whether this Italian-American Congressman
> was not even more of a clown.

At first La Guardia tried to win back silk-stocking New
York by soberly addressing himself to its concerns: the elimination of graft, municipal reorganization, regional planning. But
he was seen to be suffering under this constraint, and sounded
dull besides. In any case, his disguise of proper Republicanism
fooled no one and won him few converts from the ranks of ortho-
doxy. Some New Yorkers of national stature endorsed him—Secretary of State Henry Stimson, Columbia University President
Nicholas Murray Butler, Theodore Roosevelt, Jr., Charles Evans
Hughes—but none campaigned for him as Al Smith was out

campaigning for Jimmy Walker. When he attacked big property owners for paying less than their fair share in real estate taxes, those among them who had been regular campaign contributors, like John D. Rockefeller, Jr., closed their checkbooks in his face.

Sam Koenig later conceded that there was no money. "We didn't have any . . . and he didn't have any, either, and you know what that means in a campaign."

It meant a shortage of advertising funds and campaign literature, and headquarters stuffed into a couple of cramped rooms on the second floor of the Cadillac Hotel on Times Square. Marie La Guardia came out of her brief retirement to take over there, and La Guardia tried to stretch his 20th District organization over the city's sixty-two assembly districts. The old regulars— Windels, Espresso, Andrews—were all on board, as was the young Vito Marcantonio; but there just weren't enough of them to make up for the tepid support La Guardia was getting from the rest of the party apparatus.

Frank Freidel, F.D.R.'s biographer, says La Guardia was "weighed down by a foolish and incompetent Republican organization." He had still another problem in that his traditional appeal to progressive and liberal voters was undercut that year by the entry into the race of Norman Thomas, intelligent, earnest, forceful, the best Socialist candidate for public office since Eugene Debs.

Meanwhile Walker, still the biggest problem of all, went waltzing through the election as though the outcome were foreordained. He didn't start campaigning until the middle of October 1929, and even then didn't let it encumber his romance with musical-comedy actress Betty Compton. Every newspaperman covering City Hall knew the mayor's weakness for a pretty face and a well-turned ankle, but this time it was serious. He had packed up and left his portly wife and the family home on St. Luke's Place and now lived in a suite at the posh Mayfair Hotel on Park Avenue. The fetching young Miss Compton kept her things there too. New York rang with rumors but none appeared in the papers—the reporters, who loved Walker for his wit and Irish affability, guarding what was left of his secret.

They also screened his risqué ad libs. One day a report flew through the city that the mayor had been shot. When a newsman reached him at the Mayfair—he was still in bed though it was past noon—the ineffable Walker said, "Shot? Listen, I'm not even half-shot." That one they printed.

Another time he arrived at a Jewish fund-raising dinner wearing a yarmulke. As he walked toward the dais amid tumultuous applause, slim, jaunty, sartorially splendid, a woman embraced him and crooned, "Jimmy, circumcision next?" To which he replied, without missing a step, "Madam, I prefer to wear it off." That one they *didn't* print.

There was no animosity between the candidates. Walker once said of La Guardia, "His is the keenest political mind in many a day, but he's a great showman too. . . . The Little Flower is no shrinking violet." And La Guardia, like everyone else, knowing Walker was a rogue, still couldn't help liking him. This did not inhibit his flailing-arm assaults on the mayor's integrity, conduct, or even his clothes. But Walker was smooth as silk at turning away wrath. "Can anyone expect me to keep my good nature in this campaign? I will go as far as the gutter to defend myself. I will not go down in the sewer."

La Guardia, who was not used to being the straight man in a political campaign, tried harder. One night, in a Harlem church, he bewailed conditions in the city, and in a pointed reference thanked God that at least some people went home to sleep with their own wives. But somebody stepped on his punch line by calling out, "Yeah, and that ain't so good either."

Not until he opened up on Tammany Hall did his campaign catch fire. "There is not a Tammany politician with the exception of Al Smith who would dare to have his bank account examined," he charged, and no Tammany politician came rushing forward holding out his bankbook. Then he began asking why Walker and his police department were so obviously reluctant to press an investigation of Arnold Rothstein's murder. It was a rhetorical question; La Guardia and half the city knew the answer.

Rothstein was to crime what Henry Ford was to manufacturing: the creative wizard who advanced it from a cottage industry to the assembly line. He did not specialize; he had his hand in loan-sharking, counterfeit securities, bootlegging and narcotics. But his bookmaking empire reached across the country and he was the underworld's financial genius and banker; it was Rothstein who put up the money to fix the 1919 World Series. "He is a man who dwells in doorways," said his lawyer, William J. Fallon, "a gray rat waiting for his cheese."

For fifteen years Rothstein did everything but commit murder in Macy's window without ever suffering serious inconvenience at the hands of the authorities, which could only mean that he had friends in high places. Then, on November 4, 1928, he was shot down during a floating poker game at the Park Central Hotel and died two days later. His friends panicked. The police investigation was a textbook example of a cover-up, inept in everything but the dissipation of the evidence. Gone was the killer, until he surrendered three weeks later, when every semblance of a case against him had been undermined; gone any number of eyewitnesses and the fingerprints on the gun; gone, too, all Rothstein's carefully kept black books listing big-name clients and the high police and political figures without whose indulgence he could not have risen to such criminal eminence in New York.

This much was no secret. It was the answer to La Guardia's question: The effective prosecution of the Rothstein case would have revealed, as the Little Flower so emphatically put it, Tammany officials' "intimate, close, personal and pecuniary connections with the criminal element of this city." Now, probing around the periphery of the scandal—as close as an outsider could get—he began making some startling revelations.

La Guardia had always had good sources of private information; his obvious integrity inspired people to tell him things, and his diligent study and sifting developed many a likely lead. Now, in the face of official allegations that Rothstein had died faithful to the criminal code, saying nothing, La Guardia charged that ". . . he made several communications. He also made statements to detectives." He divulged that a chambermaid at the Park Central had been held in jail for months as a material witness in the case, "until the police and the District Attorney's office and the administration were sure she would not talk." When next seen, La Guardia continued, the woman had not only been freed, she suddenly had a new car and enough money to quit her job. And she suddenly remembered nothing about the Rothstein case.

Late in September 1929, La Guardia hit pay dirt. He produced a letter showing that City Magistrate Albert H. Vitale, a

Tammany Democrat even then campaigning for Jimmy Walker in the Bronx, had received a $20,000 "loan" from Rothstein in June 1928. Walker, virtually commuting to Boston to attend rehearsals of Betty Compton's new show, Cole Porter's *Fifty Million Frenchmen*, had no comment. Vitale came up with a convoluted story about a friend, nameless and now fortuitously dead, who had arranged the loan without his knowledge. Then he said that La Guardia's inferences were "most despicable" and made the ritual threat of a libel suit. But of course it never materialized.

But that did not help La Guardia beat Walker. It may be that in the year 1929 nothing could have helped him. In the endless summer of the paper prosperity, New Yorkers preferred wisecracks to reform. The loud, insistent La Guardia made them nervous. Give them their natty, gallant Beau James. Two weeks before the election, reported the *Times*, during ceremonies commemorating the start of work on the Triboro Bridge, "Mayor Walker was sighted afar and from that moment until he had made his way through the crowd and taken his seat in the bandstand, the audience stood and cheered him."

La Guardia, sensing that his charges and entreaties were falling on deaf ears, began swinging wildly. He told an Irish audience that Walker kept a picture of the Prince of Wales in his apartment and dressed like an English fop or a Paris gigolo. Walker was delighted to respond to *those* charges, and did so with his boundless urbanity:

> If I thought I might serve the taxpayers better by appearing at City Hall clad in overalls, or even a snood, I should do so. But until we have an ordinance to the contrary, I shall bathe frequently, as is my custom; and change my linen often, as is perhaps my eccentric desire; and patronize the tailor of my own choice.

To La Guardia, who may have been the only one in his camp expecting to win, the outcome was devastating. Walker crushed him by nearly 500,000 votes, carrying even East Harlem. With the exception of the Queens borough presidency, Tammany had taken every major contest, and with Norman Thomas polling more votes than any Socialist candidate in history, La Guardia was left with barely 25 percent of the total. He was as badly beaten as any major-party candidate in the history of Greater New York.

By 8:30 P.M. he had wired his congratulations to Walker and came out to tell his supporters and well-wishers, "Thank you all. And remember—when you go out of here, smile!" But they all saw that his own eyes were red with tears. Soon after, he and Marie were back in their own apartment on East 109th Street with Piccirilli, Windels and some others. La Guardia, his ebullient high spirits restored, ceremoniously donned his apron—on which he had pinned his war decorations—and made spaghetti. Political talk was finished.

But the editorial postmortems had only begun. The *Herald Tribune* said the people wanted four more years of Tammany; the Brooklyn *Eagle* said Republicans deserted La Guardia because of "your wet stand and foreign extraction." Perhaps both were right, and others as well. But it was crusty old Sam Koenig who summed it up for those who still believed in the La Guardia destiny. "We were too soon with the right man," he said.

He did not know—few people did—that the new era had already begun. On Tuesday, October 29, 1929, one week before the election, the bull market broke wide open: 16.4 million shares of stock sold off at ruinous prices, and Wall Street and the nation were never the same again. The speculative orgy was over, the endless summer ended. The long winter of the Depression had come to America.

PART III
NEW YORK, N.Y.

10

THE RENDEZVOUS
WITH DESTINY

The new President was Herbert
Hoover. In 1928, when the world was still young, he had won a
landslide victory over Al Smith, who was Catholic, wet, and further offended heartland America with his Lower East Side ac-
cent. But most of all, as Will Rogers put it, Smith couldn't "lick
this prosperity thing; even the fellow that hasn't got any is all
excited over the idea."

For a heady half-year, Hoover's administrative deftness won
him admiration on all sides. Even the left-leaning *New Republic*
praised the "transition from inertia to action in the directing
head of the government," and the *Magazine of Wall Street,* ec-
static, said the Hoover presidency meant that "economics, not
politics, will be the chief concern of government." But when the
crash came, Hoover was locked into his inalterable convictions:
that the American economy was not only fundamentally sound
but righteous, that any direct federal aid or intervention would
sap the national will, that occasional hard times were like a bad
cold—people just had to put up with them.

To men who had lost their life's savings, and to others who
didn't know how they were going to feed their families, the President's old-fashioned nostrums—confidence and charity, "neighbor to neighbor, community to community"—and his look of
well-fed detachment seemed hardhearted. Hoover, the man who
had organized an international relief program to feed the hungry
after the war, was not hardhearted. But he was a prisoner of out-
moded beliefs. They were not applicable to the crisis; they did not
work. The people thought he was whistling in the dark. They felt
angry and leaderless.

By the time La Guardia returned to Washington that winter of 1929, prosperity had disappeared around the corner. The
number of unemployed was 2.5 million and climbing. In four
years it would reach 13 million—of every four members of the

work force, one would be out of a job. By the end of 1933, eighty-six thousand businesses and nine thousand banks had failed, wiping out $3 billion in deposits. The national income had fallen by half. These numbing statistics translated into farmers getting 10 cents for a bushel of oats that had cost 13 cents to raise; into 100,000 New Yorkers evicted from their homes because they couldn't pay the rent; into millions of men and women all over America sleeping in parks and doorways, and millions more wandering rootlessly across the land looking for work and the self-esteem that was the Depression's invisible toll, and finding on locked factory gates wherever they went the same hope-killing notice: NO HELP WANTED. It was as though the lights were going out all over the United States.

There remained those who believed that suffering, especially by others, was never in vain. We would have a wholesome elimination of the stock-market gamblers and carry through to a new era of prosperity, they held. Meanwhile, the people would have to tighten their belts. In Secretary of the Treasury Mellon's memorable phrase, we needed to "liquidate labor, liquidate stocks, liquidate the farmers"; then there would be no way to go but up. In June 1930, Hoover was saying this had already happened. When a delegation came to the White House to urge a federal public works relief program, he coolly replied, "Gentlemen, you have come sixty days too late. The depression is over."

If he really thought so, he was out of touch. This was no six-month shakeout of speculators and marginal enterprises. This was an economic collapse without precedent, a crisis of confidence such as the nation had never undergone and whose consequences were unpredictable. The crash had come and the way ahead was full of peril because American business, contrary to the assertions of its dauntlessly reassuring spokesmen, was fundamentally *unsound.* Five percent of the population had contrived to gather in 80 percent of the nation's wealth, using its enormous surpluses to overbuild industrial facilities at the same time that it was denying to the majority of Americans the money that could make them customers. Said Frank A. Vanderlip, a small-town banker who did his own thinking, "Capital kept too much and labor did not have enough to buy its share of things." Meanwhile, the tax and fiscal policies of three administrations kept encouraging stock market speculation, a wildly burgeoning upside-down pyramid teetering on unfounded hopes. When confidence ran out, when it finally collapsed of its own unsupported weight, it brought down not only the gamblers but thousands of solid investors, stripping them of the very resources needed to rebuild the shattered economy.

Now the letters that poured into La Guardia's office were full of personal grief and begged for help:

It is nearly seven months I am out of work. I hope you will try to do something for me. I have four children who are in need of clothes and food. . . . My rent is due two months and I am afraid of being put out.

From his district came this letter from a political aide:

Every night our club is besieged by countless unemployed men and women and their children, all looking for relief from the sufferings of starvation, the dire need for clothing and the landlord's threat of eviction for nonpayment of rent. What can this organization do? Little or nothing.

Nor was there much La Guardia could do. He worried about the deep psychological wounds suffered by millions of decent, hard-working men and women overtaken by a catastrophe for which they were blameless. He knew there were plenty of zealots out there ready to exploit the nation's desperation, and that *their* solutions to the crisis could bring down America's 150-year experiment in democracy. He heard from them regularly. To the reactionary fringe, he was a dangerous radical, the tool of Moscow; to the communists, he was a paid agent of capitalism. On the floor of the House, he spurned both:

Are we going to admit that Lenin was right? I refuse to do so. Are we going to admit that Mussolini is right, that republics and parliamentary forms of government are failures? I do not believe so. I still have hope in representative government.

When the Communist party organized a march on Washington, he told a perturbed House that its Committee on Un-American

Activities was not the answer, that "the American home, a steady job, an opportunity for the children to go to school properly nourished is the way to combat communism."

Nobody argued with his goals, but neither Congress nor the President was yet ready to accept any legislation that might make them attainable. La Guardia, who had made a crash study of past economic crises and who wanted to plan for reform as well as recovery, began working with Senator Robert F. Wagner of New York on long-term measures to fight off this Depression and prevent future ones: direct government relief because the need was so obviously beyond the resources of private or community charities, the establishment of federal employment offices, a public works program, federal loans to municipalities. He derided the cheery little reports on the nation's economic health by Secretary of Commerce Julius Klein, "the bed-time story teller of the Administration," and called for sweeping new measures, "a major operation." Finally, he wanted a national system of unemployment insurance, and responded to charges of a handout by asking why, if people could be insured against fire, theft and death, it was such a revolutionary idea to insure them against the disaster of extended unemployment. He reminded the House that temporarily idle machinery was carefully housed, oiled— and insured. "Only the human beings who operate that machinery are ignored."

In the end Congress passed an emasculated version of the Wagner bills, but Hoover vetoed them anyway. La Guardia's bill for unemployment insurance was killed in committee.

Meanwhile, with his zest for uproar and protest, he was pelting away at those he held responsible for the nation's misery. He would hardly have been the Little Flower otherwise. When Hoover proposed to provide government credit to the banks, La Guardia, beside himself with rage, bounced up to call it a millionaire's dole and accused the bankers and their cohorts of starting the Depression by selling worthless securities and gambling with depositors' money. "The bastards broke the People's back with their usury," he told his young law clerk, Ernest Cuneo, "and now they want to unload on the Government. No, no. Let them die; the People will survive."

When he discovered—after an assiduous search—that Treasury Secretary Mellon, who was his special monster, still had ties to private industry, he immediately prepared articles of impeachment against him. A few days later President Hoover rescued Mellon by appointing him ambassador to England.

Cuneo, in his wonderfully evocative memoir of La Guardia, tells how he was called in one day and given a rush assignment: La Guardia had gotten the government to build some ships at the port of New York to provide employment in the area, but now that the shipbuilding companies had the contracts safely in hand, they had cut wages. "That is, they *think* they did," La Guardia told Cuneo with a snarl of righteous indignation. "I'm going to make the government break those contracts. Go get me some legal reasons."

Cuneo, who says he felt as though he were in an enemy engagement, a stoker in a battle cruiser under fire, and knowing the captain would fight to the last shell—"while there was life in him he would fight"—tried very hard to find what La Guardia wanted. But it wasn't there; there was no precedent in the law to sustain him.

Cuneo returned to the office, sad but confident of his position. "The contracts can't be broken," he said. "There is no express provision in the ship contracts for *no* lowering of wages."

"It was implied," said La Guardia sharply. "Can you imagine me going to bat for the shipowners? They knew the deal."

Cuneo tried to emphasize that what was implied had no legal standing, only what was expressed. "Unless"—he chuckled nervously—"you're going to argue something new in the law: that it was expressly implied."

"That's it!" La Guardia cried out triumphantly. "It was *expressly implied*!"

Cuneo was horrified. "There's no such thing, Major. It's a contradiction in terms. It's absolutely ridiculous!"

But La Guardia wasn't listening anymore. He had already started lining up his support in the House and informing the newspapers that he was sailing off against the shipbuilding industry.

It didn't take long. Only a few days later he showed Cuneo a brief article in the morning paper. It told how the shipbuilders, "after a careful and thorough reconsideration of the problem, had restored the pay cut." There had never been any question of going to court. La Guardia's "expressly implied" threat had been enough. Later Cuneo wrote,

> This episode prompted me to speculate on what might happen to Fiorello if he weren't on the side of the angels. . . . He was armored with complete self-confidence. Not only was he morally certain he had the right answer; he was equally certain that no other answer was conceivable, except to crooks.

Improbable as it sounds, he became the congressional champion of the Eskimos. They were innocents, exploited by everyone who crossed their path. They *needed* someone to fight for them. He took on the job with his usual vigor and soon "La Guardia's damn Eskimos" were a recurring item on the House calendar. A story went around that he had won certain benefits for an Eskimo tribe in such a remote part of the Alaskan wilderness that the Department of the Interior couldn't even find them to break the good news. La Guardia had the last word. "That just shows how neglected they've been," he said with perfect conviction. "They can't even be found."

By this time, he was the most influential progressive in the House. His big city policies, keyed to the needs and aspirations of the working class, somehow encompassed Western populism as well, and he was the hero of Wisconsin dairy farmers and Oregon salmon fishermen. The Wisconsin Progressive Thomas Amlie said, "I don't think anyone in Congress typified the Farmer-Labor sentiment there better than Major La Guardia."

He had never had such a sense of command. Although he was the only easterner among the congressional insurgents, he was older and more experienced than most of them and they were glad to follow his lead. Holding the balance of power in the closely divided House, he reveled in his ability either to outfox or to outmuscle the failing forces of the administration. Hoover called him a demagogue, and it is perfectly true that he knew how to make an issue spectacular. But as Professor Mann points out, in his unwavering belief that the law must protect the poor against the rich, he was "the most consistent . . . moral absolutist on the Hill."

He had also begun to strike the national fancy. Short, round, his black hair forever in disarray, he did not look like anybody's idea of a United States congressman—which, paradoxically, boosted his stock in the hinterlands as it did in the city. The government was not of late famous for its beneficence, but anything anyone heard of this La Guardia was about his fight against "them"—the bankers, the landlords, the judges who issued foreclosure notices, and the politicians who lined their pockets at the people's expense.

Everything about him was exaggerated: the big western hat, the shrill overkill of his speeches, the rages, the courage, the compassion. Parlor psychologists said it was all because he was short. Social thinkers said he was revenging himself on Anglo-Saxon America for treating his people like "wops." Perhaps. Only let it also be noted that he loved as fiercely as he hated, and that for perfectly understandable reasons he identified with those struggling against odds to make a place for themselves in a sometimes terrifying world—the poor, the foreign-born, the children.

Early in 1932, faced with the prospect of an unbalanced budget, President Hoover proposed a national sales tax of 2.25 percent on manufactured goods, meant to raise $600 million. It set the stage for the most spectacular victory of La Guardia's legislative career.

He was inalterably opposed. Perhaps, he told the House, in a society where wealth was more evenly distributed, such a tax could be equitable. But to ask people who could barely afford *anything* to pay a tax on life's necessities was nothing less than asking the poor to carry the rich on their backs. Instead he proposed taxes on safe-deposit boxes and stock transfers and a surtax on incomes over $100,000.

In the beginning he stood almost alone. Newspapers across the country approved the sales tax; some called it the last chance to avert national bankruptcy. The House Ways and Means Committee endorsed it by a vote of 24 to 1. Speaker John Nance Garner, the salty Texan running for the Democratic presidential nomination, agreed to lead Hoover's fight on the floor. When the debate began on March 10, 1932, more than four hundred congressmen were ready to vote yes.

But La Guardia was not one of them. "What is this—a kissing bee?" he asked, and taking the floor, rallying his handful of supporters, he forced the steamroller to a halt with a showman's mix of eloquence, low comedy, and parliamentary razzle-dazzle. A debate that was supposed to last two days erupted into a two-week carnival. "All was serene a few days ago," complained *The New York Times,* "until Mr. La Guardia tossed a nice, new shiny monkey wrench." Mr. La Guardia was also splashing headlines across the country, picking up support, crying out that the President's bill was a conspiracy to make the poor poorer; it was "taking the milk from babies and bread from mothers."

"He really laid it on," said Cuneo. He had prepared a major speech for La Guardia on the failure of sales taxes wherever they had been tried in the past. It was full of figures and historical allusions, and as La Guardia read it, he kept dropping it, one legal-size lined yellow page after another, into the wastebasket.

Cuneo says he wasn't offended, only sick with anxiety for his captain, marching off to battle unarmed. "What are you going to say, Major?" he asked.

"Soak the rich," said La Guardia, starting for the door.

Appalled, Cuneo called for him, "Major, you are sure to be misunderstood!"

"So was Christ," echoed the reply from the corridor.

His speech was a sensation, but by this time everything he said was a sensation. As the second week opened, the leaders could no longer hold their people in line. There was turbulence on the floor of the House, members shouting, jeering, coming close to fistfights. Then the lines broke altogether. On a certain day, La Guardia had a telephone call from Garner, whom he liked and respected. "He seemed quite broken up," La Guardia later told Cuneo. "He said, 'Florio'—he always called me Florio—'I've changed my mind. You can quote me as being against the Sales Tax, and I'll stand by anything you say.'"

The battle was over. On March 24, 1932, the bill came to a vote and was rejected by a count of 211 to 178. Not in recent memory had a single member so dramatically turned the House around.

La Guardia was immediately assailed by newspapers all over the country. An editorial in an Ohio paper called him "La Guardia of New York City, a product of steerage and Ellis Island of a few years back . . . gone on an orgy which [he himself] calls 'soak the rich.' "

But there was grudging admiration too. Said the St. Louis *Post-Dispatch:*

> Among the strange aspects of a confusing situation it appeared that virtually the only member who still exerted an effective influence on both sides of the chamber was Representative La Guardia, an uncompromising Republican Progressive from the Harlem District of New York City. . . . The only leader who appears to have a program and a plan for carrying it out is La Guardia.

In the same week that the national sales tax was defeated, President Hoover signed into law the Norris-La Guardia Anti-Injunction Act. It was a landmark in American labor legislation, perhaps the one law for which La Guardia will be best remembered. It had been an eight-year battle, joined in 1929 by his old Senate ally, George Norris. Their first bill was defeated, but in 1932, a year of adversity and affliction, people began to look at some of the inequities built into the economic structure. They were willing to listen, and so were their representatives in Washington.

Specifically, the Norris-La Guardia Act outlawed the yellow-dog contract, under which workers, as a condition of employment, had to agree not to join a union; it also forbade the federal courts from issuing an injunction against legal strikes unless they turned violent or caused "irreparable harm." By taking away from employers two powerful cudgels, which some of them had used with devastating effect, the act restated and reinforced the right of working men and women to bargain collectively—a basic tenet of a free society. In that light, it is held by many to be the Magna Charta of organized labor.

That summer, when the House adjourned and La Guardia went back to New York to campaign for reelection, he had a national reputation. Columnist Heywood Broun wrote that ". . . today, in spite of all opposition, he stands as the most powerful and persuasive member of the lower House." *The New York Times* said he was its most effective leader. "His influence was sought; the House hung upon his words."

So did the nation. That July of 1932, when General Douglas

MacArthur (whose aide was Major Dwight D. Eisenhower), following the President's orders, used tear gas and charging cavalry to drive a ragtag army of 10,000 bonus marchers out of their pup-tent and tar-paper encampment within sight of the Capitol, La Guardia sent a furious—and instantly famous—telegram to the White House: "Beans are better than bullets and soup is better than gas."

He was not in favor of a soldier's bonus; others needed help more, and only 13 percent of the unemployed were veterans. But he had caught and expressed the anger of most people that the President, having refused even to listen to the bonus seekers' spokesmen, had resorted to brute force against fellow Americans. In just that way, La Guardia suddenly seemed to be at the forefront of every popular current. For once, he had real power; he had become a national spokesman.

And precisely then, the people of East Harlem voted him out of office.

What happened?

La Guardia had beaten Tammany candidates in the 20th District five straight times. In 1924, declaring for the Progressive party and Bob La Follette for President, he was denied the Republican nomination but, running as an independent on the Socialist line, won his biggest victory of all—whereupon he bolted the Socialists too. But there is another side to the story: Only in 1924 was his margin ever as high as 3,500 votes; in 1926, it was 55. And in the three-party 20th, there was never a time when the combined votes of his opponents would not have buried him.

La Guardia, well aware of the hazards, never took reelection for granted, certainly not in 1932, a year in which the Democrats, led by Franklin D. Roosevelt, were threatening to sweep everything before them. In fact, assessing the prevailing winds, La Guardia decided to try for *both* major party nominations. And most Democratic leaders were more than willing. Said one, "Mr. La Guardia, I'd like to see you made ambassador to Australia; but failing that, I'll try to send you back to Washington. Anywhere, so long as you're kept out of New York."

But the effort foundered on the refusal of a West Side Tammany boss named James J. Hines. It proved to be a spectacular irony and the worst mistake a crooked politician in New York could have made, for Hines had passed up a golden opportunity to keep La Guardia far away and occupied with congressional duties. If he hadn't been so obtuse, the history of the period might have read differently. As it was, La Guardia would eventually go to City Hall and declare open season on racketeers and their friends in high places, and Jimmy Hines, who did favors for gangster Dutch Schultz and was on godfather Frank Costello's payroll, would go to prison. But of course that didn't do La Guardia any good in the autumn of 1932.

His campaign manager and district warlord was Vito Marcantonio, then twenty-nine, slight, stoop-shouldered, brilliant and impassioned. La Guardia had taken a liking to him years before, and there developed a relationship between them that could not have been more deeply felt had they been father and son.

> ". . . Cut out your evening appointments [La Guardia wrote Marcantonio], your dances, your midnight philosophers for the next five years and devote yourself to serious hard study of the law. . . . Get a Gillette razor and keep yourself well groomed at all times . . . and for goodness' sake keep your ears and eyes open and keep your mouth closed for at least the next twenty years. Now, my dear boy, take this letter in the fatherly spirit that I am writing it. Keep in touch with me. . . ."

The time would come when La Guardia would be sorely grieved by Marcantonio, in the way only deep disappointment in their sons can grieve fathers, but in 1932 he could not have had a better or more devoted deputy in East Harlem than the fiery young man with the haunted dark eyes. He was a natural leader, a magnetic speaker and, said Cuneo, "a really tough guy."

Toughness counted. Tammany thugs disrupted La Guardia meetings by turning in false fire alarms, which brought screaming fire engines to disperse the crowd, and by aiming milk bottles—once a baby carriage—at street corner gatherings from the tenement roofs overhead. La Guardia supporters fought back; violence was common in 1932 and store windows displaying enemy campaign posters were smashed by both sides.

In the forefront of the La Guardia legion was a Robin Hood band of young Italo-Americans with a fierce and absolutely unswerving loyalty to the Little Flower. They were invaluable as organizers, lookouts and guards, and if it came to bare knuckles, they didn't shrink from that either. They called themselves *gibboni*—big apes—with affectionate mockery. The name spread and soon, throughout East Harlem, *gibboni* came to be proud shorthand for membership in the F. H. La Guardia Political Club, which eventually numbered around one thousand people. The leader was Marcantonio.

But the commander in chief was La Guardia, and the campaign of 1932 ended with his appearance at a tremendous rally at what had come to be known as "the lucky corner," 116th Street and Lexington Avenue. It was, said Cuneo, "unforgettable":

> Thousands of people were on hand, [those] who regarded Fiorello as their own champion ... There was almost a religious fervor about it. Fiorello spoke, and his soul was in every word. Never had his integrity, all his gifts, found better expression. As he concluded, a searchlight played down on him from somewhere above. And at the end the tumult of the crowd was such as must have toppled the Walls of Jericho.

"How can we lose!" exulted Marcantonio.

Less than twenty-four hours later, they had the answer: James J. Lanzetta, a young Tammany alderman who had won his first election only the year before, had unseated the best-known congressman in the United States by 1,200 votes. That night, watching from his apartment window as the Lanzetta victory parade strutted down Madison Avenue, La Guardia was full of bitterness and said he was finished with politics—"What's the good of doing anything for the people? They don't appreciate it." He was going to work for himself for a change. Later he said he would get a place in the country and raise chickens.

No one who knew him believed a word of it. By the following week, writing to his journalist friend Duff Gilfond that "I so wanted to serve in the next Congress," he had already absolved the people of the 20th District.

> ... The outcome naturally does not reflect the sentiment in my district. A vast majority of the residents of the district voted for me. I was beaten by the importation of floaters and repeaters, together with the Puerto Rican vote.

It was a good sound analysis. There was plenty of evidence of fraud. In some precincts there were more votes than residents. Men claiming to be election inspectors later disappeared and were found to have given fake addresses—but the votes they had certified were already counted. At the polling place assigned to Cuneo, a Tammany watcher brazenly paid off the first three voters, then held the voting booth curtain open to be sure he got what he paid for. When Cuneo challenged the votes and demanded that the two policemen on duty arrest the Tammany man, they told him to take it easy. Only when Cuneo took matters into his own hands—"I belted the Tammany guy on the jaw with everything I had"—precipitating an uproar that brought a carload of La Guardia supporters to the scene, did the vote buying at that particular polling place end. But of course there weren't enough Cuneos for all the polling places.

That was part of it. Those who claim the other part was the Roosevelt landslide are mistaken. It is true that F.D.R. swept East Harlem, as he swept the United States, but he ran 20,000 votes ahead of Lanzetta, who was not backed by a single New Dealer—many of whom were out campaigning for La Guardia. More than anything, the Little Flower's downfall was brought about by an abrupt population shift in the 20th District. Nearly 13,000 more people voted there than in 1930—and two thirds of them had come to East Harlem from Puerto Rico in the past two years, displacing Jews and Italians. Lanzetta, personable, hardworking, won because for two years while La Guardia was in Washington fighting national issues, he was in East Harlem, making friends among the newcomers, doing favors, forging alliances.

For La Guardia, it was time to take stock. Should he quit politics? He was fifty years old, a man with a brilliant past and no future. He was exhausted from two months of day-and-night campaigning and ten years of arguing, wheedling, pleading, mostly all on his own and to deaf ears. And though he was now married and in his middle years, he still didn't have anything more to his name than what it might take to pay last month's bills.

Did he *need* politics? There was more to his life now, with Marie, more laughter. Once, in a letter to Duff Gilfond, he said,

First off, I want to tell you that I cannot send you all the love and affection I would like to because I am dictating this letter to a certain skinny woman who was my former secretary.

He used to say, "I lost a good secretary and got a bum cook," but coming home was now an event. "Yoo-hoo, Skin-nay!" he would call out, and Marie would respond, "Okay, Colonel."

They had a tiny apartment in Washington and the four-room tenement flat on East 109th Street, and there weren't enough things in both places to furnish either properly. Creature comforts meant little to Marie; as for La Guardia, possessions, things, had no interest for him at all. Cuneo tells of the Christmas when the small office force chipped in and bought him an expensive, beautifully grained Kaywoodie pipe to replace the smelly old corncob he had lately been smoking. He seemed deeply touched. He said such a pipe was what he always wanted, that they shouldn't have done it. "He was quite right," said Cuneo, "we shouldn't." Days later, the old corncob was smoldering away again and the expensive Kaywoodie was gathering dust.

Until the adoption of the Twentieth Amendment, neither the Congress nor the President elected in November took office before the following March. And if it happened, in those dark days before the convening of the lame duck session of the 72nd Congress, that La Guardia asked himself whether he could be happy pursuing money instead of justice, whether he should retire from politics—whether he *could* retire from politics—the answer was obviously no. He went back to Washington, finishing his term in a blaze of glory, and returned to New York ready for some still-uncalled future election.

In the first months of the New Deal, when Franklin Roosevelt was fighting, most of all, against the state of shock paralyzing the nation, he told a story about Andrew Jackson dying and someone asking whether he would go to heaven. And a man who had known Jackson replied, "He will if he wants to."

"If I am asked whether the American people will pull themselves out of this depression," said F.D.R., "I answer, 'They will if they want to.'"

But time was short. No one would ever know "how close we were to collapse or revolution," said General Hugh S. Johnson, administrator of the National Recovery Administration. "We could have got a dictator a lot easier than Germany got Hitler." Sharply aware of this, and of the hunger among Americans for leadership, Roosevelt, at his inauguration on March 4, 1933, said, "This nation asks for action, and action now." Within the next three months, the fabled 100 Days, he sent to Congress, and Congress passed, fifteen major proposals for dealing with the economic crisis.

By then the 72nd Congress had moved into history and La Guardia was gone from Washington. But some of the ground for this rebirth of the national confidence, for this peaceful revolution, had already been prepared, and it was the defeated congressman from New York's 20th District who did the spadework.

He seemed so much a New Dealer that, though they were of different parties, Roosevelt had offered him the post of Assistant Secretary of Labor; La Guardia said he was too old to start taking orders from anyone. But the fact is he was already on the high ground when the New Dealers got there. He hadn't changed; history had simply caught up with him. Even repudiated by the electorate and serving out the last few months of his term in office, he did not change. Back in Washington for those last three months, he let himself be talked into going to a public-relations party at the Mayflower Hotel. He had a drink in his hand when someone quipped, "Watch out, Fiorello, the Power Trust paid for that." He put the glass down and walked right out.

During the tense days of the interregnum, with more banks closing every day and local relief funds running out, there was serious question whether there would be anything left of the economy to salvage before Roosevelt was sworn in. Congress heard the thump of America hitting rock bottom when a "hunger march" of three thousand jobless men and women reached the capital. Two weeks later, on December 13, 1932, a chilling display of the desperation abroad in the land was acted out before the terrified legislators themselves. Suddenly the drone of business on the House floor was interrupted by a shout from the gallery. When the members looked up, they saw a young man pointing a revolver at them. He cried out, "I demand twenty minutes to address the House. Whoever tries to stop me will die. Is that understood? *I want to be heard!*"

The pandemonium that followed was not edifying. Those

near the doors fled, tearing one of them right off its hinges in their panic. Some members dived under desks; one, perhaps intentionally, wound up with a cuspidor on his head, then went crawling blindly across the floor searching for cover. The rest just stood there looking up at the gun, ducks in a shooting gallery.

Two men showed their mettle. La Guardia went running for the stairs leading to the gallery while Melvin Maas of Minnesota, a husky ex-marine, began assuring the man with the gun that he would be allowed to speak, but not with a weapon in his hand. "Come on, drop it down to me," he coaxed. In the next instant, La Guardia burst into the gallery—and kept right on charging. Just as he grabbed the distraught young man and pinned his arms, the gun fell into Maas's outstretched hands. It was loaded, cocked and ready to fire. To many, the terrifying moment seemed to symbolize the state of the nation—held hostage by menacing, unfathomable forces.

To La Guardia and a few others, the job was to hang on, to keep everything from falling apart until Roosevelt took office. The President-elect already had an advance guard in Washington. Its leader was a thirty-seven-year-old law professor named Adolf A. Berle, a shrewd and cerebral member of the Brain Trust, as the press had taken to calling Roosevelt's inner circle of advisers. He had been recruited from Columbia University and put to work drafting legislation which, it was hoped, might be passed by the 72nd Congress, putting the New Deal into action even before Roosevelt took office. But a lame duck session, by its transient nature, is always unruly and sometimes rebellious, and Berle went to Speaker John Garner, now also the Vice-President-elect, for help. "Could anyone hammer that Congress together?"

"Cactus Jack" Garner, who was said to know his way around just two places in the world, southwest Texas and the House of Representatives, replied that "there is only one man who can make the House do anything: La Guardia." He referred to the Little Flower's one-man assault on Hoover's sales tax and called him "a good little wop." He said if anyone could master the cliques and crosscurrents of this "hog wild" Congress it was "Florio."

Berle had met La Guardia in New York that summer and been moved by his "tempestuous, passionate honesty." The two had taken to each other from the start—the polished, contained, wellborn intellectual who also knew his way around the arena, and the volatile son of immigrants who admired brains but really went for Berle's ability to get things done. They became friends, colleagues and allies, and stayed that way until La Guardia died. Now, Berle, who was also scouting talent for the new administration, on November 28, 1932, sent this memo for Roosevelt's attention:

> Fiorello La Guardia. You know all about him. He is going to be important in the short session. I am having him to dinner tomorrow. His career is not over by a long shot and I think he ought to be annexed.

La Guardia was already committed to the fight to halt the wild and disastrous liquidation of capital—bankruptcies and the foreclosure of thousands of farm and home mortgages. Now, working with Berle, he drafted two important pieces of legislation during the lame duck session. One, aimed at stanching the flood of foreclosures, would have provided for $200 million in government capital for a federal credit bank that could refinance farm and home mortgages at low interest. It was bottled up in the Finance Committee, but a similar proposal was passed during the 100 Days. The second bill, an amendment to the National Bankruptcy Act of 1898, empowered courts to give credit extensions to farmers and individuals, staving off forced liquidations by their creditors; another section took the reorganization of bankrupt railroads out of the hands of private bankers and put it under the jurisdiction of the Interstate Commerce Commission. This became law on the last day of the Hoover administration.

And then suddenly, too soon, it was all over. The last session of the 72nd Congress ended on March 4, 1933, and that afternoon a subdued La Guardia sat in his tiny apartment, made cheerless now with everything boxed and waiting for shipment. A few friends stopped in to say goodbye, but this only intensified his gloom. "That's politics," he said. "Here I am on my last day, without food or drinks for my friends."

The pain of departure had been eased by the thousands of letters and telegrams he received expressing regret at his defeat and gratitude for "your constant effort to see that the little fellow gets a bit of justice as he struggles through life." But in the end, the letters didn't change anything. The 20th District had a new congressman, and hours after Franklin Roosevelt took the oath of office as the 32nd President of the United States, La Guardia and Marie went to Union Station and boarded the train for New York.

No one could say that 1929 was Magistrate Albert H. Vitale's year. During the mayoralty campaign, La Guardia charged that he had been companionable enough with the late Arnold Rothstein, New York's murdered crime overlord, to have "borrowed" $20,000 from him, and Vitale's explanation sounded, to be charitable, foolish. Then, just a few weeks later, the magistrate made the headlines again, and again he should have stayed in bed. Instead, he went to a testimonial dinner in his honor in an upstairs room of the Roman Gardens in the Bronx where, near 1:30 A.M., six masked gunmen came in and robbed the guests of some $5,000 in cash and jewelry and relieved a detective present of his service revolver. This unscheduled diversion so infuriated Vitale that he took leave of what little common sense he may have had. He went charging over to his Tammany clubhouse and made some telephone calls, and by 4:00 A.M. money, jewelry and revolver had all been restored to their rightful owners.

The guests were naturally delighted, but the city Bar Association, intrigued by the magistrate's ability to reach "the boys" on such short notice, decided that his underworld connections must be exemplary. Investigators went down the guest list and found, among lawyers who advertised and bail bondsmen who went under assumed names, at least seven felons, convicted of crimes that began with burglary and ran all the way to murder.

So Vitale fashioned his own noose—but it was Fiorello La Guardia who had provided the hemp. The Appellate Division of the State Supreme Court, weighing Vitale's fitness to serve, decided to reexamine La Guardia's revelation of the $20,000 Rothstein loan, and learned, among other things, that Magistrate Vitale, earning $1,000 a month on the bench, had banked

$100,000 in the past five years. In March 1930 he was removed from office.

But Vitale was only one in an endless parade of corrupt Tammany appointees and his discharge just the opening rumble of a detonation that was to blow the old Tammany Hall out of existence. Suddenly the smell of venality was everywhere. In August 1930 the Appellate Division voted to conduct an inquiry into the magistrates' courts; the following March, Governor Roosevelt ordered an examination of charges that the Manhattan district attorney had failed to prosecute scores of indictable criminal offenses. Meanwhile, a special state legislative committee, appointed to investigate corruption throughout the city government, including the office of the mayor, was organizing for what would turn out to be twenty months of hearings.

All three inquiries, which were to be conducted simultaneously, were headed by the same chief investigator and eventually became known by a single name, his—Seabury. From then on, the aims and fortunes of Judge Samuel Seabury and Fiorello H. La Guardia would run together, their stars joined, their union in the eyes of history forged.

La Guardia was one of a kind to begin with, to be sure, but the contrast between these two was stunning. Samuel Seabury was descended from John and Priscilla Alden, who came to America on the *Mayflower;* among his other forebears were the founder of the New York bar and the first bishop of the Episcopal Church in the United States. He was the fifth Samuel in nine generations of American Seaburys, nearly all of them dedicated to the tradition of service—doctors, teachers, lawyers, clergymen. He grew up in awareness of the Seabury family motto: "Hold to the most high"; his biographer, Herbert Mitgang, said, "He bore the Protestant ethic and the Anglo-Saxon legal traditions of his ancestors, not as a burden but as an escutcheon."

He became a good lawyer who eventually made a lot of money, but until 1916, when he was forty-three, he was a rising reform politician, a Democrat, who might have gone all the way. But in that year—when La Guardia was first elected to Congress—Seabury, running for governor of New York, was abandoned by the Tammany machine, attacked by Hearst's Democratic newspapers, and betrayed by Theodore Roosevelt, who had promised to support him. Defeated, embittered, he withdrew from public life and only reappeared—nearing sixty, an immaculately tailored and thoroughly patrician figure with white hair, pince-nez and cane—to take on Tammany Hall. For in the end, there was something basically the same about the estimable aristocrat and the rough, rumpled, eternal outsider: a tenacious longing to bring decent government to the people of New York City.

From the start of the investigations in 1930, Democratic members of the legislative committee sought to obstruct or embarrass the investigators. John J. McNaboe, Tammany chief John F. Curry's man on the inside, once admitted that he had "instructions" to discredit Judge Seabury. His technique was, in the true Tammany tradition, contemptible: He told a Seabury staff member that the judge was "keeping a woman on Park Avenue," and that if the investigation didn't "cool off," he was going to produce her. When the shocked aide reported this, Seabury's amused reply was, "Tell McNaboe that if he can produce such a lady, I will put her on the witness stand."

The tactic of State Senator John J. Dunnigan, a Bronx architect whose firm had close ties to the Democratic machine, was to attack Seabury's professional integrity. At one point, without relevance to anything under discussion, he said he had heard the judge was paid a fee of $1 million for settling the Jay Gould estate. "Yes," Seabury answered, "over a ten-year period."

Feigning amazement, Dunnigan said, "But I never heard of anyone receiving such a fee. *I* never did."

"Senator, the reason is obvious," said Seabury, a study in equanimity. "You were never worth that much to anyone."

Cool, correct, but more than a little flinty, Seabury had given his nervy young lawyers, most of them barely out of law school, the motto "Old heads for counsel—young heads for war." Together they sifted a mountain of evidence and eventually questioned four thousand witnesses, producing enough transcribed testimony to fill ninety-five thousand pages. And as the damning facts piled up, detailing what one writer called the insolence of office, they exposed a spoils system hardened into ritual, and a pattern of ordinary everyday graft that reached from the clubhouse wheelhorses to Mayor Walker himself.

Seabury could not discharge anyone from office; he could not send anyone to prison. He was empowered only to bring out the particulars of wrongdoing in the city government. But he had taken on himself larger responsibilities: first, to let the investigation fire a reform movement against the existing power structure; second, to demonstrate by encyclopedic examples how Tammany bosses had turned New York into an enormous moneymaking machine for the enrichment of the faithful; and third, by so doing, to bring down Tammany, the mayor, bosses and all.

Some witnesses created instant folklore. Here is the Honorable Thomas M. Farley, sheriff of New York County and Democratic leader of the 14th Assembly District, who has just been asked to explain how, in the same six years during which his salary totalled $87,000, he had somehow banked $396,000:

FARLEY: Oh, that was moneys I had saved.
SEABURY: Where did you keep these moneys that you had saved?
FARLEY: In a safe-deposit box at home in the house.
SEABURY: . . . a tin box?
FARLEY: A tin box.
SEABURY: Now, in 1930, where did the extra cash come from, Sheriff?
FARLEY: Well, that is—my salary check is in there.
SEABURY: (*With unvarying politeness*) No, Sheriff, your salary checks are exclusive of the cash deposits which during the year you deposited in those three banks.
FARLEY: Well, that came from the good box I had.
SEABURY: Kind of a magic box?
FARLEY: It was a wonderful box.

Farley's story gave an appealing sobriquet to the Seabury investigations: the Tin Box Parade. For his blithe explanations differed only in detail from the always dignified, always outrageous testimony of other leaders.

John H. McCooey, Democratic boss of Brooklyn, had recently concluded a strikingly generous bipartisan compact. Having decided that five new supreme court judges were required in Kings County, he magnanimously offered the Republicans two, whereupon all five were swiftly endorsed by both parties. Now it having happened that one of the five was John H. McCooey, Jr.,

Judge Seabury put the father on the stand and asked him to explain how it was that his thirty-year-old son, who had had a hard time getting through law school and whose legal experience was sharply limited in both length and breadth, had gotten the $25,000-a-year supreme court nomination.

"Oh," responded the senior McCooey with alacrity, "nearly every leader in the party urged me very strongly to nominate Jack. I had no idea there was such a unanimity of opinion." The proud father leaned back and said his boy had "the poise and the character and the industry," adding, as if to emphasize just how lucky the citizens of Brooklyn had been, "Besides, he was in a receptive mood."

At work here was the organization's tradition of public office as the private property of Tammany Hall. Jobs were always needed. There were thirty-two thousand Democratic leaders and committeemen to be looked after; how else could they be persuaded to work for the party? Brooklyn leader McCooey and Queens leader John Theofel, for example, each drew $10,000 a year as chief clerks of their respective surrogate's courts, though neither knew anything about the work or had any legal training, or any education at all beyond a few grades of elementary school.

But what did that have to do with it? Everyone in the county courtroom could see McCooey's genuine surprise when Seabury raised the question of competence as a standard for public office. Competence had nothing to do with politics. "Politics was jobs," as Arthur Mann put it, "and jobs went to men who served the party."

But now there were portents of change. The relentless questions and the droll, evasive answers were building into a big mosaic with an irrefutable message, and the message wasn't funny. Tammany "fattened upon these evils," said Seabury, and the people, "who have been humbugged, swindled and betrayed," paid.

On Election Day, 1931, when young Jack McCooey won his supreme court race—with his name on both the Democratic and Republican lines it could hardly have been otherwise—a hastily put-together slate, challenging the combined pulling power of both machines, polled a staggering 100,000 votes. And from Albany there came word that Governor Roosevelt had removed Sheriff Farley from office.

On May 25, 1932, Mayor James J. Walker, the primary target of the Seabury investigation, finally took the witness stand. He had been staving off the day of reckoning since the previous August, when he was first summoned. Seabury's interrogation, which lasted two days, centered on the $300,000 given to Walker by people who did business with the city, and $1 million put into the safe-deposit box uncovered by Seabury's young warriors, jointly owned by Walker and his financial agent.

Walker, whose intelligence was questioned by no one but who played while his adversary worked, made a pathetic defense. He came to the Foley Square courthouse without papers or preparation; he could not answer questions about either his administration or his personal finances. Overwhelmed by the mass of evidence accumulated by the Seabury staff detailing neglected duty and, if not outright graft, colossal indiscretions, Walker fell back on theatrics, loss of memory, and accusations of "a Red plot." The crowds still cheered him as he came and went, but it was now clear that he had betrayed his trust as mayor. On June 8, Seabury sent a transcript of Walker's testimony and a statement of charges to Governor Roosevelt.

Roosevelt was not overjoyed. He was running for President and wanted neither the open enmity of Tammany Hall, which he would surely get if he removed Walker from office, nor the charge that he was willing to tolerate malfeasance in a fellow Democrat if he did not. But he was firm in his questioning of Walker during the two weeks of hearings that followed; he insisted that the people deserved more than evasions and unbelievable rationalizations.

On the last day of August 1932, La Guardia and Ernest Cuneo were crossing Times Square when the news trucks rolled in with the first evening editions. Cuneo bought one and they stood together on the corner of 47th Street and Seventh Avenue reading the headline: ROOSEVELT SUSTAINS SEABURY—RULES PUBLIC OFFICIALS MUST EXPLAIN PRIVATE FUNDS.

"Ernest," said La Guardia, "this is a great day for our country."

The next night Walker sent a one-sentence message to the city clerk, "I hereby resign as mayor of the City of New York," and sailed off to Europe.

* * *

When the biggest municipal investigation in American history ended, New Yorkers wondered whether anything more substantial than a few dismissals and a few resignations would come of it. After all, Tammany hadn't begun with Jimmy Walker—and, in fact, didn't disappear with him. In November 1932, as though nothing had happened, a Tammany regular won the special election to fill out Walker's unexpired term by 600,000 votes. He was John P. O'Brien, paunchy, earnest, inept—and so true to the party line that when newsmen asked who he intended to name as police commissioner, he forthrightly replied, "I don't know. I haven't had the word yet." What he had was the virtue of being Walker's opposite: a hard-working family man who went home at night and stayed there.

But the truth is that Tammany was in trouble and the more enlightened leaders knew it. O'Brien's victory was not nearly so convincing as the celebrants pretended—he had run 400,000 votes behind Roosevelt, and Joseph V. McKee, acting mayor following Walker's departure, pulled some 250,000 write-in votes. For anyone who could count, that looked like a respectable basis for a fusion candidacy in 1933. A die-hard band of civic leaders, veterans of past reform movements that had died of indifference or foundered on political infighting once the ins were out, began to dream again of taming the Tammany tiger and bringing a nonpartisan fusion government to New York.

Fiorello La Guardia, who could count and dream with the best of them, was positive he was the man to lead the crusade. He was a reformer who knew what it took to win an election, a moralist who had fought Tammany—Tammany's way—more persistently and with greater success than anyone else on the political scene. And he did not stand alone. Many people remembered that it was La Guardia's charges against the Democratic machine in 1929 that had touched off the investigations just ended. *The New York Times* wrote that only La Guardia had the right "to stand up in New York City today and say 'I told you so.'"

But there were no La Guardia fans among the members of the Fusion conference committee, organized that spring to choose a mayoral candidate. They spoke for business and good-government groups, disenchanted Democrats and conservative Republicans; there was not one representative of the unions, minority groups, women's organizations, the intellectual community or the clergy among them. And in their view La Guardia was a political freak, "Half wop, half American, half Republican," as one of them put it. Even those not moved by outright prejudice thought of him as a loud and vulgar self-promoter and shrank from the idea of such a philistine as the Fusion standard bearer. "If it's La Guardia or bust," declared one, "I say bust!"

They were looking for a "respectable" candidate but kept getting turned down—by Judge Seabury, everybody's first choice, because he did not want to jeopardize the anti-Tammany cause by appearing to capitalize personally on the investigations; by Joseph McKee, the serious and personable young independent Democrat who had run up such a fantastic write-in vote against O'Brien, because he was quitting politics to become a bank president at $50,000 a year; by others for other reasons, chief among them the lack of stomach for a bruising campaign whose outcome was dubious. To La Guardia, who kept insisting that he *wanted* to be mayor and was ready to fight for it to the extent that he promised to split the reform movement with an independent candidacy if he didn't get the Fusion nomination, the search committee turned a deaf ear.

But La Guardia did have a few influential friends and they kept the door from being closed on him altogether. One was Adolf Berle, who went to see Seabury on his behalf; although he had renounced the nomination for himself, Seabury held the power of veto over all other candidates, none of whom could hope to be taken seriously without the judge's benediction. Seabury listened to Berle's earnest account of La Guardia's effectivenes during the lame duck session of the 72nd Congress and promised to give him serious consideration.

At a dinner in Berle's home in May 1933, La Guardia met Newbold Morris, a young lawyer with a civic conscience who had just been elected president of the 15th A.D. Republican Club, the silk-stocking district. Morris was more than a head taller than the Little Flower, blond, blue-eyed, a graduate of Groton, Yale and Columbia Law School, and was descended from a distinguished colonial family—in other words, a symbolic profile of the do-gooders on the Fusion conference committee to whom La Guardia was a dirty word. But to Newbold Morris, from that first meeting, he was "this dynamo, and I was very much taken with him." He invited La Guardia to address his club the following Friday evening. It would turn out to be a crucial turning point.

Soon after the meeting notices had been sent out, Morris was peppered with letters from indignant members. They assured him that his sainted father had to be turning over in his grave because the drawbridge of their Republican stronghold had been lowered to "that filthy radical"—*and Newbold had done it!*

La Guardia arrived ten minutes late, by which time Morris was having nervous second thoughts. The controversy over the invitation had made the papers and the meeting room was packed, standees in the aisles and an overflow out on the sidewalk. Morris concluded that if La Guardia started one of his screeching, arm-thrashing attacks on "the interests," disaster was certain; the room was full of "the interests."

But the thing was, Morris knew only La Guardia the dynamo so far; he had no measure of his resourcefulness, his sheer wizardry on the platform. Introduced, the Little Flower stood up to face row after row of frozen-faced men in tuxedos and their ladies in long gowns resplendent with jewels, and he said, "I apologize for being late. Marie, my wife, sent my suit out to be pressed and it didn't come back until a few minutes ago. I couldn't leave the house until it was returned."

They hadn't come to laugh, but they couldn't help it.

"I'm very proud to be here tonight. But I don't know whether you ladies and gentlemen have decided to admit me to the social register, or whether you just wanted to go slumming with me."

That broke them up altogether. There was even a scattering of applause. When they quit laughing, they sat back in their seats to listen to what he had to say. "He had them, you see," said Morris afterward, with a remembered surge of pride.

What followed was one of La Guardia's most telling speeches, certainly among his most useful. The exposures of the past two years, he began in a deliberately understated tone, would serve the city nothing if the only result was the replacement of the Democratic machine by a Republican machine. New York needed and deserved government by professionals, not politicians. Would they let incompetent and unproductive hacks run their businesses?

So far, he was on solid ground. But he was not afraid to tell them of his other concerns, that to date the search for a mayoral candidate had excluded representatives of groups with vital interests in the city's welfare: women, minorities, the poor. The man they chose needed to speak for *all* the people. And he closed with a stunning declaration that brought the audience to its feet clapping hard. "My candidate is not Fiorello La Guardia; it is Judge Samuel Seabury."

Perhaps he was playing on his knowledge that Seabury could not be persuaded to run. But nothing is certain in politics. It was a calculated risk. But the judge did not change his mind, and as of that night, when one of the club's most outspoken conservatives offered a resolution "thanking the Congressman for his magnificent speech," and the next day, when the speech was widely reported throughout the city, La Guardia was the leading candidate for the nomination.

But he was a long way from home; those who opposed him were conceding nothing. Spring of 1933 passed into summer without a decision. Robert Moses, a Republican who had served in Albany as Al Smith's secretary of state, was proposed. But when Smith, honest but regular, said he would have to support the Democratic nominee, Moses withdrew. The next choice—and now it was the week before Fusion had to name its man—was General John F. O'Ryan, wartime commander of the 27th Division. This plunged La Guardia into one of his fits of dark despair. Dining with Berle one night during that climactic last week, he said, "You'll propose me, they'll propose O'Ryan, and then we'll both have to withdraw for some nonentity who will get the nomination."

Berle tried to cheer him up, but La Guardia was sure he was finished in politics. Walking uptown afterward in the soft summer night, he said with more sadness than bitterness, "Why is it that every time you get to a point where you can do some good, the *nice people* move in and block you? That's what drives a man like me to be a demagogue, smacking into things."

But he despaired too soon. For Judge Seabury, having talked at length with La Guardia, had come to believe in him. "Sam," his sister-in-law once asked him with genuine amazement, "how did you possibly come to pick La Guardia to run for mayor?"

And Seabury replied, "Because he's absolutely honest, he's a man of great courage, and he can win."

And all through the afternoon and evening of August 3, on past midnight, he fought off one argument after another, until the Fusion leaders, knowing they were going nowhere without Seabury and that Seabury was going nowhere without La Guardia, gave in.

All this time, the candidate was at his apartment in East Harlem, with Marie, Marcantonio and a few others, waiting, alternately tense with hope and lost in gloom, certain the prize he had longed for all his political life was to be denied him just when he could all but touch it. The telephone rang at 12:15 A.M. A desperate silence fell on the room as La Guardia answered.

"Yes, Judge . . . speaking." The others could only watch his face as he listened. Then they heard him say, "I promise you faithfully you will never regret this."

Despite the Democratic machine's never-to-be-underestimated knack of generating votes—one way or the other—La Guardia went sailing into the campaign with even more than his habitual confidence. How could anyone lose to O'Brien? The interim mayor, an amiable bumbler who had put the city even deeper into debt, kept losing his way in the vagaries of his own prose and came out sounding as though he were burlesquing a Tammany precinct leader making his maiden address. But that was no burlesque; that was John Patrick O'Brien.

> During the week [he told a ladies theater club at the Hotel Astor] I have momentous matters to attend to. I meet great people and I must go here and there to make up the addenda that goes with being Mayor of the City. Therefore, when I come here to this great forum and see before me flowers and buds, ladies, girls and widows, emotion is just running riot with me.

Anything, it seemed, could start his orations careening suicidally out of control. "Mr. President," he confided to a men's group, "and may I say brothers? When I get in a room with chairs I get the fraternal spirit." He told a Jewish audience how much he admired "that scientist of scientists, Albert Weinstein." Speaking to blacks in Harlem, he called it "the garden spot of New York." When people laughed, he beamed; he thought they were expressing their love for him. But the City Hall press corps, which had protected Walker to the end, reported O'Brien's public utterances with every devastating detail; by comparison, John Hylan came to look like a philosopher.

La Guardia, meanwhile, had gotten off to a flying start. He broke with tradition to choose running mates who represented the city's major ethnic groups; for the first time, a mayoral slate included an Italian, an Irishman, a Jew and a Protestant. This was no more a guarantee of good government than the Tammany practice of naming Irishmen for *all* political posts on the grounds that the Irish were natural leaders and New Yorkers "want to be ruled by them." But La Guardia chose no one for nationality or religion alone; the first requisite was ability.

And as he hammered away at boss rule, addressing ardent crowds and pulling ahead in the straw polls, it began to dawn on the machine that their man was in trouble. They did not know it yet but he was, in fact, already finished. The real threat to La Guardia's election was to come from a new and totally surprising quarter. On September 30, 1933, Joseph V. McKee entered the race. He had been dusted off for the occasion by Bronx Democratic leader Edward J. Flynn, persuaded to leave his lucrative bank job, and nominated by the just-invented Recovery party. The reasoning was convoluted and the idea Machiavellian, but it was all perfectly logical to the man who thought it up—President Franklin D. Roosevelt.

F.D.R.'s contempt for Tammany matched La Guardia's. He had clashed with Boss Murphy at the outset of his political career; at its climax, Boss Curry and every leader but Ed Flynn had fought his presidential candidacy. Now, with the wounds of the Walker scandal still oozing, they were offering the citizenry a hopeless incompetent for mayor, and the new commander in chief of all the Democrats wasn't having it. McKee, he reasoned, an attractive, well-spoken candidate, might just pull enough anti-Tammany votes to put an honest Democrat in City Hall, one whose politics would not embarrass the White House. And if he didn't win, he would still split the Democratic vote and assure a victory for La Guardia, a man Roosevelt had already worked with and regarded as a New Dealer in a Republican disguise.

La Guardia read the same tea leaves and came up with a much more ominous divination: he and McKee splitting the anti-

Tammany vote; McKee picking up the support of independents and conservative Republicans who could not resign themselves to La Guardia; McKee winning the election. In a flash his euphoria had been transformed to high anxiety. Once again the Little Flower was fighting for his political life.

And how he fought! One observer said his campaign was "like a Kansas cyclone" sweeping through New York every day, leaving in its wake battered, dazed opponents unable to keep up with his furious energy and lightning thrusts. With his operatic gusto—arms pumping, torso gyrating—his shirt wilted and his suit looked as though it had been stomped on, and one of his advisers warned, "Do not appear in public to speak before anybody unless you are dressed in a suit that has been pressed that day."

La Guardia paid no heed. He was too busy crisscrossing the city condemning both "Tammanyitis, a fatal municipal disease" and "Holy Joe" McKee, who, he charged, had only found the faith *after* Tammany gave the nomination he craved to O'Brien; while president of the Board of Aldermen, he had served as Jimmy Walker's willing prime minister. He had been regular as rain.

Stung, McKee tried to duck behind the shield of Roosevelt's endorsement, but suddenly it wasn't there anymore. The wily F.D.R., having arranged things so Tammany couldn't win and he couldn't lose, sanctimoniously declared his neutrality and sat back to watch.

Gone with Roosevelt's presumed backing went McKee's cool demeanor. Distraught, he cast about for ways to buoy up his sinking ship. He called La Guardia a dangerous demagogue and "a Communist at heart," but New Yorkers had heard all that before. He tried to ally himself with the popular new governor, Herbert H. Lehman, and jumped on Judge Seabury, who had been taxing Lehman with failure to root out Tammany miscreants. To La Guardia, McKee sent a telegram challenging him to repudiate Seabury's "reckless slander," which, he insinuated, was rooted in anti-Semitism.

La Guardia, who knew how the Jews idolized Lehman, the state's first Jewish governor, had tried to call Seabury off—"My God, Judge, you're ruining me. Stop attacking Governor Lehman!" Now he heaved a sigh of relief. The situation was saved—

Holy Joe McKee had come to the rescue! By his calculated smear of Samuel Seabury, the most transparently upright public servant New Yorkers had laid eyes on in a generation, McKee had not only exposed himself to ridicule, but turned a fair fight into a street brawl. La Guardia, who played *that* game, too, and had some sensational ammunition stored by for just such an eventuality, now let it fly. It was, perhaps, not his finest moment, but McKee should have known—everyone else did—that when put to it, the Little Flower could fling mud with anybody in the house.

It appeared that when McKee was a twenty-six-year-old high school teacher in the Bronx, he had suffered from a slight case of anti-Semitism himself—and it was on the record. For the May 1915 issue of a magazine called *Catholic World,* he had written a prissy, pedantic supplication for more Catholic boys to attend the public high schools. Why? Because as matters then stood, the Jews of New York, 25 percent of the population, were enrolling 75 percent of the high school students; and these young men, wrote McKee, having largely abandoned their fathers' faith and morality for "the furtherance of the Socialistic dogma," were prepared to lie and cheat in pursuit of money. "It is to such as these that our [meaning Catholic] children, who are without benefit of education, must bow in later years."

Perhaps McKee's youthful prejudice had been tempered by the wisdom of maturity—afterward, most observers thought so—but there was the article and La Guardia now chose to make something of it. To McKee's telegram demanding that he denounce Seabury, La Guardia wired back:

> Your silly effort to create a false issue ... will not be taken seriously by anyone in New York. Are you trying to draw a red herring across the cowardly, contemptible and unjust attack that you have made and published against a great race represented by our Governor? Answer that, Mr. McKee, and think twice before you send me another telegram.

The newspapers were quick to pick up this promising exchange; the *Times* printed the entire text of McKee's 1915 article. And the result—only to be expected in New York in 1933, the year Hitler came to power—was a thunder of denunciation, drowning out McKee's efforts at explanation, ending any real hope he ever had of becoming mayor.

He made an urgent last attempt to get Roosevelt to speak for

him, but the White House remained silent—and in light of
McKee's straitened circumstances, this began to be taken as a
tacit endorsement of La Guardia. Desperate, McKee tried to enlist Al Smith's support. The answer was no.

Meanwhile, eight days before the election, the best-known of
Al Smith's "boys," Robert Moses, came out for La Guardia. The
impact was terrific, for anything Moses said was front-page news,
and the bite and flair with which he said it, matched against the
general run of predictable, mind-wearying campaign rhetoric,
shone and sparkled and was repeated everywhere in the city.
Here he is in a radio address, reminding New Yorkers of "the
strange characters they have seen occupying City Hall":

> Hylan, the ranting Bozo of Bushwick; Walker, half Beau Brum-
> mel, half guttersnipe, and John P. O'Brien, a winded bull in the
> municipal china shop ... [Young voters who could not remember
> a non-Tammany mayor] must think of the great office of Chief
> Magistrate with derision and contempt.

McKee, he said, was "a pious fraud ... a synthetic character
who never actually existed on land or sea, puffed up by the press
and now in the process of deflation." But for La Guardia—whose
liberal ideas actually made him a little nervous—he had nothing
but praise. In a ringing public declaration on November 3, he
told him,

> No one has ever questioned your independence. You have no
> strings on you. You are not engaged in an obscure struggle for the
> control of a rotten political machine. You are free to work for New
> York City. Go to it.

Election Day in New York in the year 1933 will never qualify for anyone's pageant of the democratic process at work. Tammany, out to salvage everything it could from what promised to
be an epochal disaster, deployed an army of goon squads, and
these were abetted by Dutch Schultz's mobsters and musclemen;
Schultz had paid out $15,000 for the election of William C.
Dodge as Manhattan district attorney and he meant to protect
his investment. Against all this brawn, the Fusioneers had La
Guadia's *gibboni* and the flying squads of young Clendenin

Ryan, a silk-stocking blue blood, who had recruited a corps of college athletes and slum neighborhood Golden Glove boxers. Heads were cracked, noses bloodied, and arrests made all over the city.

La Guardia spent the day touring the toughest districts, chasing gangs of intimidating Tammany thugs with his unbridled fury. In the evening he went to Judge Seabury's East 63rd Street town house to await the returns. The contrasts were striking. Outside, bands of La Guardia supporters, waving green placards in the shape of Fusion's four-leaf clover, roamed the streets singing the campaign theme, "Who's Afraid of the Big Bad Wolf?" In Harlem, thousands joined a jubilant procession behind a hearse bearing the sign "HERE LIES TAMMANY—THE BIG STIFF!" Meanwhile, in the handsome Seabury library, all was calm. Occasionally the judge and the candidate exchanged a nod of quiet satisfaction, no more, although the returns were now indicating a La Guardia victory by 250,000 votes.

The victory was short of a sweep. The Democrats would still control the Board of Aldermen and—hired gunmen in their pearl-gray fedoras having guaranteed what Dutch Schultz paid for—Dodge, the Tammany candidate for Manhattan district attorney, was squeezed in by 12,000 votes.

Around 9:30 P.M. there was an emergency call from W. Arthur Cunningham, Fusion candidate for comptroller, the Number 2 spot on the ticket: His 50,000-vote lead had all but vanished in the past hour, and there had been no returns at all from some four hundred precincts. Even a political newcomer like Cunningham could tell the election was being stolen from him.

La Guardia went directly to Fusion headquarters in the Paramount Building in Times Square, where he was stormed by a swarm of shrieking, exultant supporters. It took a wedge of thirty-five perspiring policemen to clear a path for him to a small side room, where Cunningham brought him up to date on the steadily deteriorating situation. La Guardia heard him out, then said, "Come on, Arthur. I'll go get those four hundred precincts for you."

New York Police Headquarters is located on Centre Street in lower Manhattan, in an old baroque building that only grows uglier with the years. There, in a huge room on the fifth floor where Tammany still held sway, the vote was being tallied that election night. The Board of Elections, Tammany-controlled, supervised the counting; high police officials, Tammany-promoted, reported their sometimes highly imaginative tabulations with straight faces. But from the time, a little before eleven, when someone looked up and saw La Guardia and some others standing there, it was clear that a new order had come to New York.

Inspectors and captains all but fell over one another congratulating him. He cut them off with a crisp command: "I want four hundred patrolmen mobilized behind headquarters just as fast as they can get there."

"Yes, Mr. Mayor." Someone ran for a telephone.

"Get me four hundred patrol wagons. Roll 'em into the alley behind headquarters as fast as God will let you."

"Yes, Mr. Mayor." Someone else ran for another phone.

La Guardia continued barking out orders: The patrolmen were to proceed at once to each of the four hundred precincts where the count for comptroller was being held up and mount guard over the voting machines with drawn guns; the patrol wagons were to follow, load up the machines and bring them back to headquarters. "By God," said La Guardia grimly, "I am going to count those votes for comptroller myself."

He didn't have to. News of what was happening in Centre Street reached the four hundred silent precincts even before the patrolmen, and suddenly the delayed returns began pouring in. La Guardia watched them being totaled, then turned to Cunningham and said, "There you are, Arthur—you're elected. Now let's all get a drink."

But a little while later he was back in the apartment on East 109th Street with friends. "Come, Marie," said the mayor-elect as he put on an apron, "we're going to cook dinner."

11   THE FIRST 1,000 DAYS

Just past midnight on Monday, January 1, 1934, in the polished oak and leather library of Judge Seabury's town house, Fiorello H. La Guardia was sworn in as the 99th mayor of New York. All the stunning disparities that had marked his life to that moment seemed to be summarized by the setting. Here was the undersized, roughneck, first-generation son of Italian immigrants assuming the magistracy of the nation's first city in the home of a patrician jurist, portraits of whose ancestors, robed in the vestments of church and bar, stared down at him from every wall. Seabury and the handful of other men present wore tuxedos, as was the custom among gentlemen. La Guardia, who didn't own a tuxedo, wore a brown business suit.

There was no swagger or revelry such as had ushered in the administrations of his Tammany Hall predecessors, no showy inaugural address. When the oath of office had been sworn, Seabury said, "Now we have a mayor of New York," and as the newsreel cameras turned, La Guardia stepped up to a microphone and spoke with uncharacteristic solemnity for three minutes.

> I have just assumed the office of the Mayor of the City of New York. The Fusion administration is now in charge of our city. Our theory of municipal government is an experiment to try to show that a nonpartisan, nonpolitical local government is possible. If we succeed, I am sure success will be possible in other cities.

Then he and his wife went home to the apartment they'd recently rented on the unfashionable upper end of Fifth Avenue, what had come to be known as Spanish Harlem. By 8:30 the next morning, when New Yorkers were sleeping off New Year's Eve hangovers, their new mayor was on his way to work in an official limousine, a well-worn Chrysler Imperial that still bore Joseph McKee's McK-1 license plate.

He faced an unenviable task. On the first day of this new year, New York City, staggered by the full force of the Depression, bled by a decade of heedless mismanagement and knavery, was hanging by the fingernails over the abyss of bankruptcy. The budget was $31 million in deficit; short-term obligations due and past due totaled $500 million—and there was nowhere to turn for help. So low had the city's credit rating fallen that there was no market for its bonds, bankers refused to lend a dime, and even the federal government had been obliged to reject its loan applications. Meanwhile 140,000 city employees faced payless paydays and a million people who depended on the Department of Public Welfare for direct aid or work relief faced destitution.

"It distresses me greatly to see my excellent friend La Guardia on so hot a spot," said H. L. Mencken, the cynical sage of Baltimore, parading his black humor. "If he is well advised he will make his will, get a shave and a haircut, burn all the letters that he has ever received from women, and jump off the Al Smith [Empire State] building."

Instead, La Guardia, who would never deny how much he had wanted the job—"Nobody forced it onto me. I went after it!"—set in motion a whirlwind hundred days of bustle and innovation that saved the city, and he began that very Monday morning.

On his way to City Hall, he stopped at Police Headquarters and swore in the new commissioner, General John F. O'Ryan, in front of two hundred ranking officers. "Drive out the racketeers," he told them bluntly, "or get out yourselves." He notified O'Ryan that those who had attained high posts in the department through political influence were to be removed. Henceforth merit would be the basis for promotion. "I want you to see, Commissioner, that this message is conveyed to every man in your command," he said.

Arriving at City Hall, he ran a gauntlet of reporters massed on the steps and shouting questions. As he bounded by, he threw a one-sentence, all-purpose answer at them over his shoulder—in Italian: *"È finita la cuccagna."*

"What the hell does that mean?" someone asked.

"It means," said a newsman who understood both Italian and La Guardia, "no more free lunch—the party's over."

A little later, Robert Moses, who was about to be named city-wide commissioner of parks, had his first look at La Guardia in action. He would never forget it.

> He was sitting at his desk in City Hall ... tossing letters at a pint-sized secretary and shouting, 'Say yes, say no, throw it away, tell him to go to hell,' etc. The Fusion regime was warming up.

It was indeed. La Guardia called for a big wastebasket— "That's going to be the most important file around here"—and ordered the telephones removed from his desk. Thereafter, for the next twelve years, he resisted every call, and when he had to take one he walked next door to his secretary's office to do it. He preferred settling things face to face.

At 11:15 he delivered a brief inaugural statement from an NBC studio, concluding with the moving oath sworn by the young men of Athens on reaching the age of citizenship, which he recited from memory:

> We will never bring disgrace to this, our city, by any act of dishonesty or cowardice, nor ever desert our suffering comrades in the ranks. We will fight for the ideals and sacred things of the city ... and thus, in all ways, we will transmit this city, not less, but greater, better and more beautiful than it was transmitted to us.

After eating a sandwich for lunch in a cafeteria on Chambers Street, he broke precedent by addressing the Democratic-controlled Board of Aldermen. He called on the members, regardless of party, to support his economic plan for averting bankruptcy, which involved cutting salaries and pruning political deadwood from the city payroll. Later, an indignant Democrat protested that it was the duty of the majority to lead, not follow. When this remark was reported back to La Guardia, he set out the main tenet of his mayoralty. "In this administration," he snapped, "*I* am the majority."

* * *

At the heart of all his hopes for rescuing and rehabilitating the stricken city was the emergency Economy Bill, feverishly worked out in a matter of days with his main financial adviser, City Chamberlain Adolf Berle. It was a bold, sweeping attempt to restore confidence by cutting through ancient charter provisions to free New York City from the heavy hold of the state legislature, and to balance the budget by consolidating or abolishing overlapping city departments and regulating the pay of employees.

The opposition, orchestrated by Tammany hacks and hangers-on who knew they would be first to go, denounced La Guardia as a would-be dictator. He was forced to travel to Albany, hat in hand, to plead for the necessary enabling legislation. But at the same time he was fighting back as only he could, using the press and radio, and the desperate emergency, to hold his opponents' feet to the fire. With every forced layoff of city workers as money ran out, he repeated his fundamental message, that without a balanced budget New York was doomed to bankruptcy and financial ruin. When Governor Lehman declared that what La Guardia proposed violated the Constitution, he replied, "The plan to cut expenses, thereby reducing taxes of home owners . . . is more in keeping with the spirit of the American government than invoking the Constitution to protect ward heelers and payroll parasites. . . . I'd rather save a home than a politician."

All through that bitter-cold winter he held the city solvent by hand-to-mouth financing and fiscal sleight of hand. Time after time he rose before dawn to take the 7:00 A.M. train to Albany, laden with briefs and reports, once getting out of a sickbed wheezing with pleurisy to explain the crisis facing New York to a joint legislative committee. All winter and into spring he fought, yielding where he had to but holding to the essentials of what his city needed, maneuvering with skills honed in fourteen years as a congressional gadfly, winning over the governor, losing four straight votes in the legislature but coming back each time with a new version of his bill. "Wear your rubbers, Mr. La Guardia," begged the *Daily News*. "You're turning out to be too good a mayor to lose."

On April 10, 1934, exactly one hundred days after he took office, the emergency Economy Bill finally became law. The same day, New York sold a $7.65 million bond issue at 4 percent—just in time to meet the week's payroll. Those who thought of La Guardia as a reflexive liberal, preconditioned to demand the opening of the public purse for every cause, were astounded by the hardheaded industry with which he now slashed away at New York's deficit. More than a thousand officeholders were summarily discharged, and all above certain salary ranges took hefty pay cuts—none steeper than La Guardia himself, who went from $40,000 a year to $22,500. Additional taxes were levied to put the relief load on a pay-as-you-go basis. The budget was balanced, whereupon the federal government loaned $100 million for essential local improvements. Once-wary bankers began vying for New York municipal bonds. By the end of the year, the city's books showed a modest surplus of $6 million—which La Guardia promptly applied to the 1935 budget. The crisis was past. The credit of New York had been restored.

Meanwhile the new mayor had been assembling his administration and turning back the tremendous inertial thrust of Tammany Hall's sixteen-year tenure. He told his supporters, "To the victors belong the responsibility for good government." A few days after the election, he addressed a meeting of loyal Fusion workers and thanked them for their efforts. Then he said, "I don't owe you a thing and you're not going to get a thing—no jobs, no favors."

An old pro sitting next to Newbold Morris snickered, "Ain't he cute! The papers'll eat that up."

"I'm afraid you'll find he means it," said Morris.

He did. The day he took office he declared war on the spoils system and launched a revolutionary experiment in city government. "There is not a Republican or a Democratic way to collect garbage," said the new mayor, and from then on the clubhouse was out and merit, excellence and experience were in. The new commissioner of public welfare was not a friendly assemblyman or district leader, as in honored tradition, but the former president of the biggest private welfare agency in the United States. The head of the Works Division had been the chief engineer of the New York Central Railroad, the relief coordinator a Macy's vice-president; neither had ever had anything to do with politics. The new fire commissioner was a fireman—another first—and when John O'Ryan quit the police force early on because he was a prima donna and there wasn't room for *two* prima donnas in the administration, La Guardia replaced him with Lewis Valentine, an honest cop who had once been broken in rank for raiding Tammany gambling clubs.

Never before had such strikingly qualified administrators been chosen to govern a major American city. The only thing they had in common was a dedication to La Guardia's brave new concept of municipal government, their very diversity underlining their freedom from political incrustation. Paul Blanshard, the city's chief investigator, was a socialist. So was his young assistant, Louis E. Yavner; neither had even voted for La Guardia. Berle was a New Dealer; Moses and Windels, Republicans. Austin MacCormick, the corrections commissioner, came from the federal Bureau of Prisons, and Dr. John Rice had been chief of New Haven's health services before La Guardia lured him to New York.

"Visiting City Hall," said tart-tongued Robert Moses, "was like opening a box of animal crackers. You never could tell what kind of beast would come out of the Ark."

Bright as his managerial stars were, La Guardia was their sun. All authority radiated from City Hall. He insisted that every department head report to him personally, regularly and in detail. He showered them with endless directives. He was simply incapable of letting a man loose to do a job.

By every theoretical test, this ought to have turned the La Guardia mayoralty into an administrative nightmare. But it worked because he knew what to do with every string in his hands; he had mastered the city and knew its innards better than any of his commissioners. By putting in sixteen-hour days, by his awesome ability to absorb, synthesize and call up vast stores of information, some of it irrelevant and just plain petty, and by suddenly appearing in the unlikeliest places to cross-check what he had been told, he could violate all the rules and—in terms of results—still inspire the most effective administration in the history of New York.

The price was high. He had come to an office described as second in complexity only to the presidency at the age of fifty-one, vigorous and with a seemingly inexhaustible store of energy. But sometimes the energy ran low and the strain showed in slumped shoulders and a sagging gray face. Just after the first hundred days, he wrote to his friend Senator Robert F. Wagner, "I am so tired at times I can hardly stand it." Late one night he told Adolf Berle that life would be much easier if he could say yes to everything that was asked of him; the hard part of being mayor was honoring his oath of office. "The devil is easy to identify," he said. "He appears as your best friend when you're terribly tired and makes a very reasonable request which you know you shouldn't grant."

Few even suspected this introspective side of him. How could they? The only La Guardia on public view was a day-long sensationalist who could turn a playground dedication into high drama. Invited to make an address and drive the first rivet for a new pier on the Hudson River, he said, "This is an administration of action, not words. Give me the riveting gun." Equipped with a two-way radio, his limousine became a mobile City Hall, speeding him from an inspection tour of a Brooklyn construction site to a gas-main explosion in the Bronx. He was the most highly visible chief executive New York had ever had, forever swooping down on some far corner of his domain. One of his magistrates said, "It seemed as though the town had been invaded by an army of small, plump men in big hats; he was everywhere." And La Guardia said, "What the hell—how else are you going to get people excited about a sewer?"

An obscure statute empowered New York's mayors to sit as judges; none of them had ever paid the slightest attention to it. But at 8:30 one morning, La Guardia walked into the West 100th Street Police Station, told the dumbstruck magistrate to go find a seat in the courtroom, and himself sat down to preside at the bar of justice. It was a hard day for pimps and gamblers.

One defendant, charged with operating a string of slot machines, stepped up confident of receiving the usual admonition or, at worst, a fine. La Guardia sent him to jail. Later, to underline the point, he posed for press photographers wearing a menacing scowl and holding a sledgehammer poised over a heap of slot machines about to be dumped into the East River. It became one of the best-known photos in a gallery that included

La Guardia twirling a six-shooter, conducting the Sanitation Department band, and hobnobbing with the King and Queen of England.

He also became famous for turning up at murder scenes, automobile accidents and railroad wrecks. He had a standing order with the fire commissioner to be called at any time of the day or night that a fire went out of control or threatened human life. No ordinary fire-chaser, he felt a compulsive need to share hazard with his men. He accepted the reality that firemen and police could be injured or killed in line of duty, but believed strongly that whenever it happened, wherever it happened, that's where the mayor's place was.

His sense of responsibility for the city and everyone in it was also especially engaged by the army of the unemployed. In 1934, faced by the worst winter weather in years, he ordered regimental armories opened so the homeless would have a warm place to sleep and at least one hot meal a day. But when he presented his record-breaking relief budget, some aldermen judged it a profitable line of attack. At a meeting of the Board, one member, with appropriate expressions of shock and lament, said he understood that common prostitutes were receiving relief funds. The sharp, sudden silence that fell on the chamber was soon pierced by the high-pitched agitation of the mayor: "I thought that question was settled two thousand years ago, but I see I was wrong." Then, jumping to his feet so he would be in full view when he administered the coup de grâce, he shouted, "Mr. Sergeant-at-Arms, clear the room! Clear the room—so this big bum can throw the first stone!"

One day he turned up at a Lower East Side relief station and found interviewers gossiping and reading the morning papers while a long line of applicants stretched out into the cold street, waiting. As he pushed toward the director's office, an underling wearing a derby and smoking a fat cigar grabbed his arm and bellowed, "Where the hell do you think you're going?"

La Guardia smacked the cigar out of the man's mouth with one hand and the hat from his head with the other. "Take your hat off when you talk to a citizen!" he commanded.

By the time he had flung open the director's door and found him absent, the others, horrified, realized who he was and rushed to make amends. What could they do for His Honor? He ordered a secretary to summon the welfare commissioner at once. "And let me see how fast the rest of you can clear up this crowd of applicants."

It didn't take long. But it was too late for the offenders. When Commissioner William Hodson arrived, La Guardia ordered them fired, then instructed Hodson to wait there until the director appeared. "If he doesn't have a good excuse—and I mean a doctor's certificate—he's fired, too."

Those who lost their jobs that day would always remember Mayor La Guardia as despotic and unforgiving, which was not entirely untrue. But on the other hand, as he walked out of the relief station, the welfare applicants who had witnessed the little drama broke into a spontaneous cheer.

He had to know everything. At 3:00 A.M. one night during that first winter, he telephoned William Carey, the sanitation commissioner, and demanded to know whether he had a snow-alarm plan. "Sure," was the prompt reply. "I'm called as soon as the first flake falls."

"Wonderful," said La Guardia, voice dripping sarcasm. "Stick your head out of the window." Then he hung up.

When the hapless Carey looked, he saw nothing but snow; a full-fledged blizzard was under way. That week he won the mayor's least-coveted trophy—a highly-polished sheep shank relentlessly bestowed on commissioners who pulled a certifiable boner. Other notable awards went to the commissioner of licenses for seating La Guardia next to an infamous racketeer at a public function, and to the fire commissioner when he burnt himself setting off illegal fireworks on the Fourth of July.

Only afterward did any of them love him. "Working for La Guardia," said Bea Himmel, one of his secretaries, "was nerve-racking. Even when things quieted down you walked around with the feeling that something traumatic was about to happen. And it always did."

He freely conceded his shortcomings—"I'm an inconsiderate, arbitrary, authoritative, difficult, complicated, intolerant and somewhat theatrical person," he warned a young assistant district attorney coming to work at City Hall—but if he ever made any effort to reform he failed spectacularly. He expected daily deliveries of the impossible and assumed if he called you on a Sunday afternoon, or in the middle of the night, that you would be standing by the telephone, just waiting to hear from him. He was forever firing commissioners—"absolutely and permanently, goddam it!"—then flying into another rage when they weren't on the job next morning.

Some commissioners took it in stride. Henry Rosner, a key officer in the Welfare Department, said, "Being fired by La Guardia meant you were really in—he'd noticed you. If you hadn't been fired a few times, you probably weren't doing your job."

But young Louis Yavner, who had been with La Guardia from the beginning and became a tough and effective investigations commissioner, was devastated when it happened to him and went stumbling out of La Guardia's office with tears in his eyes. An hour later, as he was clearing his desk of personal belongings, he was summoned back. The mayor wanted to discuss an investigation by Yavner's predecessor, William B. Herlands. Dazed, Yavner returned to find La Guardia beaming over the Herlands report. There then ensued the following dialogue of the deaf:

LA GUARDIA: (*Brandishing report*) Ah, there was a commissioner who knew how to conduct an investigation.
YAVNER: Major, if you'll look at the footnote on the first page, you'll see that *I* conducted the investigation.
LA GUARDIA: And what a report! Have you read this report carefully?
YAVNER: (*Louder*) Mr. Mayor, *I* wrote that report. It was my investigation. It says so . . .
LA GUARDIA: Herlands could really do his job. (*Tosses report across desk to Yavner*) Here—study this: You'll learn something for next time.
YAVNER: (*Stupefied, gropes for words. La Guardia is suddenly immersed in something else, signalling dismissal, but Yavner persists*) Major, you just fired me.
LA GUARDIA: (*Without looking up*) Oh, don't be foolish—get back to your work.

Some couldn't stand the pressure and left him. But one, Robert Moses, gave as good as he got. Brilliant, overbearing, self-centered and driven, Moses once held twelve city, state and fed-

eral jobs at the same time; before his long career ended in 1968,
he had served under five mayors, six governors and five presi-
dents—and bullied them all. But La Guardia didn't give much
ground and their battles shook the rafters at City Hall.

Moses believed government leaders should be measured by
their works, not their words. He was enraged by men of small vision who contributed a bottomless store of reasons why a thing
could not be done, but little else. Nor did he have any use for theoretical planners and professional idealists, forever hatching
vast social programs that came to nothing. To Moses, a social
program was a park that ordinary people could get to.

"If your head is wax, don't walk in the sun," he used to say,
quoting Benjamin Franklin. But he said it with an arrogance
Franklin never intended. He *was* arrogant. "There are people
who like things as they are," he once said. "I can't hold out any
hope to them." And this scorn for other viewpoints, this outspoken vanity, troubled even a generally approving press and a
public grateful for his bridges and beaches and miles of parkway
without a single defacing billboard. In 1934 he ran for governor
and lost by the biggest margin in the history of New York. Whatever he achieved and was yet to achieve would depend on his
having a patron in high office. At first it was Al Smith, a Democrat and the only public official to win Republican Moses's unqualified admiration. Thereafter, during the twelve years when
the master builder changed the face of the city and the state, his
patron was La Guardia.

Once the mayor said—no doubt through gritted teeth—"No
law, no regulation, no budget stops Bob Moses in his appointed
task." He might have added that not even the President of the
United States did, and that he, La Guardia, at the risk of losing
federal millions for public works in the city, had to protect his
park commissioner from a vengeful Franklin D. Roosevelt. Their
enmity went back many years, and Roosevelt, now in a position
to exact tribute, demanded as the price for continued federal
grants to New York that the mayor dismiss Moses from the Triborough Bridge Authority, the linchpin of his power. Moses, of
course, flatly refused to go quietly, and thereafter La Guardia
kept stalling for both practical and political reasons: Moses, besides being absolutely irreplaceable, would never let the world

forget it if the Little Flower knuckled under. And so La Guardia kept assuring Washington that he was handling the problem, which in fact he was assiduously not. It brewed on and on—until Moses, diabolical to his fingertips, leaked the President's order to the press. Then the whole thing boiled over in such a wrathful protest against the White House effort to drive "one of [New York's] ablest public servants" out of office that F.D.R. had to back off. As for La Guardia, he was greatly relieved to be able to quit defending Moses's 360-degree virtue and take up his own feuds with the irascible park commissioner.

He spoke of him privately as His Grace, a reference both to Moses's imperial manner and his sense of his own infallibility. And when La Guardia wasn't within earshot, Moses called him "Rigoletto"—unless he was more than normally agitated by the Little Flower, in which case he called him "that dago son of a bitch." When the Triborough Bridge was opened in 1936, he asked La Guardia to discontinue an unneeded East River ferry because he wanted the land on which the Manhattan terminal stood for a park. Then, deciding that La Guardia wasn't being quick enough, he sent in a wrecking crane and pile driver to tear the dock apart—while the ferry was in mid-river. La Guardia, who turned red with rage when he heard the news, had to send in the police to stop the mayhem. But Moses got what he wanted. Ten days later the ferry was retired and the wrecking crew came back.

The tactic of threatening to resign one or all of his offices had been perfected by Moses to wrest concessions from the mayor, but he began using it so often that La Guardia sent him a note saying, "Enclosed are your last five or six resignations; I'm starting a new file." Moses didn't think that was funny, so La Guardia tried again. He had a pad of forms printed to read, "I, Robert Moses, do hereby resign as————, effective————." The next time Moses came in threatening to quit, La Guardia whipped out the pad and handed over one of the forms with a flourish. "Here, just fill in the blanks," he said with a leer.

Moses took one look, grabbed the pad off the desk, and threw it across the room. But it was a good three months before he used the resignation ultimatum again.

Of course, what their explosive confrontations revealed to

anyone who had the insight to appreciate it was that they were kindred spirits, made arrogant and authoritarian by the central imperative of both their lives: getting things done. There was never personal hostility between them, despite the highly flavored language with which they assaulted one another; only disagreements about *what* should be done, and how. "You'd see the two of them in the goddamnedest argument," said Moses aide Jack Madigan, "and then five hours later they could go and have a drink together and you'd never know they had fought."

And sometimes, wittingly or otherwise, they revealed their secret admiration for one another. "Robert Moses couldn't survive in a Tammany administration for three good reasons," La Guardia once said. "First, he knows his job; second, he is honest; third, he has opinions of his own."

During one argument between them, the mayor yelled, "You can't get away with riding roughshod over things!"

To which Moses shouted back, revealingly, "Why not? That's the way *you* get things done!"

With La Guardia's support, Moses created hundreds of playgrounds; he linked the five boroughs of the city with bridges and tunnels, and built a network of landscaped parkways that led to immaculately maintained parks and sparkling beaches. Even Robert Caro, whose pioneering reevaluation of Moses's achievements is sharply critical of their ultimate effect on the city, wrote:

> In the five years after he became Park Commissioner, in a city in which the parks had been barren for decades, he made the parks bloom. In a city in which not a mile of new arterial highway had been built in fifteen years, he built fifty miles of arterial highway. In a city in which a new bridge had not been built in a quarter of a century, he built not only three new big bridges—Triborough, Henry Hudson and the Marine Parkway—but 110 smaller ones to carry local streets across the parkways.

Shortly before he died in 1981, Moses was asked by this writer what La Guardia's most enduring legacy would be. "The public works," he replied, "the tangible things. He stood up for them. He has to get the credit."

*　*　*

There are some long-retired cops in New York who still gloat over the story of the doctor, a casual friend of the mayor, who came upon a rookie patrolman sticking a ticket under his windshield wiper for illegal parking. The doctor tore it in two under the policeman's nose and warned him not to be so stupid again. The young man, still unschooled in the labyrinthine ways of power and pull, placed the physician under arrest and took him directly to the police station, where he had to pay a stiff fine. Fuming, the doctor rushed right over to City Hall to complain to the mayor about the flagrant insult.

La Guardia listened, then instructed his secretary to call the station house and get the young policeman on the phone. But when he took the call, the precinct captain was on the line, distraught, full of apologies that one of his men should have ticketed a friend of the mayor. Could the mayor find it in his heart to excuse the man, since he was only a rookie?

La Guardia's face reddened, a very bad sign. "You idiot!" he shrieked. "That rookie is a better cop than you are! I called up to tell him I was sending him a box of cigars. He's the kind of cop I want—and you're not!"

The rookie got the cigars—delivered by the mayor's car— and the mayor's "friend" got an invitation to leave City Hall before he was thrown out. And the story, running through the Police Department like sheet lightning, did more for morale than a pay raise.

La Guardia was a newspaperman's delight in those first years, always ready with a wisecrack for the next edition. During the December days when half the world was holding its breath waiting to hear if the King of England would give up his throne to marry a twice-divorced American, New York's mayor interrupted the harangue of a Board of Estimate doomsayer to ask, "Excuse me, my friend, but by chance were you the guy who introduced the King to Mrs. Simpson?"

It was also the time when the First Lady of the land became famous for her whirlwind travels and frank pronouncements on all subjects. When someone suggested to the mayor that he call on Mrs. La Guardia to dedicate one of the city's new playgrounds, the response was, "Hey, wait a minute—my wife's name is Marie, not Eleanor."

He often took the conductor's baton at public concerts—and,

being his father's son, knew how to handle it. Wrote *Times* music
critic Howard Taubman, "We *like* his conducting. He knows
what the brasses are for—to be heard. He knows that band music
should make the blood tingle." Once, when he was to conduct the
combined Police and Sanitation Department bands at Carnegie
Hall, the nervous stage manager went to City Hall for final instructions. Did His Honor want anything special? Spotlights,
perhaps, following him down the aisle? "Hell, no. Just treat me
like Toscanini," La Guardia instructed him.

An aide who was to meet him at ceremonies opening a new
public market arrived late. Typically, La Guardia "raised hell."
But that wasn't the end of it. Months after, the offender received
a newspaper clipping from City Hall; it told how a Japanese official who came late to a public function had committed hara-kiri.
In the margin La Guardia had scrawled, "That's what I call
class."

He was immensely proud of cleaning up the city's markets.
When he took office, thousands of pushcart peddlers operated in
the open streets under unsanitary, unsightly conditions, creat-
ing traffic problems for miles around, and were themselves vic-
timized by weather, thieves and gangsters. It was not uncommon
for peddlers to sleep on their carts so their curb space wouldn't
be stolen from them. It all changed, dramatically, under the new
mayor. La Guardia instructed Markets Commissioner William
Fellowes Morgan to expand and enclose the major markets, provide running water, rail facilities and loading platforms. The
Bronx Terminal Market, an unfinished $17 million white ele-
phant under Tammany, was completed and showed a $200,000
profit in six months.

The public was delighted, and the peddlers—able to operate
every working day even if it rained, snowed or froze outdoors;
assigned a permanent place and protected from thugs and extor-
tionists by the Market Department's anti-racketeering division—could hardly believe the sudden shift in their fortunes.
When La Guardia came to dedicate the modern new municipal
market under the New York Central tracks between 111th and
116th streets, they stood proudly by their stalls in crisp white
coats and listened adoringly as he said, "I found you pushcart
peddlers; I have made you merchants."

The day of reckoning was at hand for the likes of Socks

Lanza, who terrorized the Fulton Fish Market, and Arthur (Tootsie) Herbert and his brother Charlie, who monopolized the poultry business by going after aspiring competitors with sawed-off billiard cues. La Guardia did not always observe all the niceties of the law when he set about rooting out the racketeers who had had years to fasten themselves like leeches onto the body of the city's commerce. Ciro Terranova, the infamous Artichoke King, was driven out of New York by the threat of instant arrest. When a civil liberties group protested this infringement of a citizen's constitutional right, La Guardia said they were absolutely correct. He turned to Police Commissioner Valentine and told him that Terranova was to be allowed to come into New York City. "Wait until he gets to 125th Street," he added, "and *then* go to work on him."

Driving Terranova out of the artichoke business, a $1 million-a-year racket, called for more finesse, but La Guardia was up to that too. Terranova "handled" all the miniature artichokes—a delicacy among Italians—that came into New York. He performed no service; he did not grow, deliver or unload artichokes. But by graft and terror he forced municipal market dealers to sell the entire crop to a spurious Terranova company, which tacked 100 percent on the price for itself and then resold them to retailers.

All this was known, but how to stop it? La Guardia's answer was so stunningly theatrical that he might have been laughed out of town—except that it worked. Well before the sun rose on December 20, 1935, the mayor, his markets commissioner, the Bronx district attorney, and two policemen with bugles suddenly appeared in the Bronx Terminal Market. The mayor climbed up on the back of a truck, and the policemen, like heralds of an earlier day, summoned the astonished populace with a clarion call from the bugles. Whereupon La Guardia—and this must surely have been one of the most satisfying moments of his life—unfurled an enormous scroll and read a proclamation: Under a colonial law which empowered the mayor to forbid the sale of certain food in an emergency, he was herewith banning the sale of artichokes in the public markets. While he leaned into the swelling crowd of dealers and retailers and exhorted them to help him drive out the racketeers, assuring them he would protect them, policemen were posting the proclamation throughout the city markets.

The afternoon headlines were all La Guardia's, but some of the editorials were caustic. Where did he get the idea that New York could be run by proclamation? cried the aggrieved *Post*. But the Little Flower was not relying on proclamations alone. Show business was for winning the hearts of the people. He crushed Terranova by sending his law secretary to Washington to persuade the Agriculture Department to cancel the gangster's license to sell perishable commodities. Between the two, and in a gratifyingly short time, Terranova was out of business and the price of artichokes had dropped spectacularly.

Meanwhile Governor Lehman had appointed thirty-three-year-old Thomas E. Dewey special prosecutor to investigate crime in New York, launching a career that was to make Dewey district attorney, governor of New York, and twice the unsuccessful Republican candidate for President. Now the headlines were his, and La Guardia was required to accommodate Dewey's insatiable appetite for more funds, more office space, more furniture. "Compared to Tom Dewey's love affair with himself," said an inside observer, "Romeo and Juliet could be classed as a couple of neighborhood acquaintances." But La Guardia provided everything that was asked for and ordered his police and magistrates to give the prosecutor full cooperation. His personal, passionate hatred of the underworld overrode any other consideration. He once told his police, "I want you to put so much fear into the heart of every crook in New York that when he sees a cop he'll tip hat." It never quite came to that, but by the end of his first term, major crime in the city was down by 20 percent.

But he was not perfect. For it was La Guardia, the mayor who brought the City Center for performing arts and $2 opera tickets to New York, who also drove the Minsky brothers and their inimitable burlesque shows out of town. His puritanical streak, that sense of moral outrage, was so highly developed that he could make no distinction between a truly original theatrical genre, only one part of which featured the unadorned female breast, and ordinary prostitution; or between a work of literature with some four-letter words, and magazines with flagrantly lewd cover illustrations publicly displayed; or between church bingo and the numbers racket. To him they were all the same, and he railed away at them with fine impartiality, sometimes making himself look silly.

On April 30, 1937, a time when the six Minsky burlesques in New York starred such wonderful entertainers as Phil Silvers, Red Buttons, Abbott and Costello, and Gypsy Rose Lee, when New York theater critics from A. J. Liebling to Brooks Atkinson were celebrating the genius and genuine good fun of burlesque, La Guardia refused to renew the Minsky theater licenses, banned the very use of the words *Minsky* and *burlesque* in theatrical advertising, and so put them out of business. And throughout this favored land there are men with long memories, now well into their middle years, who have never forgiven him.

"No, he was not perfect," Louis Yavner said in reflection. "He could be cynical, churlish, hot-headed, petty and just plain wrong. At one time or another he antagonized everyone who ever worked for him. But he also gave us all a standard of excellence, a sense of adventure in government, pride in what we were doing. He was actually making New York a better place to live—and he made us part of the excitement."

He took everything that came his way, the huzzahs and the Bronx cheers, without deviating from the course he had set. Nor did he shrink or agonize over the tough decisions. Absolutely determined that welfare had to be financed on a pay-as-you-go basis, he needed $65 million that he knew could never be squeezed out of current revenue. As a congressman, he had won a national reputation fighting Hoover's national sales tax; now, as mayor, he levied a 2 percent city sales tax (lowered to 1 percent in 1941) to pay for his welfare program. He did not explain, recant or apologize. He just did it because it had to be done. As it happened, there was no great outcry, but he would not have changed his mind if there was. "The sales tax is wholly wrong except for one thing," he said. "It raises the money we need."

12
THE SECOND
BEST-KNOWN AMERICAN

The four-room apartment at 1274 Fifth Avenue had to be expanded. In 1933, Marie and Fiorello La Guardia adopted two children, Jean, seven, the daughter of Thea's sister, and Eric, a year younger. La Guardia, who responded to all children and became a warmhearted, devoted and—to no one's surprise—demanding father, experienced a great fulfillment finally from having his own, though he fussed and worried about them with the anxiety of a man entrusted with some evanescent treasure. That year, he prevailed on the landlord to let him take over a room from the then-vacant apartment next door, and this became the children's bedroom. But it could be reached only from the door cut through the La Guardia's bedroom, and the mayor's old friend and doctor, George Baehr, noting that the children would have to pass alongside his bed to go to the bathroom at night, asked if they didn't waken him. They did, he replied, but he liked it. "I like to see them, even in the middle of the night."

However, in May 1942 he let himself be persuaded to move the family into Gracie Mansion, a handsome white eighteenth-century building on a bluff over the East River at 89th Street, owned by the city and lately designated as the official residence of New York's mayors. Neither of the La Guardias was overjoyed; it was not their style. Marie wondered how she would take care of such a big house, and La Guardia worried that New Yorkers would think he had gone high-hat. But they agreed that the children would enjoy the two-acre grounds and adjoining Carl Schurz Park and decided to go ahead.

Again the family expanded. Moving in with them were the young son (and namesake) of La Guardia's brother, Richard, who had died in 1935, and the La Guardias' black cook, Juanita, with her son—also Richard. Thereafter, on most fair Sundays, East End Avenue neighbors and passersby could look through the high iron picket fence and see their mayor playing catch with his son and the two Richards, or standing on the bluff with Jean, an arm around her shoulders as he talked about the ships and barges and sailboats that passed on the river below.*

Those were some of his rare moments of leisure. John Gunther, who devoted a chapter to La Guardia in his 1940s best seller *Inside U.S.A.,* spent a typical work day with him. It started at 9:12 A.M., and though Gunther quit at 8:00 that night, the mayor didn't. It was a "desk day," that is, one in which no tunnel openings or fish-market inspections were scheduled—just an ordinary day in which La Guardia administered the affairs of the City of New York.

Here are some of the matters he dealt with: crime prevention; zoning regulations; a broken water main in the Brooklyn Children's Museum; a meeting with his Committee on Race and Religion (to whom he said with sly irony, "Now let's all be good Anglo-Saxons. Let's not lose our heads like all those Latins up in Albany"); a forthcoming trip to Washington to see the President and the Secretary of the Interior; professional gambling on college basketball games (which provoked a rage; "The tin-horn chiselers, the big-mouths, the procurers!"); reprints of modern classics for the public schools (for which the mayor dictated an introduction on the spot: "Ever see a movie that was a bit over your head? Well it was because you haven't read enough."); the coal supply for Broadway theaters (World War II was in its fourth year and critical materials were rationed); plans for the international airport at Idlewild (since renamed John F. Kennedy); the fact that liverwurst was on sale at the municipal cafeteria though it was meatless Tuesday—which touched off another rage.

In occasional thirty-second intervals between appointments and other activities, Gunther squeezed in questions and elicited these pearls of apocrypha from the La Guardia anthology:

On his famous temperament: "When I get excited and blow off, it was all planned two days ago."

On files: ". . . the curse of modern civilization. I had a young secretary once. Just out of school. I told her, 'If you can keep

---

* Jean, a diabetic, died in 1967 at the age of 34, Eric is a professor of English literature at a West Coast university.

these files straight, I'll marry you.' She did—so I married her."

On the essence of municipal government: "Housekeeping—to make a city clean and keep it that way."

On why the politicians always oppose him: "I keep them on a strict diet. You know what it is to starve?"

One exchange, spontaneous and heartfelt, went this way:

GUNTHER: Whom do you hate most?
LA GUARDIA: Hitler.
GUNTHER: What do you like most?
LA GUARDIA: Music.
GUNTHER: What do you believe in most?
LA GUARDIA: Children.

La Guardia worked in the seventy-foot-long Blue Room—which was white—a chamber of such heroic proportions that civic ceremonies had once been held there. The little mayor, hunched over his desk at one end, was all but lost to the view of anyone entering from the other. Close up, he was seen to be in perpetual motion, swinging violently around in his chair, pouncing forward, throwing himself back so far his feet left the floor. Dictating to two, sometimes three, stenographers—one couldn't possibly keep up with him—he shoved his glasses up on his head, frowned, grimaced, snorted and shook his fist as though the recipient of the letter were standing in front of him. In the more than eight hours that Gunther spent alongside his desk, La Guardia got up only three times: to take a telephone call, to swear in a new member of the Board of Health, to go to the bathroom. Lunch was a cup of coffee. The author had never seen anyone expend so much energy sitting down.

La Guardia tried to see that everyone at City Hall worked as hard as he did. David Rockefeller, who served him as a dollar-a-year-secretary in 1940 and 1941, says the staff was limp with weariness by the time the mayor left in the evening—whereupon he would call back from the phone in his limousine with some things he had overlooked. Rockefeller's own assignments covered a wide range of activities, from answering mail for La Guardia's signature to raising fellowship money for Latin Americans studying in New York. Once the mayor sent him out to generate some revenue in the almost empty terminal building at La Guardia Field. So it came about, thanks to Fiorello La Guardia, that the young man who was destined to head the Chase Manhattan Bank, perhaps the single most powerful financial institution in the world, started his commercial career flogging rental space and display cases in an airport terminal building.

Someone once asked the mayor how he relaxed from work. "More work," he replied succinctly. He worked even in the limousine, which was now equipped with a swing-out desk and telephone, only taking a break for a whiskey and soda at the Advertising Club on the way home. Gunther wrote, when he left La Guardia at Gracie Mansion that winter day in 1945, "The mayor was going to have a bite of supper and then deal with paper work until midnight and beyond."

La Guardia's three terms as mayor coincided closely with F.D.R.'s twelve years in the White House. They became friends; not close friends—they had lived too long in separate worlds for that—but sharing the progressive spirit and a zest for the political arena. Their hearts were as fully engaged as their minds. They forged an undeclared alliance that was no secret to any politician, Democrat or Republican, operating on the New York-Washington axis. They crossed party lines in four elections to endorse each other's candidacies; in a fifth, the President offered benevolent neutrality.

The relationship was based on more than mutual admiration. Both derived real and practical benefits from it. To La Guardia, the Roosevelt administration was a reliable source of financial support for the city, which gave him a certain independence from local naysayers, and in the President himself he had a constant and powerful benefactor in the otherwise unpredictable political swirls and eddies. To Roosevelt, already in debt to the Little Flower for his efforts on behalf of the New Deal during the last days of the 72nd Congress, the mayor proved a brave and resourceful ally in the enemy camp. With one foot firmly on the neck of the Tammany tiger, he many times saved the President from embarrassment by his own party in New York City.

So it was that from the outset La Guardia found a sympathetic audience whenever he went to Washington to plead the city's cause. In a time when the experiment of federal aid to localities was being gingerly tested on a case-by-case basis, the mayor of New York rarely came home without a commitment for funds: $20 million for low-cost housing, $1.5 million toward completion of the Triborough Bridge, $25 million to put three thousand men to work on subway construction—all in his first year on the job.

More than once his impulse for controversy appalled Cabinet officers and presidential aides, but Roosevelt himself always seemed to be amused and invigorated by La Guardia's temperamental outbursts. When the Little Flower spoke out against the depravities of Hitler and the Nazi dictatorship as though New York City had a foreign policy of its own, it was much to the irritation of the State Department, then trying to maintain a "correct" attitude toward Germany. But La Guardia, who regarded Hitler and Mussolini as international racketeers—tinhorns!— could not keep still. Addressing a meeting of the American Jewish Congress, he called Hitler "that brown-shirted fanatic now menacing the peace of the world" and suggested that he be enshrined in a chamber of horrors at the forthcoming New York World's Fair.

An international uproar followed, the German press and Nazi sympathizers all over the world heaping abuse on the head of "that Jew, La Guardia" and on the United States generally. Secretary of State Cordell Hull felt compelled to offer "very earnest regrets," and when La Guardia next appeared at the White House, the press corps flocked around, eager for the condemned man's last words. "You're going to catch it now, aren't you?" said one reporter, expressing what they all believed.

La Guardia, who had no final words and certainly no regrets, marched right on and went into the President's office. As soon as he had closed the door behind him, Roosevelt's right arm shot forward in a mock Nazi salute. "Heil, Fiorello!" he said with a grin.

La Guardia immediately snapped to attention and thrust out his own arm. "Heil, Franklin!" he responded.

Then they had a good laugh and no more was said about the episode. Later, though, F.D.R. told Hull he wished he could pin a gold medal on La Guardia for saying what everyone in the administration was thinking.

One summer, when the Roosevelts and the La Guardias were

together at an official function in New York, Mrs. Roosevelt spontaneously invited the mayor and his wife to come to Hyde Park for lunch. Marie said they had no one to leave with the children. Eleanor said to bring them. But there was Richard, the cook's boy; he always played with the children and . . .

And what?

And he was colored, said Marie.

Mrs. Roosevelt beamed. She was a woman who never passed up a chance to live out her commitments, and she told the La Guardias they *must* bring Richard. So they did, and everyone had a marvelous time. However the little family outing touched off a flurry of criticism in the national press. How could La Guardia have brought a black child into the President's home? To his luncheon table! How could Roosevelt have countenanced such impudence? But thoughtful Americans were pleased, and F.D.R., lining up with the Little Flower on the side of the angels, was delighted.

By the early 1940s, when La Guardia had been twice re-elected mayor and appointed by Roosevelt to national posts as director of the Office of Civilian Defense and chairman of the Joint United States–Canadian Defense Board, he was regularly sitting in on Cabinet meetings at the White House, taking the midnight train from New York and flying back in time to be at his desk at City Hall by the following afternoon. This did not necessarily summon forth cheers from administration stalwarts, among whom competition for the President's ear was already hot. In a spasm of petulance, Secretary of the Interior Harold L. Ickes, usually a La Guardia booster, confided to his diary, "After all, Fiorello is not God and he has to eat and sleep like other human beings."

But the Little Flower was riding high in those years and there was no stopping him. As the perennial president of the U.S. Conference of Mayors, he was the acknowledged spokesman for municipal concerns—"the Andrew Jackson of the cities," someone dubbed him. Next to Roosevelt himself, he had become the most colorful and invariably newsworthy personality in the country. Adolf Berle, who was called to Washington in 1938 and moved steadily upward in the administration, later said, "I suppose the two best-known names throughout the entire world in this generation are Franklin D. Roosevelt and Fiorello La Guardia."

*   *   *

In 1936 a longstanding boundary dispute between the Bronx and the Westchester County town of Mount Vernon was resolved by a referendum of the seventy-four householders on the contested land: They voted to remain in the Bronx. Taking note, the mayor of the City of New York dispatched the Police Department band to serenade them and hand out proclamations expressing His Honor's pride in their decision. It was vintage La Guardia. Through the years, no matter how many extraterritorial assignments he took on, no matter how much there was to do, he never lost his instinct for the small dramatic gesture.

Or for the annihilating phrase. When he was denounced for leaving City Hall on federal business, his answer was, "I can do more work for New York in an hour than those deadbeats can do in a whole year." It was not his most far-fetched exaggeration. In their seminal work, *Governing New York City,* political scientists Wallace S. Sayre and Herbert Kaufman wrote,

> Under a lesser Mayor . . . the Democratic majority might have been able to assume a larger role in making governmental decisions. . . . La Guardia, however, was so agile, so politically astute, so energetic, and so immensely popular, that they were no match for him. With his unexpected and continually shifting alliances (including some with influential Democrats), explosive temperament, talent for invective, genius for ridicule, and with a press that loved his outbursts because they made such colorful copy, he beat the Council majority into submission—when he was not circumventing [it] altogether.

He governed as though no goal were out of reach. Slum clearance; the substitution of an integrated bus service for a tangle of obsolete trolley lines in Queens; the elimination of darkening, deafening elevated subway lines in Manhattan—undertakings no previous administration had attempted now were pressed forward. In the ninety-two months between the time La Guardia assumed office and when wartime restrictions ended all nonessential construction projects, New York City built ninety-two new schools, giving it the biggest and best public education system in the world. In 1944 the mayor introduced an inclusive health insurance plan for city employees earning less than $5,000 a year; it was the first in the nation.

The level of his appointments was the highest by far in New York history. He chose blacks, women, political opponents—color, sex and political preference weighing next to nothing on his scale of excellence. Nor did he pay much heed to the requests or recommendations of those who might have assumed a certain influence. When the dean of the New York University law school, his alma mater, wrote suggesting a qualified staff member for "a judicial career," La Guardia replied that he would give the letter serious consideration, but cautioned

> [This] does not mean very much. I have a long list of applicants for judicial appointment. You can check the list any time. Just take the "Red Book" under the heading "Attorneys." Omit the letter X and you will get a pretty good idea.

His standard for all appointments was breathtakingly straightforward: Was the candidate the best available for the job? But he was not infallible and when he made a mistake . . . well, he coined a phrase for it, and now it is immortalized in Bartlett's *Familiar Quotations*. This is how it came about:

In 1936, against sound advice, La Guardia appointed Herbert A. O'Brien, an eccentric, authoritarian figure, to a ten-year term as judge of the Queens Domestic Relations Court. He proved to be an unrelieved disaster, enraptured of reactionary causes, stirring racial antagonisms with his decisions and public statements, even traveling to Washington to warn the Senate Foreign Relations Committee solemnly that civil war was imminent between "the foreign-born elements in New York City." La Guardia, testifying before the same committee, was asked if he placed any credence in Judge O'Brien's dire forecast:

> LA GUARDIA: I didn't know the committee would be interested in stories of that kind. If I had thought so, I could have given you several better ones from the psychopathic wards.
> SENATOR CLARK: But wasn't it you who appointed this man to the bench?
> LA GUARDIA: (*Chuckling grimly*) Senator, I have made a lot of good appointments, and I think I am good. But when I make a mistake, it's a beaut.

New York owned a radio station, WNYC, over which John Hylan once tried to read his autobiography. It is questionable whether any other mayor even knew of its existence. But La Guardia and WNYC were made for each other. It was not love at first sight; the Little Flower used it only for an occasional report until the Japanese attack on Pearl Harbor, when he went on the air at once with an emergency address. But a few weeks later, on January 18, 1942, he inaugurated a series of Sunday afternoon programs, *Talk to the People*, that continued without interruption, even when he was far from New York, until the day before he left office four years later.

No professional performer could have duplicated the fascination of those broadcasts, or attracted their audience. In an era when television was unknown and radio still groping for its place as a medium of information, as many as 1.8 million New Yorkers tuned in—25 percent of the city's population. "This is a new kind of government," wrote drama critic John Mason Brown, "this government by microphone. With a flip of the dial, he turns the metropolis into a small town."

All week he would tear items out of the newspapers, or write little reminders to himself. On Sunday, these, together with memoranda and reports from his commissioners, were dumped in a heap in front of the two microphones on his desk. Precisely at 1:00 P.M., as the opening bars of the *Marine Hymn* faded and an announcer introduced him—"And speaking to you from his desk at City Hall . . ."—La Guardia was tearing open his tie and unbuttoning his collar.

"Patience and fortitude," he always said, but that was absolutely the only predictable part of the next thirty minutes. He might start with late news from the fighting fronts, interrupting himself to address a little homily to, say, Winston Churchill, as though the Prime Minister of Great Britain, like all sensible people, was tuned to WNYC:

"Mr. Churchill, over here we believe that the Atlantic charter is a rule, not a guide. And so, Winston, if I may use the language of Shakespeare or Browning or other British classicists, please don't louse it up."

Glancing at a slip of paper on the desk, bouncing in his chair, he might then discard the role of grand strategist to tell something that had happened to Jean or Eric that week, or explain the current status of the meat supply. "Remember I told you last week that lamb would be plentiful and all you had to do was sit tight and not buy and the price would come down? ... Well, you know, the black market was forced to sell at ceiling price because you listened to me. We struck right where it hurts most—right in their perishable stock. Ha ha ha!" (slamming the desk for emphasis).

Suddenly he would be brandishing a clenched fist at the microphones, yelling, "Again I warn you, chicken dealers. I'm not fooling. No more monkey business!" Another slip of paper, some more bouncing, some more homely advice: how to help children with homework, how to cook fish—once meat rationing was imposed, he championed the use of fish so often and so vigorously that New Yorkers began referring to him as the Little Flounder.

He shared his problems. One winter he confided, "This year we broke even on snow. I'm so grateful for that. Did I pray and pray! We just got under the wire with $1,169,000. We cannot have any more snow because we have no more funds."

Soon after, something reminded him to say, "Ladies, I want to ask you a little favor. I want you please to wear your rubbers when you go out in this weather. If you don't wear your rubbers, you may slip and fall and hurt yourself. ... Now another word about fish."

It was pure corn, but it was all in the family; it was between the people and their mayor. For a little while each Sunday afternoon, he helped them believe that someone was looking after things, that what was right would prevail. And in the dark days of the war, that was not a small matter.

During a 1945 newspaper deliverers' strike, La Guardia read the Sunday comics to the children and assured himself a kind of immortality. He did it with such slam-bang gusto— "Ahh! What do we have here? The gardener! Stabbed! ... But Dick Tracy is on the trail!"—that the live audience in the Blue Room burst into applause. La Guardia paid no attention. He still had a moral to impart: "And say, children, what does it all mean? It means that dirty money never brings any luck."

The reading was such a sensation that when the strike went on and La Guardia repeated his performance the following Sunday, newsreel cameramen came in to film the fire-and-brimstone extravaganza, and years afterward people who couldn't pronounce his name would hear it and somehow remember, "Oh, yeah, he was the guy who read the comics on the radio that time."

One winter evening in 1934, a TWA flight from Chicago landed at Newark Airport and the passengers disembarked. All but one; he refused to budge. "My ticket reads Chicago to New York," he told the stewardess, then the copilot, then the pilot. "This is only Newark. I'm flying to New York."

He was, too. The most earnest persuasion failed to change his mind, and eventually the airliner climbed back into the night sky and delivered him to Floyd Bennett Field at the foot of Flatbush Avenue in Brooklyn. "Thank you," said the mayor of New York as he fixed his wide-brimmed black hat on his head and stepped off the plane. "And remember, Newark is not New York."

He never let anyone else forget it either. Almost exactly five years after striking that first gaudy blow toward bringing his city's airport back across the Hudson River from New Jersey, La Guardia won the war. At North Beach in Queens, a smelly marshland was transformed—only biologists knew what ecology meant then—into a $40 million commercial airport, only twenty minutes from the heart of New York (population 7 million) when traffic permitted. From Newark (population 500,000), it took more than twice as long, even in the middle of the night.

No one but La Guardia, not even Robert Moses, could lay claim to any of the glory for the new airport. It had been his dream and it became his baby. When construction began, Marie later recalled, "I think he spent every Saturday and Sunday out there watching every bit of sand that was put in. Just nurtured it like a plant."

He nailed down $28 million in federal funds toward the final cost. At one time 23,000 men, most of whom would otherwise have been unemployed, were on the construction payroll. And he faced down the derisive charges that "Fiorello's Folly," as critics called it, was too big, too grand, too expensive.

La Guardia, who started flying in aviation's infancy and was now a constant commercial air traveler, felt in his heart that the air age had barely begun. A year after its opening, the New York Municipal Airport, as it was first called, had become the busiest in the world, with two hundred flights carrying three thousand passengers a day. Soon that much traffic would be generated in a single hour, and La Guardia, who sensed what was coming, wanted New York to be ready.

He was not alone. On the day he stood up before 325,000 proud citizens to dedicate the gleaming runways and futuristic hangers to the service of the city, three skywriting planes flew overhead and spelled out the words, "Name it La Guardia Airport." The mayor took, or pretended to take, no notice. But a few weeks later such a resolution was passed by the City Council. "Never," editorialized the New York *Herald Tribune,* "was there a more fitting tribute to a man than La Guardia Field."

He wasn't finished. Barely was the new field operational before he bulled through the purchase of a polluted bathing beach known as Idlewild Point on the south shore of Queens and began the long and controversy-ridden work of turning it into the international air terminal for North America. The opposition stormed onstage exactly on cue—how many airports did New York need, for God's sake?—but the work went ahead. It was not to be completed until after La Guardia's death, but by then it needed no defense. Idlewild, covering five thousand acres, an area equal to all of Manhattan south of Central Park, became operational in 1948—when 6 million passengers entered or left New York—barely in time to relieve overburdened La Guardia Field of its international traffic. It was the first of the super terminals, the greatest airport the world had ever seen. It remains the first port of entry to the United States.

Had it not been built in Queens it would have been built somewhere else, outside the city, for the need for a second airport soon became apparent to everyone. If that had happened, if Fiorello La Guardia hadn't foreseen aircraft then not even in the design stage, and a time when they would all but replace ships and trains as passenger carriers, the city's international air travelers, of whom there were 30 million by 1980, would have had a far longer journey to and from their planes, and New York would have lost one of its most important sources of revenue and employment.

In the spring of 1941, President Roosevelt named La Guardia director of the Office of Civilian Defense. He accepted willingly, prepared to serve without pay and to govern New York on a part-time basis. But it was not the job he wanted. Less than a year before, when Roosevelt decided to appoint a Republican as Secretary of War to emphasize the nation's unity in foreign policy, he dispatched one of his Brain Trusters, Rexford G. Tugwell, to sound out La Guardia. The Little Flower was all for it; as the Nazi blitzkrieg overtook France, and Japan moved to dominate southeast Asia, he longed to be at the Washington command center. "Fiorello's hopes were so high," said Tugwell, "his eagerness so apparent that his ambition became more and more evident to others."

But the job went to staid Henry Stimson. Ironically, one reason that La Guardia did not get the appointment was because of his enthusiastic support of Roosevelt in the election of 1940; it made his already pallid Republican credentials all but worthless. Another was the burden he could never shed outside New York: his rambunctious, wild-swinging, "little wop" image.

Around the same time, before F.D.R. had declared his willingness to run for an unprecedented third term in 1940, there was considerable enthusiasm in some quarters for giving La Guardia the first or second place on the national ticket of a realigned party of Progressives. Ickes was for him. Adolf Berle thought there was no one in the country better qualified to be President after Roosevelt retired. In the Illinois primary that spring, four thousand people signed a petition to nominate him. But La Guardia withdrew in deference to the President, and the President bluntly listed for Berle all the reasons La Guardia couldn't win, harking back to the prejudices that had defeated Al Smith in 1928 and adding in that La Guardia would be condemned not only by those who thought, mistakenly, that he was a Catholic, but by those who knew his mother was Jewish, two apparently invincible liabilities in 1940. And then, of course, Roosevelt decided to run himself.

A year later, a Gallup poll measuring the strength of those considered likely candidates in 1944 put La Guardia in fifth place. But, as we know, Roosevelt ran still another time, and then any aspirations La Guardia may ever have nurtured for the presidency or vice-presidency were crushed.

He pitched into the civilian defense job with all his fierce energy, although he wasn't really quite sure what to make of it.

He was charged with mobilizing a force of volunteers in all the
cities and towns to protect life and property in an air raid or
other emergency; but somehow the OCD was also given the duty
to invigorate drives for the conservation of food and the collection of scrap metals, and to boost civilian morale. Not that La
Guardia objected to this multiple and disparate array of assignments. But he was already under fire from two flanks: from those
who didn't want to hear anything about possible American involvement in the war, and from those who thought he had spread
himself too thin. Now he became the target of still others, who
demanded to know what planned physical-fitness clinics and rec-
reation centers had to do with OCD's main mission: to organize a
network of air raid wardens and shelters so people would have a
reasonable chance of surviving an air attack.

Perhaps La Guardia didn't know either. In any case, he
tried to solve the problem by naming Eleanor Roosevelt as his
first assistant and handing over to her all OCD activities not specifically related to the defense and safety of the civilian population. But their personalities were radically different, the Little
Flower caught by the pyrotechnics of the task—fire-fighting
equipment, air raid warning tests, practice blackouts—and the
First Lady concerned with gaining the understanding and interest of the people; and their collaboration was an uneasy one. Mrs.
Roosevelt, who was famous for never complaining, complained
that La Guardia always seemed too rushed to discuss anything
thoroughly, and that he furthermore foisted off on her everything about the job that bored him. As for the rowdy Little
Flower, he must have found Mrs. Roosevelt's above-the-battle
temperament and her too-good-to-be-true forbearance something
of a trial. Once, when there was something she particularly
wanted to discuss with him, she invited him to lunch in her small
Greenwich Village apartment. Afterward, as La Guardia was
leaving, he said to her, "My wife never asks me where I have been
nor whom I saw, nor what I did, but she always asks me what I
had to eat. Today I can truthfully say I did not have too much!"

For a time it appeared that the underlying high regard each
had for the other's innate decency and ability would enable them
to overcome differences and work together toward fulfillment of a
difficult job. Mrs. Roosevelt conveyed something of this feeling in

an account of a trip they made to the West Coast on the day after Japan struck at Pearl Harbor. Their purpose was to buck up the fragile civil defense apparatus there and to calm hysterical and loudly voiced fears that the Japanese were about to overrun California. As they flew westward through the night, Mrs. Roosevelt working on, La Guardia climbed into a berth aft and went to sleep. Then the copilot came back with stunning news: A San Francisco newspaper had announced that the city was being bombed by Japanese aircraft.

As their plane began its descent for a midwestern refueling stop, the First Lady woke La Guardia. He poked his head through the compartment curtains, "looking for all the world like a Kewpie," but when she gave him the report he took charge at once.

> ... He asked me to get off when we landed and telephone the Washington airport for verification, saying, "If it is true we will go direct to San Francisco." It was so characteristic of him that I glowed inwardly. One could be exasperated with him at times, but one had to admire his real integrity and courage. I telephoned and found that it was a rumor without verification, so I went back to the plane and the mayor decided we should continue to Los Angeles.

She admired the way he took hold and inspired everyone, but she "did not know and never have known how much all our plans, both his and mine, really helped," since so much essential equipment was lacking. On La Guardia's return to New York, the criticism intensified. Earlier, he had been ridiculed for his shrill efforts to stir the people into action against a danger the isolationists said didn't exist; now he was flayed because the danger was all too real and the country was still not prepared to deal with it.

But some of the criticism was justified. No one, not even La Guardia, could adequately handle national civil defense and the city of New York at the same time. In February 1942, both he and Mrs. Roosevelt resigned their posts. La Guardia, a stranger to failure, was deeply depressed, reduced, as he put it, to "keeping the streets of New York clean" in the midst of a war on which the fate of the whole world hung.

He exaggerated somewhat. As it happened, he continued with a unique contribution to the Allied effort, but the trouble was it had to be kept secret. Beginning before Pearl Harbor, he had been making regular shortwave broadcasts to Italy, telling the people that the Nazis were stealing away their pride as well as their food. That his words stung the Fascists was apparent from the calumny heaped on his head by their propagandists. "That false Italian and authenticated Jew, Fiorello H. La Guardia," they called him.

The name meant something different to ordinary Italians. Afterward, when the war was over, a G.I. from Brooklyn sent the mayor a snapshot he had taken in a town near Naples. It was a picture of a wall with three names painted on it in big, defiant white letters: F.D.R., Churchill, La Guardia.

Reform is a political high-wire act, but what do you do for an encore? In 1937, La Guardia won reelection with more votes than any candidate for mayor had ever received. In 1941, running for a third term, he squeaked through by the narrowest margin since 1905, a bare 130,000 votes. Early in 1945, another election year, the great guessing game began: Would La Guardia run again? Many simply assumed it. He had served longer in City Hall than any predecessor. Children had become voters knowing no other mayor. He was part of the peripheral life of so many New Yorkers, taken for granted, like the city itself, as much a fixture as Roosevelt was in the White House.

For weeks La Guardia wouldn't answer the question. Dropping hints yea and nay, he pretended to be too busy to think about politics. But as the war moved into its final weeks, he thought about little else. He had nowhere to go, but the prospects of succeeding himself and staying where he was were not encouraging. He used to like to boast that he had never been a member of any political party for more than fifteen minutes; now his cantankerous independence was coming back to haunt him. Three times the Republicans had given him their mayoral nomination, keeping the old fusion coalition intact. But during his twelve years at City Hall he had spurned every Republican candidate for top state or national office, and finally the leadership had had enough. They went shopping for another candidate for mayor.

"I could run on a Chinese laundry ticket and beat those political bums," La Guardia responded defiantly, and maybe he
could have. But there were other considerations.

He was a desperately tired man by now, perhaps already fa-
tally ill. Newbold Morris said, "I know that he was frequently in
great pain. He would sit in his chair holding on to his back. [He]
seemed to have a premonition that he wouldn't last long." Now
there was a bottle of white pills amid the litter of papers and
corncob pipes on his desk.

Nor had he rallied from the desperate disappointments of
the past months. Failing to win a Cabinet post, he had talked
with Roosevelt about a role in the military government of liberated Italy. The President encouraged him to believe he was to
become civil affairs director and have the rank of brigadier general. "I saw the chief yesterday," he wrote White House aide
Harry Hopkins, "and I am so happy I can be of service to my
country—besides cleaning the streets of New York City. I expect
to get my medical exam next week."

But once again fate—and La Guardia's reputation for dis-
ruption—intervened and the appointment was finally denied
him. It was a body blow and a great embarrassment because the
newspapers had all but dressed him in uniform and shipped him
out. But he faced up to it with a kind of wistful gallantry. "I'll
carry on," he told reporters. "I've got a uniform of my own up in
New York, a street cleaner's uniform. That's my little army."

In April, Roosevelt died. La Guardia, deeply shaken, sat before the WNYC microphones thirty minutes after hearing the
news and spoke of the great loss suffered by peace-loving people.
He urged New Yorkers to carry on the unfinished work. But
later he told George Baehr that F.D.R. was lucky to have died on
the job.

The old order was passing; all within a few months, Al
Smith, George Norris and now Roosevelt, had died, and La
Guardia must have felt the chill as the end of his political career
suddenly rose up before him. Eulogizing Norris, his old congressional colleague and hero in a Sunday broadcast the previous
September, he recalled how the great Progressive had been defeated by the people of Nebraska because young voters didn't
know him and old voters had forgotten him. There were tears in
his eyes as he said,

You see, he was an insurgent, and the life of an insurgent in American politics is an unhappy one. He draws opposition from every side. He is always open to attack. . . . I guess [Norris] will get his reward in heaven and his credit in the history books.

And now that was all he could hope for himself. On May 5, 1945, he ended the guessing game by opening his Sunday broadcast with the announcement that he would not be a candidate for mayor. He tried to keep the mood light. He was leaving, he said, because people who stay in office too long tend to become bossy, "and they tell me I am sort of inclined that way at times." But his private feelings come clear in a poignant story told by Julius Isaacs, assistant corporation counsel.

Years before, Isaacs, whose wife was a New Zealander, had gone to a reception for Dr. Herbert V. Evatt, the Australian statesman. Suddenly, unexpected, uninvited, La Guardia appeared. When he had paid his respects to the astonished Australian and left, Evatt asked Isaacs what had brought La Guardia to such an obscure function. "He's the mayor," Isaacs replied. "He knows everything about this city."

Moved, Evatt said, "You know, Mr. Isaacs, we in Australia know only two men in America—Roosevelt and La Guardia—both very great."

As things worked out, Isaacs did not get a chance to repeat this tribute to La Guardia until just before he left office. The Little Flower listened without expression, then said, "Yes, Roosevelt and La Guardia—and both dead."

But he was far from dead. He couldn't even bring himself to retire. He signed up to do two Sunday radio programs and a twice-weekly newspaper column, but still paced his new Rockefeller Center office with time on his hands. It did not take long before he was back in the familiar waters of controversy. *Liberty Magazine,* one of his broadcast sponsors, which had previously agreed that his fifteen-minute commentary would be free from outside interference, suddenly released him from his contract for what they claimed were "reckless and irresponsible" statements. "I have lost *Liberty,* but I retain my soul," the irrepressible Little Flower shot back.

In March 1946 he was appointed director general of the United Nations Relief and Rehabilitation Administration,

charged with feeding, clothing, and bringing some small measure
of hope to millions of the war's victims. Somehow he geared himself up to the old enthusiasm one last time, exhorting an audience of midwestern farmers to go all out producing food for
nations in need:

> I want plows, not typewriters. . . . People can't eat resolutions and
> even the people in our own country have learned through a period
> of depression that ticker tape ain't spaghetti.

But UNRRA was soon mired in international politics, and
in December, after England and the United States withdrew financial support, La Guardia resigned.

By spring 1947, the pain in his back was so insistent that
George Baehr put him into Mount Sinai Hospital. There were
endless tests, exploratory surgery, and a diagnosis, as Baehr told
it to the press, of "chronic pancreatitis." But of course it was
cancer, and Baehr was never convinced that his perceptive old
friend didn't know it before the doctors.

But the charade was acted out to the end. La Guardia went
home to the heavily mortgaged house he and Marie had bought in
Riverdale, a pleasant enclave in northernmost New York City.
Those who came to visit were appalled by what was happening to
him. Robert Moses climbed the stairs to the second-floor bedroom
that summer and came down a shaken man.

> When the Mayor sent for me, I was shocked at the change in him.
> He was in bed, so shrunken, so chapfallen and yet so spunky, and
> so obviously on the way out. To tell the truth, I felt like crying.

But the old fires burned on and sometimes, by sheer grit, he
could pull himself free from the clutch of death long enough to
put on a good imitation of his old self. Newbold Morris tells of the
September day he brought his wife's mother and father to see
him, unaware how far the Little Flower had slipped. But La
Guardia insisted they come in. Recalled Morris,

> At what great cost in pain I dared not guess, La Guardia had
> pulled himself together and was standing to greet us, a big smile
> on his face. . . . He launched into a discussion of conditions
> abroad, denouncing those who failed to support the United Na-

tions and its humanitarian work. He lectured us all, rolling his eyes, wagging his fingers and pounding his hands together as if from some depth within his emaciated body he had summoned the old brimstone. I never saw him give a better performance.... When we left, La Guardia grinned at me mischievously as if to say, "Well, we gave them a show, didn't we?" Then he gave me a salute, a salute that I knew was farewell.

On September 16, 1947, he slipped into a coma that lasted four days. Early on the fifth day, the kind of bright blue autumn morning New Yorkers glory in, police stations hauled their flags down to half-mast, firehouse gongs began sounding the 5-5-5-5 signal that means a fireman has died, and the city's newspapers remade their front pages: Fiorello La Guardia, sixty-four, the best mayor New York ever had or is likely to get, was dead.

Thousands came to see him one last time at the Episcopal Cathedral of Saint John the Divine, and thousands more lined the streets as his hearse wound through Harlem on the way to Woodlawn Cemetery in the Bronx. The obituaries were full and generous. The *Times* recounted his achievements as mayor and said, "He did much of this in an uproar of controversy but he did it." *Time* magazine remembered that he had given the city more than "material benefits; he had stamped on the serpent of municipal corruption until it moved only faintly; he had proved that 'reform mayors' need not end their careers in hopeless frustration."

President Truman wrote Marie that he was as "incorruptible as the sun," which was one measure of La Guardia's personal priorities. When Newbold Morris went with Marie to open the Little Flower's safe-deposit box; there was $8,000 in United States war bonds inside, and this, plus the house in Riverdale, constituted his entire estate.

What no one said, what no one had yet comprehended, was that the empty place he left would never be filled. He believed in a uniquely American way, and it was embodied in everything he did, even in his excesses and crudities. Alien as his antecedents were, La Guardia was an American original. And with every mayor of New York who would like to think of himself as "another La Guardia," we learn better just how terrific the original was.

ACKNOWLEDGMENTS

I want to say something about my sources and thank those who contributed to this book and encouraged me in the writing.

Earlier works on La Guardia were obviously of considerable help, although, surprisingly, the Little Flower has received only spotty biographical attention since his passing. Two books published early in La Guardia's second term, those by Lowell Limpus and Jay Franklin, are now nearly five decades old; they are wholly uncritical. Bella Rodman's more recent *Fiorello La Guardia*, a sometimes touching account directed mainly at younger readers, deals primarily with the landmarks of his life. And William Manners's breezily written 1976 biography is entertaining but similarly fragmented. La Guardia's own book, the autobiography cut short by his death, seems guarded and, in any case, carries the story only to his return from the Italian front in World War I.

Arthur Mann's two-volume work is essential for anyone with serious interest in the life and times of Fiorello La Guardia; it is balanced, comprehensive, and lucidly written. Unfortunately, it ends with the mayoral election of 1933. On the other hand, August Heckscher starts with La Guardia at mid-career and gives us a strong narrative account—but only of the mayoral years. Howard Zinn has been praised, deservedly, for his careful study of La Guardia's congressional period, and Charles Garrett has written the best book about the governance of New York City when La Guardia was mayor. Two memoirs of the Little Flower ought to be noted, one by Robert Moses, the other by Ernest Cuneo; both are moving and candid, but highly personal.

La Guardia was so central to his era that he figures in books by or about nearly every major public figure of the time. The most relevant of those consulted for the present work are included in the bibliography. I acknowledge my indebtedness to all these authors, as well as to the journalists who wrote about the living La Guardia in innumerable magazine articles and newspaper stories.

Judge Eugene R. Canudo has been of inestimable help to me. Son of La Guardia's early law partner Raimondo Canudo, member of both the Little Flower's congressional and mayoral staffs, and later, keeper of the flame as president of the La Guardia Memorial Association, Gene Canudo knows both the La Guardia story and the trove of documentation in the New York City Municipal Archives better than any single person I encountered in my seven years of research and writing. For his patience and guidance and encouragement, I offer my sincerest thanks.

I am also grateful to all the others who took time to share their memories of La Guardia and to answer my questions, foremost among them Mrs. Marie La Guardia, Louis E. Yavner, and the late Robert Moses. And special thanks to the following as well:

Joey Adams, Dr. George Baehr, Judge Francis J. Bloustein, Ernest Cuneo, James A. Farley, Judge Anna M. Kross, J. S. (Sandy) Hand, Beatrice Resnick Himmel, Goodhue Livingston, Alice Roosevelt Longworth, Walter S. Mack, James Marshall, William Fellowes Morgan, Morris Novik, Peter Pascale, Maurice G. Postley, David Rockefeller, Henry Rosner.

The Fiorello H. La Guardia Papers in the Municipal Archives—hundreds of cartons and scrapbooks—contain more raw material toward a La Guardia biography than is to be found anywhere else. Yet there are riches that cannot be ignored in the files of the New York Public Library; the Houghton Library at Harvard (the Oswald Garrison Villard Papers); the National Archives; the Franklin D. Roosevelt Library at Hyde Park, N.Y.; and the Columbia University Library (the Frederick C. Tanner Collection). Thomas Kent Gulley helped me research most of these materials; for his careful and intelligent assessments, for his volumes of notes and perceptive ideas, I am deeply appreciative.

The reminiscences of the La Guardia era in the matchless Oral History Collection at Columbia University were invaluable to me. To the writer who comes poking around the theater decades after the stage has gone dark, there is nothing to compare with these interviews. They infuse the past with contemporary color; they are a new kind of primary source material, conserving human experience in the words of those who lived it. I took full advantage of the opportunities offered by the Collection and I will always be grateful to the late Louis M. Starr, the director, for his kind and knowledgeable assistance.

I also owe particular thanks to Maurice A. Crane, director of the National Voice Library of Michigan State University in Lansing, who took time to make me cassette copies of all La Guardia's radio broadcasts. I have had similar personal help in all the many public and private libraries where I gathered material for this book, but I must note my special gratitude to the librarians at Columbia-Greene Community College in Hudson, N.Y., who, through the marvelous interlibrary loan network, provided me with books available nowhere else; and to Robert J. McVeigh, assistant to the president of the Fiorello H. La Guardia Community College, Long Island City, N.Y., who gave me free access to the school's growing collection of La Guardia materials; and to Mrs. Ethel Gold, reference librarian of the New York Institute of Technology in Westbury, N.Y., who was somehow able to produce all the magazine articles, even the most obscure ones, I needed to see. Let me here also acknowledge the silent cheers and special efforts on my behalf by Harrison Stewkesbury, Mrs. Gold's deft assistant, for which warmest gratitude.

I want to express appreciation to Mrs. Camilla Saadoun, who took on the chore of typing the manuscript and did a superlative job. And to my wife and son, who lived with this book for such a long time (for Nicholas, it was very nearly all of his eight years) and to whom, during the final six months, it must have seemed that a short round man with a black hat had moved in with us—for bearing with me: my loving thanks.

—LAWRENCE ELLIOTT
Aix-en-Provence
October 21, 1982.

BIBLIOGRAPHY

Adams, Joey. *From Gags to Riches.* New York: Frederick Fell, 1946.

Berle, Beatrice Bishop, and Travis Beale Jacobs. *Navigating the Rapids, 1918–1971.* New York: Harcourt Brace Jovanovich, 1973.

Blanshard, Paul. *Personal and Controversial.* Boston: Beacon Press, 1973.

Blum, John Morton. *From the Diaries of Henry Morgenthau, Jr.: Years of Crisis, 1928–1938.* Boston: Houghton Mifflin, 1959.

———. *V Was for Victory.* New York: Harcourt Brace Jovanovich, 1976.

Burns, James MacGregor. *Roosevelt: The Lion and the Fox.* New York: Harcourt, Brace, 1956.

Caro, Robert A. *The Power Broker: Robert Moses and the Fall of New York.* New York: Alfred A. Knopf, 1974.

Caruso, Dorothy. *Enrico Caruso.* New York: Simon & Schuster, 1945.

Connable, Alfred, and Edward Silberfarb. *Tigers of Tammany.* New York: Holt, Rinehart & Winston, 1967.

Corsi, Edward. *In the Shadow of Liberty: The Chronicle of Ellis Island.* New York: Macmillan, 1935.

Cuneo, Ernest. *Life With Fiorello.* New York: Macmillan, 1955.

Curran, Henry H. *Pillar to Post.* New York: Charles Scribner's Sons, 1941.

Davis, Kenneth S. *FDR: The Beckoning of Destiny, 1882–1928.* New York: G. P. Putnam's Sons, 1971.

Dewey, Thomas E. *Twenty Against the Underworld.* New York: Doubleday, 1974.

Farley, James A. *Behind the Ballots.* New York: Harcourt, Brace, 1938.

———. *Jim Farley's Story.* New York: McGraw-Hill, 1948.

Federal Writers' Project. *New York City Guide.* New York: Random House, 1939.

———. *The Italians of New York.* New York: Random House, 1938.

Fitch, Willis. *Wings in the Night.* Boston: Marshall Jones, 1938.

Flynn, Edward J. *You're the Boss.* New York: Viking Press, 1947.

Fowler, Gene. *Beau James: The Life and Times of Jimmy Walker.* New York: Viking Press, 1949.

Franklin, Jay (pseudonym of John Franklin Carter). *La Guardia.* New York: Modern Age Books, 1937.

Freidel, Frank. *Franklin D. Roosevelt: The Apprenticeship.* Boston: Little, Brown, 1952.

———. *Franklin D. Roosevelt: The Ordeal.* Boston: Little, Brown, 1954.

———. *Franklin D. Roosevelt: Launching the New Deal.* Boston: Little, Brown, 1973.

Galbraith, John Kenneth. *The Great Crash: 1929.* Boston: Houghton Mifflin, 1954.

Garrett, Charles. *The La Guardia Years.* New Brunswick, N. J.: Rutgers University Press, 1961.

Gelfand, Mark I. *A Nation of Cities: The Federal Government and Urban America, 1933–1965.* New York: Oxford University Press, 1965.

Glazer, Nathan, and Daniel Patrick Moynihan. *Beyond the Melting Pot.* Cambridge: Massachusetts Institute of Technology, 1963.

Gluck, Emma La Guardia. *My Story.* New York: David McKay, 1961.

Gunther, John. *Inside U.S.A.* New York: Harper & Brothers, 1947.

Hamburger, Philip. *Mayor Watching.* New York: Rinehart, 1958.

Handlin, Oscar. *The Uprooted: The Epic Story of the Great Migrations That Made the American People.* Boston: Little, Brown, 1951.

———. *Al Smith and His America.* Boston: Little, Brown, 1958.

Heckscher, August. *When La Guardia Was Mayor.* New York: W. W. Norton, 1978.

Hoover, Herbert. *The Memoirs of Herbert Hoover: The Great Depression, 1929–1941.* New York: Macmillan, 1952.

Howe, Irving. *World of Our Fathers.* New York: Harcourt Brace Jovanovich, 1976.

Hurst, Fannie. *Anatomy of Me.* New York: Doubleday, 1958.

Hylan, John Francis. *Autobiography.* New York: Rotary Press, 1922.

Ickes, Harold L. *The Secret Diary of Harold L. Ickes: The First Thousand Days, 1933–1936.* New York: Simon & Schuster, 1953.

———. *The Secret Diary of Harold L. Ickes: The Inside Struggle, 1936–1939.* New York: Simon & Schuster, 1954.

———. *The Secret Diary of Harold L. Ickes: The Lowering Clouds.* New York: Simon & Schuster, 1955.

Josephson, Matthew. *Sidney Hillman.* Garden City, N. Y.: Doubleday, 1952.

Kempton, Murray. *Part of Our Time.* New York: Simon & Schuster, 1955.

Kobler, John. *Ardent Spirits.* New York: G. P. Putnam's Sons, 1973.

La Follette, Belle Case, and Fola La Follette. *Robert M. La Follette,* (2 vols.). New York: Macmillan, 1953.

La Guardia, Fiorello. *The Making of an Insurgent, 1882–1919.* Philadelphia and New York: J. B. Lippincott, 1948.

Lash, Joseph P. *Eleanor and Franklin.* New York: W. W. Norton, 1971.

Leuchtenburg, William E. *The Perils of Prosperity, 1914–1932.* Chicago and London: University of Chicago Press, 1958.

Limpus, Lowell M. *This Man La Guardia.* New York: E. P. Dutton, 1938.

Lombardo, Joseph. *Vincent Piccirilli: Life of an American Sculptor.* New York: Pitman Publishing, 1944.

Lundberg, Ferdinand. *Imperial Hearst.* New York: Modern Library, 1937.

McCullough, Esther Morgan. *As I Pass, O Manhattan.* North Bennington, Vt.: Coley Taylor, 1956.

MacKaye, Milton. *The Tin Box Parade.* New York: Robert McBride, 1934.

MacNeil, Neil. *Forge of Democracy: The House of Representatives.* New York: David McKay, 1963.

Mann, Arthur. *La Guardia: A Fighter Against His Times, 1882–1933.* Chicago: University of Chicago Press, 1969.

———. *La Guardia Comes to Power: 1933.* Chicago: University of Chicago Press, 1969.

Manners, William. *Patience and Fortitude: Fiorello H. La Guardia.* New York: Harcourt Brace Jovanovich, 1976.

Martin, George. *Madam Secretary: Frances Perkins.* Boston: Houghton Mifflin, 1976.

Mitchell, Broadus, *Depression Decade.* New York: Holt, Rinehart and Winston, 1962.

Mitgang, Herbert. *The Man Who Rode the Tiger: The Life and Times of Judge Samuel Seabury.* Philadelphia and New York: J. B. Lippincott, 1963.

Moley, Raymond. *The First New Deal.* New York: Harcourt, Brace & World, 1966.

Morris, Newbold. *Let the Chips Fall.* New York: Appleton-Century-Crofts, 1955.

Moscow, Warren, *Politics in the Empire State.* New York: Alfred A. Knopf, 1948.

Moses, Robert. *Working for the People.* New York: Harper & Brothers, 1956.

––––––. *La Guardia: A Salute and a Memoir.* New York: Simon & Schuster, 1957.

––––––. *Public Works: A Dangerous Trade.* New York: McGraw-Hill, 1970.

Nearing, Scott. *The Making of a Radical.* New York: Harper, 1972.

Nevins, Allan. *Herbert H. Lehman and His Era.* New York: Charles Scribner's Sons, 1963.

Norris, George W. *Fighting Liberal: The Autobiography of George W. Norris.* New York: Macmillan, 1945.

Northrup, William B., and John B. Northrup. *Insolence of Office: The Story of the Seabury Investigations.* New York: G. P. Putnam's Sons, 1932.

O'Connor, Richard. *The First Hurrah: A Biography of Al Smith.* New York: G. P. Putnam's Sons, 1970.

Page, Thomas Nelson. *Italy and the World War.* New York: Charles Scribner's Sons, 1920.

Parsteck, Bennett J. *A Rhetorical Analysis of Fiorello H. La Guardia's Weekly Radio Speeches: 1942–1945.* Ann Arbor, Mich.: University Microfilms, 1970.

Rankin, Rebecca B. *New York Advancing: A Scientific Approach to Municipal Government.* New York: Municipal Reference Library, 1936.

––––––. *New York Advancing,* World's Fair Edition. New York: Municipal Reference Library, 1939.

––––––. *New York Advancing,* Victory Edition. New York: Municipal Reference Library, 1945.

Rodman, Bella. *Fiorello La Guardia.* New York: Hill and Wang, 1962.

Roosevelt, Eleanor. *This I Remember.* New York: Harper & Brothers, 1949.

Salter, J. T. *The American Politician.* Chapel Hill: The University of North Carolina Press, 1938.

Sayre, Wallace S., and Herbert Kaufman. *Governing New York City.* New York: W. W. Norton, 1965.

Schafer, Alan. *Vito Marcantonio.* Syracuse, N.Y.: Syracuse University Press, 1966.

Schlesinger, Arthur M., Jr. *The Age of Roosevelt: The Crisis of the Old Order.* Boston: Houghton Mifflin, 1957.

––––––. *The Age of Roosevelt: The Coming of the New Deal.* Boston: Houghton Mifflin, 1959.

––––––. *The Age of Roosevelt: The Politics of Upheaval.* Boston: Houghton Mifflin, 1960.

Seidler, Murray B. *Norman Thomas.* Syracuse, N. Y.: Syracuse University Press, 1967.

Sherwood, Robert E. *Roosevelt and Hopkins.* New York: Harper & Brothers, 1948.

Smith, Richard Norton. *Thomas E. Dewey and His Times.* New York: Simon & Schuster, 1982.

Soule, George. *Prosperity Decade.* New York: Holt, Rinehart and Winston, 1962.

Spalding, Albert. *Rise to Follow: An Autobiography.* New York: Henry Holt, 1943.

Swanberg, W. A. *Citizen Hearst*. New York: Charles Scribner's Sons, 1961.

———. *Norman Thomas*. New York: Charles Scribner's Sons, 1976.

Thomas, Norman, and Paul Blanshard. *What's the Matter With New York: A National Problem*. New York: Macmillan, 1932.

Tucker, Ray, and Frederick R. Barkley, *Sons of the Wild Jackass*. Boston: L. C. Page, 1932.

Tugwell, Rexford G. *The Democratic Roosevelt*. Garden City, N. Y.: Doubleday, 1957.

———. *The Art of Politics: Franklin Delano Roosevelt, Luis Muñoz Marin, and Fiorello H. La Guardia*. Garden City, N. Y.: Doubleday, 1958.

Valentine, Lewis J. *Night Stick: The Autobiography of Lewis J. Valentine*. New York: Dial Press, 1947.

Walsh, George. *Gentleman Jimmy Walker*. New York and Washington: Praeger, 1974.

Wecter, Dixon. *The Age of the Great Depression*. New York: Macmillan, 1948.

Whalen, Grover A. *Mr. New York*. New York: G. P. Putnam's Sons, 1955.

Zinn, Howard. *La Guardia in Congress*. Ithaca, N. Y.: Cornell University Press, 1959.

———. *The Politics of History*. Boston: Beacon Press, 1970.

INDEX

DATE DUE

DATE DUE			
MAR 2 '88			
MAR 22 '88			
GAYLORD			PRINTED IN U.S.A.